Career Education:
What It Is and How to Do It
Second Edition

Career Education:
What It Is and How to Do It
Second Edition

by Kenneth B. Hoyt
    Rupert N. Evans
    Edward F. Mackin
    Garth L. Mangum

Olympus Publishing Company Salt Lake City, Utah

Contents

Preface to the First Edition   *page* 7

Preface to the Second Edition   *page* 11

1   Career Education: What It Is   13

        A Philosophy for Career Education   16

        Concepts, Components, and Phases of Career Education   22

        Career Education Issues   32

2   Career Education: Why We Need It   45

        Education and Social Ills   46

        Achievements of Education in the United States   56

        Deficiencies in American Education   58

3   Career Education: How It Developed   81

        Changing Objectives in Career Preparation   82

        Precursors of Career Education   85

        Implementation Efforts of the Office of Education   94

4   Career Education: How to Do It   100

        Exploring the Definition of Career Education   100

        Implementing Career Education's Components   104

        Changes Required   158

        A Question of Commitment   167

5   Career Education: How to Get It   168

      Need for National Leadership in Career Education   169

      State Boards and State Departments of Education   180

      Action Steps for Implementation   188

6   Potential Contribution of Career Education   216

      Some Basic Ingredients   216

      Obligations of the Schools   219

      Educational Innovations   220

      Changing the Community's Role   223

      Summary   225

Selected Bibliography   *page* 229

Index   *page* 233

LIST OF FIGURES

1   Career Education's Place in Education   35

2   One Page from a Set of Guidelines for Middle/Junior High School Teachers   113

3   Ten Action Steps for Implementing Career Education   189

4   Community Resources Questionnaire   201

5   The Career Education Implementation Process   214

Preface to the First Edition

Career education is "in" in American education. The National Education Association has endorsed it and also the National Association of Chief State School Officers, the American Vocational Association, and the National Advisory Council on Vocational Education. The Association of Secondary School Principals has acclaimed it, and the concept is attractive to the National Congress of Parent-Teacher Associations. The American Association of School Administrators is holding conferences on career education through its National Academy of School Executives. The American Association of Junior Colleges has joined the favorable chorus. Outside education, responses from organized labor, the U.S. Chamber of Commerce, and similar groups have been equally approving. Nowhere does one find organized opposition. Though the higher education associations have shown no interest, many individuals are skeptical of any significant change, and few groups are beginning to have second thoughts on particular points.

Why the sudden interest in the concept? The immediate source of interest in career education is clear. A high official of the U.S. Office of Education, Sidney P. Marland, Jr., has made career education the password of his administration. Not only that, he has allocated some of the discretionary money available to him through various education appropriations to implement the concept. State and local education agencies seeking additional funds, U.S. Office of Education staff ambitious for the inside track, consulting firms after business — all know the key word for grantsmanship and advancement.

The lingering skepticism is the fruit of experience. Career education is on the tongue of educators as often as the "right to read" movement was a few years ago and the "life adjustment" education just after World War II. Sloganizing is a familiar pastime among educators, but the durability of the slogans is not impressive.

If career education is a personal crusade only of Assistant Secretary Marland, its life is likely to be short. The Office of Education has experienced five commissioners of education in eleven years. Most have made a contribution, but few have been able to pass their priorities on to their successors.

Whether local education decision makers should underwrite the new advocacy with major investments of funds, staff, and political credit requires a judgment of the value and durability of the concept. Since so many slogans have come and gone, what reason is there to think this will be more durable? As a matter of fact, no new concept has yet been introduced in the current discussion of career education. Though there have been new applications of familiar concepts, no concept is included which has not been discussed by leaders and scholars in vocational and other education for years. The immediate source of the present stir is that the man with the power to allocate federal education funds has made a commitment. That is career education's current strength and part of its vulnerability.

Another source of vulnerability is the verbal nature of many of the accolades career education has attracted. Not very many of its advocates have "put their money where their mouths are." Though the concept would both "generalize" vocational education and "vocationalize" general education, the development efforts thus far have been financed largely with vocational education funds. Other units within the Office of Education are anxious to be part of the policy-making process. Vocational educators are beginning to ask when they are also going to pick up more of the tab.

This growing skepticism of vocational educators is representative of possible threats from misunderstanding and confusion about what is meant by the phrase "career education." There are at least three areas of misunderstanding, partly generated by inexactness and occasional inconsistency in Office of Education pronouncements:

(1) What is career education's relation to the present scope of education? Is it a new name for vocational education? Is it a substitute for all other education? Does it fit somewhere between

WHAT IT IS AND HOW TO DO IT

the academic and the vocational in education? Is it exclusive of higher education, or does it include it?

(2) Where is the funding to come from? Will it use general education funds, vocational funds, or will there be a separate career education budget forthcoming?

(3) Is it a shortcut of second-class education for the disadvantaged or minority groups? (The latter, just getting a hold in higher education, suspect it as another device to relegate them to an inferior role.) Is it good for "someone else's kid," or for mine as well?

Despite some confusion and some shortage of volunteers in reallocating existing budgets, there are reasons to believe career education is more than the personal logo of one commissioner of education, likely to last only as long as he. A confluence of forces appears to make it a concept whose time has come.

This book provides answers to four questions:

(1) What are the key concepts of career education?

(2) Why is career education needed?

(3) How is career education being implemented in practice?

(4) What are the appropriate strategies of implementation for a school system interested in the concept?

This book was begun in the process of preparing *Career Education: A Handbook for Implementation* (in 1971) to accompany a film and a slide-tape presentation as the basis for a national series of Office of Education-sponsored conferences to introduce the career education message to lay audiences. We found ourselves in our personal commitments and enthusiasm writing far too much to be included in that brief document. Convinced that the material necessarily deleted had value to a broader audience, we resolved to take the quickest and most direct route to public attention. We express gratitude to James L. Reid, Warren Smeltzer, Nancy M. Pinson, and E. Niel Carey of the Maryland State Department of Education and to Mary Allen of the American Vocational Association who served as an advisory group in the earlier project. We take full responsibility for what we have subsequently done.

Though the authors all share the convictions expressed, the reader may find some advantage in knowing who was primarily responsible for which portion of the manuscript. The definition and components in chapter 1 around which chapter 4 is structured are Hoyt's, as is most of chapter 4 and parts of chapters 2 and 6. Evans wrote most of chapter 2 and parts of chapters 3, 4, and 5. Most of chapter 5 is Mackin's, whereas Mangum was primarily responsible for chapters 1 and 3, wrote parts of chapters 2 and 6, and took overall editorial responsibility.

MARCH 1972

Preface to the
Second Edition

Career Education: What It Is and How to Do It passed through seven printings in its first eighteen months, remaining nearly to the end of that time the only book written as a coherent formulation of the principles and practical applications of the developing concept. The response has been gratifying. It attests to a dual phenomenon: the enthusiasm with which the concept of career education has been endorsed within normally slowly changing public education and the substantive void into which the idea was dropped.

That career education emerged as a concept whose time had come was closely related to the current demand for accountability. The public had increased its investment in education tenfold in a quarter-century and wanted to know what it was getting for its money. Previous over-promises of education as the universal cure to social ills were painfully coming home to plague educators who, lacking clearly defined objectives, were hard put to demonstrate measurable results. Career success was an objective to which the public could relate. It had become clear that education could not continue to be its own justification. It had to be preparation for something.

The career education concept began with little more substance than the notion that preparation for life's work deserved higher priority among education's many objectives and that accomplishing this goal would require bridging the traditional chasm between vocational and academic education. By the spring of 1972, it had accumulated two additional points of substance. Deliberately restrained by career education's major champion, Assistant Secretary for Education in the Department of Health, Education and Welfare, Dr. Sydney P. Marland, Jr., from offering a definition, the U.S. Office of Education had agreed that (a) at the elementary school level, career education was to emphasize career awareness; at the junior high school level, career exploration; and at the senior high school level, choice and implementation; and (b) all of this was to involve study of the world of work through the instrument of fifteen career clusters under which all occupations could be subsumed.

Our own involvement leading to the publishing of *Career Education: What It Is and How to Do It* grew out of our conviction that an idea without operational substance will soon die out. Our contribution was a definition and five components which we were forced to derive as we tried to describe the substance of what career education was to mean or to be. These, we are gratified to find, have become broadly accepted among advocates of career education, though this acceptance could stem from a lack of alternative formulations.

Our definition has gained considerable acceptance, though it does have competition. It has also sparked some strong opposition. As a statement of philosophy and goals rather than a description of substance, our first edition provoked most objectors to single out its unabashed endorsement of work as an economic necessity and a social good. For this we make no apology. Work is far from being all there is to life, but no individual's life can be satisfying without a feeling of self-worth, and such feelings rarely come without some sort of achievement. The oft-stated premise that work is disappearing is nonsense . . . as Levitan and Johnston have titled a recent book: *Work Is Here to Stay, Alas*. We disagree only with the last word, as of course do the authors.

This second edition of *Career Education: What It Is and How to Do It* contains no change in philosophy and little change in substance. Its only purpose is to correct minor errors, clarify obfuscations in the original, and add an index. In doing this, we have expanded only the number of pages. No new major concepts have been added.

We believe the first edition made a significant contribution to career education. At the time of its first printing, there was a boundless need to know "what it is." Now the need is for "how to do it." Fortunately, materials are now flowing into the market to make career education "do-able."

FEBRUARY 1974

1 Career Education: What It Is

Few concepts introduced in the policy circles of American education have met such instant acclaim as career education. However, it is not unusual to have seeming agreement at a high level of generalization dissolve upon more careful definition or as specific steps to implementation are taken. This book is designed to be as specific as possible about what career education is and how it can be done.

Defining career education is not easy, and there are nearly as many definitions as definers of it. A few samples will illustrate the range of consensus and divergence and provide a background for our definition.*

The U.S. Office of Education has refrained from providing an official definition. However, Dr. Sidney P. Marland, Jr., formerly Assistant Secretary for Education in the U.S. Department of Health, Education and Welfare, who was the concept's chief promoter, has described it as:

> . . . a concept that says three things. First, that career education will be part of the curriculum for all students, not just some. Second, that it will continue throughout a youngster's stay in school, from the first grade through senior high and beyond, if he so elects. And third, that every student leaving school will possess

---

* All of these definitions are quoted by Kenneth B. Hoyt in "The Counselor and Career Education," *SRA Guidance Newsletter* (November-December 1972).

the skills necessary to give him a start in making a livelihood for himself and his family, even if he leaves before completing high school.

An official but draft publication from the Office of Education's Bureau of Adult Vocational and Technical Education describes career education as "a comprehensive educational program focused on careers, which begins in grade 1 or earlier and continues through the adult years."

To quote three prominent academic experts:

> Career education consists of all the extensive and comprehensive educational efforts that are directed to motivate, train, counsel, and improve an individual in his life's work experiences (Norman Stanger, Los Angeles State College).

> Career education is an approach to education which stresses the *instrumental value* of all education in helping an individual become a participating, contributing, and fulfilled citizen (Keith Goldhammer, Michigan State University).

> Career education has as its mission the attainment of an optimum level of work proficiency for each individual within the context of the social, individual, and work systems. Career education (1) facilitates the acquisition and processing and integration of information by the individual; (2) enhances the decision-making process; (3) provides alternatives for action through programs that are designed to equip the individual with salable skills to start his/her career; and (4) provides for continuous recycling of information, decision making, and action through retraining and upgrading of skills (John Coster, North Carolina State University).

A prominent vocational educator adds his definition:

> [In] career education . . . youth at all grade levels in the public schools will . . . acquire useful information about the occupational structure of the economy, the alternatives of career choice, the obligations of individual and productive involvement in the total work force, the intelligent determination of personal capabilities and aspirations, the requisites of all occupations, and opportunities to prepare for gainful employment. Career education is the shared and unending responsibility of all professions in education, and involves input from — and relationship to — all subject-matter disciplines and all supportive educational services. In short, it is a priority objective of public education, with achievement measured by employability in occupations, both gainful and useful, that are a reasonable match of both talent and the ambition of every citizen (Wesley Smith, former director of vocational education in California).

A random selection of definitions gleaned from a variety of sources provides other illustrations:

> Career education is a comprehensive and organized instructional program that enables public school youth, in accordance with their interests and abilities, to acquire the knowledge, skills, and attributes necessary for developing viable personal plans for lifelong learning, and for productive, personally rewarding employment in a rapidly changing society.

> Career education may be described or defined as a comprehensive educational program which gives attention to preparing all people for satisfying and productive work in our society.

> Career education is that part of the total educational process which focuses on the successful adaptation of the individual to the world of work.

> Career education encompasses all education in that it is that part of a learning experience that assists one to discover, define, and refine his talents and use of them in pursuit of a career.

> Career education encompasses those experiences which lead a person to successful occupational performance. Successful occupational performance includes self-satisfaction based on life goals of the individual and/or family as well as economic success. The experiences which lead to the attainment of occupational goals are a combination of both in-school and out-of-school situations.

> The purpose of career education should be to help people develop human resource competence along with a holistic understanding of the world of work or wage-employment system — that is, the socioeconomic institution of working for pay in a modern industrial society — to become *competent* as workers and *comprehending* as men and women.

Our own definition is not sharply different, but it emphasizes points we consider essential: *Career education is the total effort of public education and the community to help all individuals become familiar with the values of a work-oriented society, to integrate these values into their personal value systems, and to implement these values into their lives in such a way that work becomes possible, meaningful, and satisfying to each individual.*

Definers seem to agree that (a) career education has to do with preparation for work, but that (b) it involves more than training for job skills, that (c) it should be experienced by all students, and that (d) it is the responsibility of other institutions as well as the school. There appear to be some differences, even among its strongest advocates, as to (1) whether it encompasses all or is only a part of education, (2) the extent to which it should precede kindergarten and extend beyond grade twelve, and (3) whether it should extend beyond preparation for and pursuit of careers to encompass the entire process of self-actualization and character development.

Our own definition emphasizes community involvement and work values for reasons we explain in the following section of this chapter. It is oriented to the goals rather than the content of career education, requiring us to describe the latter as well. The objectives which mark the way to that goal — familiarity with alternative work values, development and integration of self-chosen work values into a personal value system, and implementation of these values into life — should help all individuals:

- Have reason to want to work
- Acquire the skills useful for work
- Know how to obtain work opportunities
- Enter the world of work as a productive contributor
- Continue to grow in a productive and satisfying career

Incorporated into our definition, its goals, and objectives are some strongly held personal convictions about the nature of our society, of the economy, and of human beings. This philosophy is stated as a guide to understanding the premises which follow.

A Philosophy for Career Education

Two basic assumptions underlie our advocacy of career education and structure our judgment of what it should be. The first is that the quintessence of human happiness is a feeling of self-worth, with work being an essential ingredient to this feeling for most of us (Maslow, 1954). The second is that success in working life requires not only the skills required to do a job, but also the attitudes, values, and general abilities which lead one to want to work productively and which influence one's ability to function as a productive member of society over a lifetime.

Few of us are self-sufficient in developing and maintaining that necessary inner assurance of self-worth. For most of us it is a reflectio

vocation defined as one's primary work role and job as one's primary work role in paid employment.

Leisure is even more difficult to define. It is more than rest or pleasure. It carries with it the connotation of discretion — what a person chooses to do with his time when he is under no economic or other compulsion from outside himself. Thus part of leisure may be spent as volunteer work. On the other hand, commuting to work is hardly leisure — or pleasurable.

By work values, we mean all of those attitudes, positive or negative, which an individual or a society develops toward work. How is work in a general sense valued by the individual or the society? What does it mean in his or their lives? Work values emerge from within the individual and may well be contrasted with a work ethic which is imposed on the individual from outside by societal norms. A work ethic carries the connotation of "oughtness." "For these reasons," society tells the individual "you *ought* to work." To say with some that the Protestant (or Puritan) work ethic which allegedly built this country is disappearing is not to charge that no other work ethic is taking its place. The previous work ethic was allegedly instrumental in the rise of capitalism because (1) it justified accumulation of wealth — salvation was by grace of God, not by act of man, but the elect of God could prove their position by demonstrating God's blessing to them in financial ways; and (2) it encouraged work and saving and discouraged conspicuous consumption — a perfect recipe for capital formation and economic development. For a consumer economy as contrasted to a capitalist one, excess saving can do positive harm. "Work and enjoy," "work and spend," or "serve through work and work to serve" are forms of the work ethic. One *ought* to go to college and become a professional is as much a work ethic as one *ought* to work hard, save his money, and become a capitalist, or one *ought* to go to work early and work hard as a craftsman or industrial worker.

Career education, then, attempts to help students understand the work ethics imposed by society, develop their own work values based on their own personal interest (but in full awareness of society's demands), become aware of the world of work and its values, explore the alternative occupations and careers available, and choose, prepare for, and ultimately begin and pursue a career, including the possibility of changes of occupation and of productive use of leisure during that career.

The importance of career education emerges from this philosophical base and these definitions. Career education is preparation for all meaningful and productive activity, at work (whether paid or volunteer), as employer or employee, in private business or in the public sector, or in the family. Beginning with that conviction, the fundamental concept of career education is that all types of educational experiences, curriculum, instruction, and counseling should involve preparation for economic independence, personal fulfillment, and an appreciation for the dignity of workers. It seeks to give meaning to all education by relating its content to the job world. Under career education, every student (young woman or young man) should leave the school system with attributes attractive to a potential employer or abilities to serve as the underpinning of self-employment. Employers may be attracted by specific job skills. They also seek employees who have the appropriate attitudes and broad general abilities to learn on the job and become quickly productive. The schools cannot be responsible for the availability of employment, but they must become accountable for the employability of their products. However, career education is a concept not just for youth but must also include adults who need to upgrade their skills, update their knowledge, and if necessary or desirable, retrain for a new job. It may emphasize the needs of the majority of women who choose to divide their careers between the home and employment, and the increasing number who choose employment as the primary focus of their productive lives. But it should not neglect the preparation required by those for whom "homemaker" and "parent" are their preferred career. It also should not neglect the fact that those two words are descriptions of important aspects of male careers as well.

Career education cannot be described as academic or vocational for it must include both to provide all of the attitudes, knowledge, and skills necessary for successful careers. Early childhood education and college education are as much a part of the concept as elementary and secondary schools — wherever youth and adults can find learning relevant to the world of work. It should become part of the student's curriculum from the moment he or she enters school, and should relate reading, writing, and arithmetic to the varied ways in which adults live and earn a living. As the student progresses through school, the skills, the knowledge, and above all, the attitudes necessary for work success should be stressed and phased into every subject for every student, not just in separate classes designed for those who are "going to work."

However, career education should not merely precede participation in society, but should provide an integration of learning and doing that merges the worlds of the home, the community, the school, and the work-place into a challenging and productive whole. It should involve no once-and-for-all decisions, no ceilings or locked doors. It should encour-age early tentative choices to give meaning and motivation to study and experience, but encourage delay of permanent choice until all the facts are in about self and jobs. It owes its participants the opportunity to present a salable skill at any port of entry into the job market, yet keep the doors open to return for further upgrading and progression or change of career direction. Rather than a locked-step, kindergarten through twelfth grade — or fourteenth or sixteenth grade — ladder, it is better thought of as a broad freeway with convenient exits and reentries as interests and needs change.

Therefore career education should be viewed as a total concept which should permeate all education, giving a new centrality to the objective of successful preparation for and development of a lifelong, productive career. Yet it must in no way conflict with other important educational objectives. Its beneficiaries can still become good citizens, parents, and cultivated and self-aware human beings because career success can augment all other sound educational objectives.

Career education must increase the relevance of school by focusing on the learner's perceptions of work and of himself or herself as a worker. It recognizes the variety of individual learning styles — that some learn better from "hands-on" experience and others from abstract concepts. For this reason, career education is not to be limited to the classroom. It relates to all learning environments and learning experiences from early childhood throughout the productive life of an individual. In early childhood it should provide an awareness of the nature of the world of work as well as the importance of work itself in our society. As the child moves through the school years, he increases his familiarity with the world of work and acquires the knowledge necessary to obtain meaning-ful employment upon leaving school. He should be able to resume his schooling at any time throughout his lifetime to improve his capacity to meet changing job requirements or to enrich his personal life.

In our view, an objectively oriented, responsible, and accountable education asks for each student at every age: What does he want to be and how can he get there? It then supplies what he needs to progress from wherever he is to wherever he has the potential ability and motivation to climb. Above all, it must aid him in developing his own sense of work values and incorporating them into his personal value system.

To achieve a truly career-oriented education will require major changes in the way we now conduct the business of education. It will require new structure and innovations; new relationships among that which is now academic, general, and vocational in education; and a greater interaction among home, school, and community. Yet it should still be possible to preserve all that is presently sound practice in education and in career preparation. Above all, it will require more specific objectives, a change in philosophy, and a new set of values. Career education's goal is to make work possible, meaningful, and satisfactory to every individual, for the best measure of the human being and the best assurance of his happiness are likely to be found ultimately in what he achieves and how he serves. This is the philosophical base from which we approach the subject of career education.

Concepts, Components, and Phases of Career Education

Our intent in this section is to identify the major concepts and components of career education and to identify important issues not yet resolved within the apparent general consensus.

The Concepts

From the philosophy declared in this chapter and the examples in chapter 4, we can derive the following key concepts of career education:

(1) Preparation for successful working careers should be a key objective of all education.

(2) Every teacher in every course should emphasize the contribution that subject matter can make to a successful career.

(3) Hands-on, occupationally oriented experiences should be used, where appropriate, as a method of teaching and motivating the learning of more abstract academic content.

(4) Preparation for careers should be recognized as involving and interrelating work attitudes, human relations skills, orientation to the nature of the workaday world, exposure to alternative career choices, and the acquisition of actual job skills.

(5) Learning cannot be reserved for the classroom. Learning environments for career education should also be identified in the home, in the community, and in employing establishments.

(6) Beginning in early childhood and continuing through the regular school years, allowing the flexibility for a youth to leave for experience and return to school for further education (including opportunity for upgrading and continued refurbishing for adult workers and including productive use of leisure time and the retirement years), career education's time horizons extend from "womb to tomb."

(7) Career education is a basic and pervasive approach to all education, but it in no way conflicts with other legitimate education objectives such as citizenship, culture, family responsibility, and basic education.

(8) Career education is for all individuals — very young children and the adults of the community, the intellectually able and the mentally handicapped, males and females, those who will attend college and those who will not, the economically affluent and the economically disadvantaged, and those from rural and those from urban settings.

(9) Career education seeks to help individuals become familiar with the wide variety of work values now present in society. It imposes no single standard form of work values on any individual, but seeks to help each individual adopt some set of work values which will be personally meaningful.

(10) Career education is vitally concerned with helping individuals *implement* their own personal work values. To do this demands that in addition to *wanting* to work, individuals must also acquire the skills *necessary* to work, and having done this, must then find work that is both meaningful and satisfying to them. Thus jobs, in a generic sense, are not career education's goal. Rather, work as productive activity that holds personal mean-

ing and satisfaction for the individual is the ultimate goal of career education.

(11) The schools cannot shed responsibility for the individual just because he or she has been handed a diploma or has dropped out. While it may not perform the actual placement function, the school has the responsibility to stick with the youth until he has his feet firmly on the next rung of his career ladder, help him get back on the ladder if his foot slips, and be available to help him onto a new ladder at any point in the future that one proves to be too short or unsteady.

From these concepts it should be apparent that career education is not to be conceived of as a time segment of education such as elementary, secondary, or post-secondary education, or as a separate subject matter such as vocational education or academic education. Yet it encompasses all of these and more as a basic part of all education. It provides a specific objective — successful career performance — which is practical, achievable, and measurable and not exclusive of other legitimate objectives. It treats all honest and productive human activity as honorable and legitimates preparation for it. It requires identification of those attributes which make for lifetime career success, whether as employee or employer, laborer or professional. It involves analyses of the entire educational process to design appropriate timing and ways in which the identified attributes can be furthered. It replaces the continued postponement of consideration of career goals with encouragement of the choice of tentative goals which can be changed whenever necessary but which serve both to motivate learning and to foster maturity of purpose. It denies to the school any monopoly as a learning environment, yet gives the school a key role in identifying and coordinating all learning environments which can further the career goal. It offers accountability because its objectives are clearly defined, and its success or failure can be measured in the employment, earnings, and job satisfaction of its recipients.

The Components

Our definition at the beginning of the chapter stated the goals and contributors to career education rather than its substance. This substance should be constructed around five basic components through which the individual progresses continually throughout life. Each is equally essential, but they are listed and treated here in order of the extent to which they are a primary responsibility of the schools:

(1) The classroom in which all possible learnings are articulated in terms of their career application for both understanding and motivation

(2) The acquiring of vocational job skills, whether they are learned on the job, in a structured classroom situation, or from general life experiences

(3) Career development programs for exposure to occupational alternatives and for derivation of a work ethic and a set of work values, allowing the individual to visualize himself in various work settings and to make career decisions which appear to promise the preferred life-style

(4) Interaction among the training institutions, employing institutions, and labor organizations to provide more fertile learning environments than the schoolroom

(5) The home and family from which the individual develops initial attitudes and concepts

First Component

A clear responsibility of the school, the first component requires every classroom teacher in every course at every level to emphasize, where appropriate, the career implications of the substantive content taught. This component is twofold: It provides more effective job skills while giving meaning and relevance to otherwise abstract academic subject matter. Its goal is to make clear the importance and contribution of such content as preparation for making a living. Such an emphasis can provide positive educational motivations that will help make school a meaningful experience for all students. In brief, this component aims to help students see some relationships between that which they are presently studying and the possible careers they may choose to follow at some future time. As such, it represents a form of educational motivation for the teacher to use *in conjunction with* any other motivational devices that have worked effectively in the past.

Career education does not seek to use this form of educational motivation to replace other effective motivational procedures that classroom teachers have always used. However, this form of motivation should appeal to all students some of the time and to some students almost all of the time. If it is incorporated with all other forms of educational motivations, students could learn more substantive content. For the teacher to emphasize the career implications of substantive content holds great potential for helping all students discover reasons for learning that are directly related to the world of work outside education.

Career implications are inherent in every learning experience from preschool to graduate school and beyond. Day-care centers can begin the process and even make up for some deficiencies in the home. Helping individual children acquire a set of meaningful work values should become a major goal of the elementary school teacher. It is as easy to learn to read from primers which expose the child to the community and the world of work as it is to absorb meaningless combinations of words or to concentrate on the antics of pets.

Math teachers can use occupational examples without "watering down" the concepts, and the principles of physics can be taught while integrating their occupational applications. What better way to drive home the importance of geometry than to show that not only the mechanical engineer and the draftsman but the crane operator determining the safe lifting capacity of his machine depend upon its principles. As an illustration, a carpenter marking and cutting a rafter is applying trigonometry, and conceptually, a youth could be taught to cut a rafter as a way of demonstrating trigonometry's practical applications. If the salesgirl cannot operate the cash register without conventional arithmetic, where better to learn it?

This form of educational motivation is not intended to detract from the actual amount of time students spend in absorbing substantive content. Rather, the *time* required for providing this motivation comes from the total pool of time and effort available to every teacher for student motivation. Thus career education in no way seeks to depreciate the substantive content of the school. Instead, it seeks to assure that *more* such content will be meaningfully assimilated by the individual student.

Second Component

The second component of career education is represented by vocational skills training that will provide students with specific competencies required for successful entry (or reentry) into the occupational world. The goal of this component is to maximize the quality, appropriateness, variety, and levels of vocational skills training from which the individual can choose. Such training must be demonstrably related to existing and anticipated occupational openings and organized in ways that will allow training opportunities to change with the needs of the occupational society. This component does not require that such skills training occur in any particular institutional format. High school-level vocational classes, classes not usually thought of as vocational (art for the artist, music for the musician, and so forth), post-secondary vocational or regional vocational schools, colleges, graduate schools, apprenticeship, and on-the-job training are all routes to specific job skills.

The goal of this component is to provide students with occupational skills required to work successfully. The phrase "vocational skills training" rather than "vocational education" is used in part to emphasize the fact that any class may be vocational skills training for one or more of its students. That is, a mathematics class is vocational skills training for the prospective engineer or mathematician or skilled worker, just as a machine shop class is vocational skills training for the prospective machinist. In part, this phrase is used to emphasize the direct and substantial contributions of basic educational skills to occupational competence. That is, both students and teachers should recognize that when students learn to read, they are acquiring skills that will be required for and useful in the work they will eventually pursue as adults.

We must rid ourselves of the false notion that students do not begin to ready themselves for work until after they leave the elementary school. Moreover, we must rid ourselves of the equally false notion that in the secondary school, only those activities called "vocational education" exist to prepare students for work. Most importantly, we must rid ourselves of the false notion that only students who lack the potential for successful college completion are readying themselves for work while they are in our elementary and secondary schools.

Education as preparation for work must become an important goal of all who teach and all who learn. To provide this emphasis adds to the meaning and meaningfulness of all education without in any way detracting from any other worthy educational goal.

Third Component

A comprehensive career development program which involves the active cooperation and participation of both school and nonschool personnel is the third component. This component, involving the efforts of all educators and those of many persons outside education, aims to help students understand themselves in terms of their values, interests, abilities, and accomplishments. Moreover, it seeks to help students see relationships between these kinds of self-understandings and understandings of possible educational-occupational opportunities that are likely to be available to them. Finally, it seeks to help students make some occupational or career decisions based on these kinds of understandings. In short, it represents career education's attempt to emphasize and make meaningful the inherent right of each individual to lead his own life, to control to the maximum extent his own destiny, and to see himself as the worthy and worthwhile person he is. It includes the provision of a variety of means, both cognitive and experiential in nature, for helping students understand and reflect upon the values of a work-oriented society. In addition, this component includes systematic and continuing assistance to students in the educational and occupational choices each must make in the process of his or her career development. This assistance must encompass helping students to understand themselves, to understand the educational and occupational alternatives available to them, and to choose wisely, based on all such understandings, in ways that fully protect individual freedom of choice. Finally, this component includes helping students implement the choices they have made in ways that will bring personal satisfaction to the student and benefit to society.

Career development is a lifelong process. It may involve several successive occupational choices. As each choice is made, the individual should derive a sufficient understanding of both himself and the available alternatives so that he may choose wisely among all such options. Few decisions in life are more important than the choice of a marriage partner and the choice of an occupation. Yet what two choices are more casually made or are based upon less information?

Many in the modern urban society grow up in homes without a working household head to emulate. Others have no means of observing the workday experiences of their successful parents. Thus the school has increasing responsibility to guide the experience and exposure while protecting the freedom of meaningful choice. The school is obligated also to protect the right of the student to make a choice (rather than to defer career choice until adulthood) and to ensure that choices, once made, are not regarded by parents, teachers, and counselors as immutable.

Fourth Component

The fourth component emerges because achieving the others requires the cooperation and positive involvement of private and public employers, labor organizations, and other institutions outside the school and the home. This component assumes that neither students nor educators can learn what they need to know about work or about the relationships between education and work by insulating themselves from the real world of work outside education.

In many ways the classroom is the most sterile of possible learning environments, useful for learning abstract concepts, but with little opportunity to demonstrate "real world" applications. This component includes the provision of work observation, work experience, and work-study opportunities for students and for those who educate students in public school settings. It also involves provision of consultative and advisory services to school officials regarding the nature and needs of the occupational society. It includes training programs conducted in the business and industrial community as well as cooperative school-government-business-labor programs designed to assist students in making a successful transition from school to work. But it goes farther than that. A knowledge of the economy and its workings, of production processes, of human interaction, of the role and impact of technology, and of the complex and growing problems of the physical environment can best be learned as they are experienced. The coordination of such learnings must be accepted as the joint responsibility of formal education and the business-labor-industrial community.

Fifth Component

This component recognizes and capitalizes upon the interrelationships among the home, the family, the community, and the occupational society. The home itself is a work setting. It is also the basic consumption unit of the products of the economy and the services of the community. Basic attitudes toward work and productivity are developed in the home. Family experiences are a major influence on occupational aspirations. The school can identify and point up the meaning of the seemingly ordinary experiences from which lifelong attitudes are formed. Parents can be brought to recognize the impact of their attitudes upon the personal value systems of their children.

A wide array of potential vocational skills as well as construction and mechanical skills can also be experienced and tried out in the home — food service, interior decorating, clothing design, and so on — if these opportunities are used constructively. Students can be helped to make wise personal decisions concerning their roles as family members, as potential parents, and as members of the outside world of careers and service. Girls and women need particular help in preparing for and carrying out the complicated dual role of homemaker and careerist which is increasingly the lot and the choice of many of them. They need also to be made aware that homemaker and parent are admirable career roles, just as a career outside the home which involves neither is admirable. The choice is theirs. Young men need to learn that homemaker and parent, except for the obvious biological specialization, is as much a male as a female challenge and responsibility.

This component recognizes both the right and the responsibility of parents to care about and to influence attitudes which their children develop toward work, toward education, and toward the relationships existing between work and education. It sees the home as a place where work values and the dignity of all honest work can be taught. In addition, it recognizes that if we help students get ready to earn money, we must also help them get ready to spend it, and so assigns a consumer education role jointly to the home and the school. Finally, it recognizes the need to help parents develop and apply means of positively assisting in the career development of their children in ways that will enhance rather than detract from the goals of career education.

The Phases

The five components of career education discussed above act as intervention strategies, beginning no later than kindergarten and continuing through the adult years, to provide positive assistance to persons in their career development. Thus career education, in the continuing process of making work possible, meaningful, and satisfying to the individual, gives special attention to assisting persons as they move toward vocational maturity and the choice (and likely rechoosing) of a primary work role. Thus we can speak of vocational maturation as an integral part of the total process; vocational maturation can be pictured as occurring in growth stages which, in sequential order, include:

(1) Awareness of primary work roles played by persons in society

(2) Exploration of work roles that an individual might consider as important, possible, and probable for himself or herself

(3) Vocational decision making (which may go from a highly tentative to a very specific form)

(4) Establishment (including preparing for and actually assuming a primary work role)

(5) Maintenance (all of the ways in which one gains — or fails to gain — personal meaningfulness and satisfaction from the primary work role he or she has assumed)

Career education theorists generally see the awareness, exploration, decision-making, establishment, and maintenance stages as coincidental to and consistent with what tends to be occurring in the broader maturation of youth at the elementary, the middle/junior high, and the high school levels of the education system. The U.S. Office of Education has designed and promulgated fifteen occupational clusters — as one of many devices to focus on this sequence — into which all occupations can be conceptually subsumed:

(1) Agri-business and natural resources

(2) Business and office

(3) Communications and media

(4) Consumer and homemaking education

(5) Construction

(6) Environmental control

(7) Fine arts and humanities

(8) Health

(9) Hospitality and recreation

(10) Manufacturing

(11) Marine science

(12) Marketing and distribution

(13) Personal services

(14) Public services

(15) Transportation

The Office of Education's proposal is that elementary school children be exposed to all fifteen clusters when they are developing awareness of the world of work, that they choose a narrower, more circumscribed focus on fewer clusters for deeper exploration at the junior high school level, and that they select and train in an occupation at the senior high school or beyond. Although there are many alternatives to the cluster approach and to these particular clusters, some such conceptualization is vital as an aid to awareness and understanding of the concept of the world of employment.

The five-step process is a continuing one which most individuals will experience more than once in their lives. Indeed it must occur whenever the individual is faced with choosing or changing his or her occupation. It is tied as intimately to why an individual chooses to work as to why he or she chooses one form of work over another. It is a concept appropriate for all students at all educational levels and in almost all kinds of educational settings. It is not a process that can be assigned to any one part of the educational establishment, but rather must involve all educators at all levels in all kinds of educational settings. Similarly, it is not a process that education, as part of the total society, can accomplish by itself. Rather, it demands the active involvement of the total community of which the school system is a part.

Career Education Issues

Despite the general endorsement of career education's objectives, a number of unresolved issues remain. A few are sufficiently serious to be a source of potential opposition. The resolution of others will determine the workability of career education. On most, though not all, we are prepared to state our convictions, and do so here and in later chapters.

Scope of Career Education

Some have shrugged off the career education enthusiasm with the judgment that "it's only vocational education with a new name." Others have reacted with more alarm that "the vocational educators are trying to take over the whole of education." Support for both views can be found in various statements emanating from the U.S. Office of Education, probably because different individuals there have different views and because an idea in formation is not necessarily fixed consistently even in a single mind. In his first widely noticed statement on career education (made before the National Association of Secondary School Principals in January 1971), Dr. Marland stated: "All education is career education — or should be."

A subsequent statement (*American Education,* November 1971) put it differently: ". . . Career education should be part of the curriculum for all youth, not just some. . . ." Unfortunately, his original and other similar statements have been taken by many persons as career education's intent, though the November 1971 statement is much more accurate.

First, career education as the focus and substance of all education is untenable. Education as preparation for work was, after all, only one of the seven basic purposes of American education stated so eloquently in 1917. The other six purposes should not disappear with the advent of career education! Career education deserves attention now primarily because education as a preparation for work has been neglected for so long. Elevating the importance of that purpose neither demeans nor detracts from any of the other worthy purposes that American education has championed for so many years.

Second, to acknowledge that one's work affects his or her entire lifestyle in no way justifies contending that all education is career education. There would be equal justification for saying that all education is citizenship education, all education is health education, or even all education is sex education. To point out that one's work affects esthetic, religious, recreational, and family interests and activities only emphasizes the obvious. The emphasis tends to detract attention from the importance career education is trying to bring to the significance of education as preparation for work. To whatever extent one departs from the central and crucial importance of the four-letter word *work* in career education, he misses the essential meaning of the concept itself.

In the third place, the general public would reject the contention that all education is career education. The business-labor-industry community, on the other hand, while willing to support and participate in that part of education concerned with preparation for work, sees no vital or urgent reason for participating in all of education. Thus opposite but equally strong objections could be raised to career education by parents and labor market institutions. Why build unnecessary obstacles? Career education demands not only the support but also the involvement of the community if it is to be successful.

In the fourth place, no new educational thrust claiming to constitute all of education has ever survived. There is no reason to believe that career education has any better chance than had, for example, progressive education or life-adjustment education. The truth is, there are certain basic academic disciplines — English, mathematics, the natural sciences, the social sciences, and the humanities — that have successfully resisted every attempt of every new movement in education to assert itself as more important than the subject matter itself. There are powerful and persuasive reasons justifying the teaching of English in our school system; for example, simply because of the importance of the subject matter per se. Career education advocates may be successful in promoting it as an additional reason for studying subject matter. They will surely lose by pretending that the subject matter exists in order to impart career education concepts.

A final pragmatic reason for opposing the concept that all education is career education arises from the inevitability of some other slogan replacing career education as the number one priority of the U.S. Office of Education. If career education concentrates on picturing itself as only one of many worthy purposes of education, it is more likely to survive along with whatever new priority comes along.

Conceptually, it is as if a variety of monitors were installed within the education system. One representing the career objective would comb the entire education experience to identify those segments which could usefully contribute to career success. Other monitors would have the same assignment for citizenship, culture, family life, self-awareness, and other educational objectives. None would compete, all would cooperate, and each objective would be strengthened by pursuit and achievement of the others.

Figure 1 illustrates our image of career education's place in the education scheme of things. Career education is far more than traditional vocational education, though the latter is certainly a vital part of it. Career education is one of, but only one of, education's high priorities. We see no reason to establish priorities among careers, culture, citizenship, family life, and self-awareness as educational objectives, since none are mutually exclusive, and in fact all, if correctly understood, contribute to each of the others. The difference has been that careers, other than professional, have never been a significant objective of education in this country. However, adequate career preparation, along with vocational skills training, can never occur in the school system alone. It requires the contributions of other institutions of the total community of which the education system is only a part.

Relationship to Post-secondary Education

Because literature from the Office of Education frequently expresses the dichotomous goal of "either achieving a salable skill or being prepared for further education" at each juncture of the school system, the conclusion appears to be warranted that career education ends before

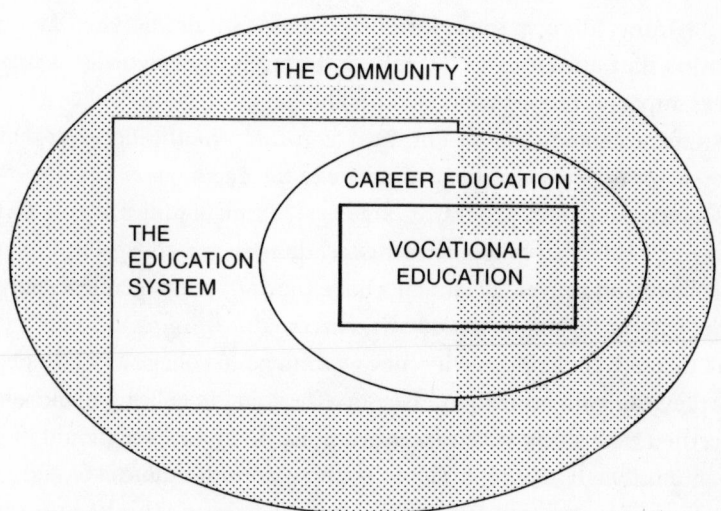

FIGURE 1. Career Education's Place in Education

college begins. It is this implication which some minority group leaders have interpreted as an intent to foreclose college attendance — and therefore access to professional, technical, and executive jobs — to the poor, the visually different, and other groups against whom society has often discriminated in the past. Their fears arise also from the reiteration of career educationists that college is not necessarily the best career preparation for everyone. "Just as we begin to get access to college education, you say it isn't needed." The concern is understandable. Any educational program can be used as an agent of discrimination. Career education's intent is to open options, not to close them. It does not argue against college training, but only against the notion that other options and those who choose them are somehow lower class.

One of the goals of career education is destruction of the societal myth that worships the baccalaureate degree as the best and surest route to occupational success. It is an educational truism that more education can lead to greater occupational success. This truism has been misinterpreted by many to mean that those with the greatest number of years of education are the most successful in our occupational society and are somehow more worthy than the others. Career education seeks to correct this misinterpretation and help all individuals see educational opportunities as differing in *kind*, not in intrinsic worth or value. It intends to enable the individual to *choose* from a wide variety of educational options rather than to settle for one of those remaining when he or she discovers that attainment of a college degree is unlikely or is undesired. It is as important to help some youth choose *not* to go to college as it is to help others choose to go. The goal is to help in the decision-making process, not to predetermine the nature of the decisions.

Career education programs have a vital and significant role to play in serving both high school students headed toward college and in helping college and university students once they arrive on a college campus. In the case of high school students, career education seeks to help them think through the reasons why they want to go to college as well as figure how they can gain admission. Reasons for going to college, while seldom concerned exclusively with career decisions, do involve, or should involve — for most high school students — these considerations. Once a student is enrolled in a four-year college or university, it is both natural and, for most, inevitable to think about how his or her college education may someday be used in the occupational society. Career education on the college and university campus seeks to help students consider career implications of their selections among courses and majors throughout their college life, rather than simply at the point when they are ready to graduate.

Some seem to feel that as career education emphasizes the career implications associated with college choices, it must simultaneously be denigrating other reasons for going to college. Nothing could be farther from the truth. Career education merely asks those students with other goals and objectives to specify them. Students have a right to know what they can gain from any kind of educational experience, be it liberal arts or career oriented in nature. They also need to know relationships that exist between education as preparation for making a living and education as preparation for living itself. Career education seeks to help students at all levels gain a better understanding of the reasons they are going to school and the ways in which their education will be useful to them after they have completed school. It in no way seeks to convince students that skills required for occupational success are more important than other kinds of educational skills.

Relationship to Vocational Education

Concern of some that career education is but a subterfuge for the expansion of vocational education is based primarily on a misunderstanding. It should be clear by now that career education is far more than vocational education. In fact, as chapter 4 points out, vocational education as now known is a part of the vocational skills training component of career education. However, the goals of career education can never be met until and unless vast improvement comes to the American system of vocational and occupational education. Career education is *not* a simple subterfuge for the expansion of vocational education. Rather, it *demands* the expansion of vocational education for both its immediate and long-run success. The fact that this is so should in no way detract from a broader conceptualization of the entire career education movement. Nor should it turn off academic educators who see no concurrent increase in funds for expanding their program. There is at present a great imbalance in the American education system. If career education is to correct that imbalance, a relatively greater amount of the education dollar must be spent for vocational and occupational education.

There is no point in emphasizing that too many high school students are enrolled in the college preparatory curriculum unless viable curricular alternatives are made available to them. There is no point in saying that too many community college students are enrolled in the college transfer program unless the students have other attractive choices for use in decision making. There is no point in lamenting the increasing problems of midcareer changes being faced by adults today unless some means is provided for helping them cope with such problems. In each instance, the most viable and obvious need is for expansion of the variety, quality, and levels of vocational and occupational education.

The Crowded Curriculum

Many teachers argue that the curriculum is already so full they have little time to teach the substantive content they know students need. They are bombarded with requests to incorporate concepts of environmental education, drug education, sex education, citizenship education, and even global education into their teaching. How (they ask) can they possibly add career education to all these other concepts and still teach the real subject matter associated with their academic field? When one adds the many interruptions that occur during the school year — special assemblies, athletic events, career days, class days, religious holidays, and so forth — one cannot help but sympathize with them.

However, career education enthusiasts emphasize that, in asking that time be devoted to discussing career implications of the subject, they are *not* asking that less time be devoted to study of the substantive content. Rather, the time they request is a portion of the time every good teacher devotes to motivating students toward studying the course content. To let students learn something with respect to how they might use that knowledge in their later vocational lives is to motivate many students to try harder to master the course content. Those teachers who are concerned about making their subject meaningful to the student are not content with simply imparting knowledge.

Career education does not ask teachers to substitute emphasizing the career implications of the subject matter for any other form of educational motivation that they have found to work in the past. It simply asks that this form of educational motivation be *added* to others that a particular teacher has found to be effective. It does not ask them to include a discussion of career implications in every daily lesson plan. There will be many days when a discussion of career implications is not appropriate and, if inserted, would be distracting and a waste of time. This form of educational motivation is one that should appeal to *all* of the students *some* of the time. The fact that it may appeal to some of the students almost all of the time is something that teachers can deal with as they become better acquainted with their students.

The goal in asking teachers to emphasize career implications of their subject matter is to help students learn more, not less, of the substantive content the teacher is trying to get across to them. If this is done correctly, students should be better prepared for college than if this form of educational motivation were to be unused. The assumption is that if students are made aware of the career implications of their subjects, increased learning will take place. This assumption has already been tested and verified in many classrooms with various groups of students. It can indeed be easily tested in any school.

Originality of Career Education

It is a natural consequence of political and bureaucratic pressure to claim originality for whatever new policies are adopted by any administration. No criticism of this practice is implied by the frequent reiteration throughout this book that career education concepts are not new. The motivation for our statement is the recognition of growing skepticism concerning sloganizing. The Office of Education's priorities in recent years, for better or worse, have made little lasting impression on American education. Innovations as well as slogans arise from other sources as well, flower briefly, and die in the tough testing ground of traditional practice. Those who must commit funds in substantial investments at the local level must be assured that the new emphasis is no temporary fad, but has a long history which is finally being recognized as a means of solving some contemporary problems. For that reason, it is important to recognize that career education has been under experiment and development for many years. Many of its applications have been in place in many locations for some time. It is arriving sooner and with more coherence because of the national leadership, but there is reason to be confident that trends will continue whatever happens to the tenure and commitment of that leadership.

Source of Funding

Vocational educators have been frequently criticized for their deliberate separateness from the rest of American education. Yet their attitudes have been responses to the generally supercilious attitude of the rest of education toward preparation for any occupation not requiring at least a bachelor's degree. To be submerged within the totality of education, they feared, would mean complete domination by academic interests. It should be noted that in attempts to bridge the gulf between the two wings of the house of education, the extended hands have been primarily vocational. To date, most of the federal funds which have been invested in the development of career education concepts have originated in vocational education appropriations. Yet vocational education commands only $1 billion of the total $85 billion annual U.S. expenditure on education. To simultaneously "generalize" vocational education and "vocationalize" general education, larger funds must be tapped, special appropriations must be supplied, or current general education funds must be reallocated. Career education emerges at a time of stringency and disillusionment with public expenditures. The traditional path to education reform by foundations and the federal government has been to supply new and additional money to be available only if used for the prescribed innovation. All too often the new departure lasted only as long as the money. Career education has a harder but, it is hoped, more durable road to follow. Its growth and survival depend upon conversion of education policy makers and reallocation of federal, state, and local funds — primarily the latter — to the pursuit of career education concepts. Career education *can* be implemented without vast amounts of new dollars. The biggest single initial expense called for is that required for in-service education of teachers, counselors, and school administrators. A second sizable financial cost will be found in the need for some school systems to expand and improve their vocational education offerings, but vocational education funds are available to help defray such costs. Career education does not, however, demand large expenditures for new materials, buildings, or staff.

It is true that in a fully implemented and comprehensive career education program, additional financial costs will eventually be required, perhaps to compensate the efforts of the business-labor-industry community and certainly to inaugurate year-round schools operating six days a week and eighteen hours a day, and serving adults as well as youth.

From a strategic viewpoint, this is no time to be asking for passage of a national career education act. In recent years, many school systems used federal funds to do still more of what had failed to work in the past. The wisest strategy now is to devote energies to building the expertise and knowledge required to make career education programs successful at the state and local levels. Once that expertise is demonstrated, Congress may be ready to consider career education legislation.

Changing Significance of Work

Some find it anachronistic that education should raise the priority of employability and productivity among its objectives just when, as they perceive it, work is of declining importance in the economy and in life. They misread the signals. Leisure has increased slowly as the fruits of productivity have been divided between higher incomes and more time off the job. But the threat is that productivity will decline, not accelerate. The four-day week is a repackaging of the standard forty hours, not a decrease of work time. Much of the rising productivity which allowed the choice between income and leisure was a product of the transfer of many workers from low-productivity agriculture to high-productivity manufacturing. The transfer of labor to service industries often has the opposite effect.

The nature of work and the work ethic is changing. Much of what was once done by hand is now done by machine. It is also true that many additional things now done by human labor could also be automated, were it not that people are willing to do these tasks cheaper. Nevertheless, it remains true that, economically speaking, "there ain't no free lunch." Individual incomes and national strength still rest upon productivity. Some can live without work only by lowering the standard of living of all. We are wealthy enough as a society to afford to support those who cannot work for a variety of reasons. We also have the wealth to support many who contribute — that is, work — in ways not measured by wages and salaries in the labor market. Still it remains true that no society can survive without work. Moreover, he who does not contribute in some way to society's welfare is a parasite, a situation more harmful to himself than to the society. If the school prepares people for life, it must prepare them for work and help them develop their own work values.

Dignity of Workers

Career education argues that all productive and honest workers should have equal dignity in their own minds and in the minds of those who receive the benefits of their work. Certainly the garbage collector's contribution to social welfare is no less necessary than that of the teacher or the lawyer, even though the focus of supply and demand may measure their market worth differently. But having said it, how many really believe it? Being told that sending their children to college is not necessary for labor market competition may do little to deter the parents who send a daughter there primarily to "catch" a white-collar or professional husband. Abolition of the present hierarchical social evaluation of the worth of various occupations will be a slow process, doubtful of achievement. But if all work cannot have equal dignity, at least all workers can gain in dignity and respect.

Timing of Career Choice

Guidance counselors have generally in recent years advocated delay in career choice until the individual has been exposed to most of the relevant alternatives and has a well-developed self-image. The career education literature advocates early tentative choice, believing it adds to motivation and to the development of decision-making skills. Achieving these values without discouraging thorough exploration of each individual's needs and capabilities requires that choice be kept tentative, options be kept open, and experimentation and change be encouraged. That overenthusiastic career education advocates may not remember this warning is illustrated by a chart in an Office of Education publicity brochure, "Career Education," which has the student examining fifteen occupational clusters in grades kindergarten through six, narrowing to three clusters for grades seven through ten, and choosing between a specific occupational area and post-secondary education by grade ten. Certainly a tenth grade view of life will be narrowly constrained, and means for constant reassessment of career choices must be built into the system both before and beyond that time.

Need for Skills Training

It is frequently argued that specific skills training should be an employer's responsibility, since he profits from the application of the skills. Given a choice, the employer will generally prefer the skilled to the non-skilled, but, it is alleged, he would have trained a person or persons for the skills if none were available. Therefore, it is argued, when an individual trained at public expense obtains a job, it is at the expense of one who would otherwise have been hired. Undoubtedly work attitudes, human relations skills, the standard communications and computation ability, knowledge of alternative career choices, and other work skills which are needed in most employment should have priority in education over skills limited in application to one employer or industry. Often the latter should be provided at the employer's expense. But there are economies of scale in skills training for employers whose businesses are too small to allow training to be conducted economically. Trained workers are also an attraction to economic development, and supply, to an extent, may create the demand. Most skills are transferable. Lack of skills training is an important contributor to the competitive disadvantages many experience in job market competition, and skills-training programs have been shown to be effective in remedying this disadvantage and offsetting others. The exact boundary between the public and private responsibility for skills acquisition should differ among locations, industries, and circumstances. But so long as employee and employer are taxpayers, they pay publicly as well as privately.

Need for Change in Traditional School Practice

Most everyone is for change until he has to do some of it. Career education, to realize its full potential, will require more change in educational practice than is often realized. The cherished Carnegie unit which uses time as the primary measure of achievement must be replaced with an objective measure of performance. The philosophy that teachers and administrators know best what is good for the student and that the customer usually doesn't know what is good for him is threatened by an open-entry/open-exit, multiple-option system. Teacher certification practices are attuned to the classroom, to lecture, to abstract subject matter, and to verbal and written learning processes, not to realistic learning environments outside the school. Teacher training institutions will experience the greatest changes. In fact, if career education succeeds, nearly every teacher and administrator will have been retrained and nearly every course prospectus and curriculum guide rewritten. New relations will exist between home, school, and work, and, to reach full effectiveness, even facilities will have to take new forms. At the same time, career education has the advantage that it can be introduced in the present classroom by a committed teacher. In a time of uncertainty in educational development, it is compatible with most presently proposed innovations. It can work in open or traditional classrooms, with or without team teaching, graded or ungraded. It lends itself to accountability. It is part of the demanded change in traditional practice, but it need not wait upon all of the other needed changes for its implementations.

Will Career Education Work?

Strong claims are being made for career education's efficacy. To the extent that the concepts are not untried, there is already evidence in experiment and demonstration. But given the high mortality rate of panaceas in recent times, it is wise to leave room for uncertainty. Some of it may not work because of being improperly done. In such a broad concept, some applications are likely to be unsuccessful. But the current experience is sufficient to promise reasonably high success probabilities to major aspects of the notion where they are carefully thought through and well administered.

Later chapters will seek to shed some light on these issues. But first, in order to demonstrate a need for change in current education practice, we must review the present social and educational scene and identify the reasons for current dissatisfaction with education's products and methods.

2 Career Education: Why We Need It

Among the reasons for believing that career education is a concept whose time has come are: (a) it has emerged at a moment when dissatisfaction with educational practices and outcomes are at a peak, and (b) it promises to attack and improve some of the apparent sources of that dissatisfaction. Whether it is successful will depend upon whether the diagnosis has been correct, the prescription proper, and the treatment competent.

A useful exploration of the demand for educational reform must identify the reasons for that dissatisfaction, test their reality, and assess their relationship to what career education reasonably can be expected to offer. It must be recognized that:

(1) Most of the dissatisfaction directed toward education is in reality frustration with social ills for which the schools bear little fault and to the solution of which they have been able to make only modest contributions.

(2) Many of American education's problems are the consequences of success, and its strengths outweigh its weaknesses.

(3) The atmosphere is permeated with demands for educational reform, and career education must be viewed in its relationship to these demands.

45

EDUCATION AND SOCIAL ILLS

The frustrations which appear to permeate the consciousness of American society are remarkable — and have been frequently remarked upon. A nation whose economy has produced wealth beyond the imagination of any people in history and has disseminated it more broadly and equally than wealth has ever been distributed appears to find little satisfaction in that relative affluence. A nation at the peak of its power is disillusioned by the uses it has made of that power. Some of these frustrations are unjustified, growing from overexpectations which could not be realized; others are valid regrets for sins of omission or commission. Few are caused solely by education, but most could be helped by its appropriate applications. Career education is specifically applicable to several.

Sources of Social Unrest

Many of our frustrations are consequences or penalties of success. We have pursued economic growth until the average American has available to him individually from twenty to forty times the goods and services available to the average Asian, African, or Latin American. But the fact that poverty by U.S. standards would be affluence elsewhere is no comfort to the 25 million American poor who compare with the affluent majority they can observe, rather than with the invisible poorer about the world. For the more affluent among the rest of us, our consciences may plague us subliminally because we know that reallocation of a fraction of our annual average increase in income could wipe out poverty in the United States within a handful of years. The launching of the minimal "war on poverty" in the first place was motivated by the fact that in that pre-Vietnam year, 1964, it was seen necessary to cut taxes and increase public expenditures by several billion dollars in some combination each year to keep the economy growing.

Those only moderately above the poverty line are frustrated, not by conscience, but by the fact that they still haven't achieved the standard of living television informs them it is their right to expect. The downtrodden historically have been notoriously docile. Violent revolutions have occurred only when people were tempted and then frustrated by real gains tantalizingly near but just beyond reach, or when they were threatened with loss of the little they had. Across the world, it is the former, not the latter, that poses the "revolution of rising expectations."

The United States finds itself at the cutting edge of a worldwide revolution in technology, living standards, and values. It is not necessary to accept everything written about it to agree that we are the first to enter a postindustrial age. The primary characteristic of the economic stage which preceded the industrial revolution was the involvement of most of the labor force directly or indirectly in agriculture. The Civil War marked the close and perhaps the immediate reason for the demise of that period in this country. The primary determinant of an economy's productiveness in that preindustrial agrarian world was the fertility of the soil. It was a natural resource-based economy in which men adapted to their environment without attempting to change it, and in which the primary source of income, wealth, and power was land ownership.

It was replaced over the following fourscore years by the industrial stage in which most of the labor force was engaged in the production and distribution of manufactured goods. Man now used the machine, both to augment his meager physical strength and to change the environment when it didn't suit him. In that world, capital resources were the most important and the "shakers and movers" were the owners of industrial capacity.

The term "postindustrial society" has become so intertwined with spectacular projections of wealth and technological impacts that realists often reject its use. Nevertheless, the number of white-collar workers in the U.S. labor force has exceeded those with blue collars for more than fifteen years, and the number providing services, governing, and processing information is now surpassing those engaged in producing and distributing foods and fibers and manufactured goods. Such an economy can hardly be accurately described too much longer as industrial. Already some outlines of this postindustrial society are clarifying. Human resources are becoming the critical ones. The wealth, power, and prestige of individuals in society are more and more determined by what these individuals know and what educational credentials they have, rather than what they own. Both the farm and the factory are controlled less and less by owners and more by professional managers. Highly trained people move freely among posts in education, government, and industry, and the boundaries between those sectors and between the private and the public sectors increasingly blur. Even the so-called energy crisis, which has reminded us all of our ultimate dependence on the endowments of nature, is a human failure — a failure to plan, ensure, and use wisely. It is no return to a preindustrial age.

But such is the human condition that growing wealth and technological power does not promote general happiness. There is no reduction in the number of problems, though there is a change in their nature. Education has been a moving force in some of these developments; its importance has been vastly augmented, but it has not changed in pace with the changes to which it has contributed.

The ramifications of this transition from preindustrial through industrial to postindustrial are pervasive, and only those most relevant to the need for career education can be treated here. Children who absorbed the accumulated "how to do it" lore of agriculture while working beside their parents were one step removed from the industrial world of work, but at least they had some idea of what "Dad did at the plant." Increasingly the world of work is some incomprehensible place to which both parents go daily, with little notion available to children of what, if anything, occurs there. While the alternative career choices have multiplied, noninstitutionalized exposure to those choices may have narrowed.

Simultaneously, there has been a shrinkage of the family structure from the extended family of the preindustrial society to the nuclear family which has increasing difficulty maintaining unity and stability in the emerging postindustrial setting. It has been in the home that children developed their basic attitudes toward work. Structural changes in the family have impinged upon the work ethic. For the labor market, one of the most deleterious impacts has been the lack of a working breadwinner as a role model in the broken homes that are the childhood and youth environments of increasing numbers.

Also characterizing the transition in the way people earn their livings is the increasing specialization of the urban society which has largely eliminated the economic role of both youth and the aged. Greater longevity and a larger proportion of aged in a society still following a policy of earlier and earlier retirement are phenomena likely to continue through the foreseeable future. It was coincidental that exploding numbers of youth struck the labor market during the 1960s just as the postindustrial trends were becoming obvious. Even had their preparation for work been adequate, it would have been unlikely that labor markets could have successfully swallowed and digested the swollen influx of youth stemming from the postwar "baby boom." That too many were obviously not prepared for the world of work made it possible to blame the schools for more than their share of the high unemployment of youth which characterized the 1960s and continues into the 1970s — a situation in which the unemployment rate of teenagers is persistently triple the average unemployment rate.

Specialization within a sophisticated technology cannot but make the workers' means of livelihood more vulnerable to change. And this sophistication increasingly means that most, not just a few, will require some formal training. Some argue cogently that we have gone too far in an assumption that more and more education is required for every job. Employers often require a high school diploma of new employees, not because the job requires such training but because they assume that the graduate is, on the average, a better employment risk than the nongraduate. Still, with growth most rapid in professional, technical, and clerical occupations, there can be no question that the proportion needing formal preemployment preparation for the job market has risen dramatically.

Urbanization has been made possible by the application of modern technology to agriculture, freeing human resources for the economy's newer thrusts. For most, the result has been higher material incomes, but the result has not always been positive for those attempting to compete in an urban labor market with a deficient rural education. Urbanization brings the advantages of close human interaction, but it also adds the irritations of congestion which is only in part a product of population growth. The source of the remainder is the inherent tendency to congregate in the most economically attractive areas — attractive, that is, within the incentives of a private enterprise system which fails to measure social costs adequately. In the wealthiest of societies, the threat is not starvation, but a loss of sense of community as populations compete irritably for space.

Among the many paradoxes of our society is the fact that the traditional work ethic encouraged development of a technology in pursuit of profit which produced abundance; this abundance in turn threatens the work ethic which was its source. Beyond the creature comforts, the consequences of wealth appear to be a revolution of rising expectations among the poor, a growing sense of ennui among the well-to-do, the threat of consumerism to the environment, and the temptations of power in the political process. Each of these deserves brief comment.

Those with low incomes, though usually remarkably docile, occasionally lash out in frustration at their inability to grasp wealth seemingly just out of reach. Even those who are the middle income group are frustrated because they cannot afford the standard of living which mass communications media intimate is the norm, while those in the upper 5 percent of income earners consider themselves the middle class. The last mentioned can take pride in having pursued material wealth and achieved it, but their offspring, having never been without it and deprived of the challenge of achievement, find in it little satisfaction. All three groups are "up tight" about education. The evidence is that the poor are far from apathetic; they just don't know how to help their children at home or to manipulate the political system which maldistributes educational resources. Those with earnings actually in the middle of the income distribution — around $8,000 to $12,000 — rightly see education as a prerequisite for upward mobility. Without recognizing it, the higher income groups are "up tight" because they are the first wealthy people in history with no way of guaranteeing wealth for their children. Those who attained wealth in land or industrial capacity could leave it as an inheritance. Those whose high incomes accrue to their personal talents and specialized knowledge can offer no bequest other than similar education and training to their children. Yet the education which brought material comfort to the parents may be inadequate for or even unwanted by the children.

Even the segregation of housing in modern U.S. cities has a base in education. To the extent that education determines income, while land prices and zoning laws insist that housing be strictly segregated by price, the children of the educated and the uneducated will grow up knowing and competing with no one but their peers. The Coleman report has demonstrated the penalties of this phenomenon. Recent court cases have documented the differences in property tax revenues which help perpetuate the inequalities in education and income.

The listing of social ills, most of them penalties of success, could continue almost endlessly. Take a few more examples:

(1) Wealth and technological power back the temptations of many politicians to overextend in international affairs.

(2) Relative poverty (more frustrating than its absolute level) continues because the affluent are unwilling to even narrow the margin of their prerogatives. As an oversimplified example, if the nonpoor were willing to accept 2.5 percent rather than 3 percent as their average increase in living standards and could find an effective way to allocate the one-half of 1 percent to the poor, poverty in the United States by present standards would be wiped out in our nation in less than five years. But since we will not or cannot share, we insist on elevating the whole income structure in order to boost the incomes at the bottom. To do so has two fallacies. It maintains or expands the relative poverty, and it multiplies the gross national product, adding all the threats of excess consumption with its depletion of natural resources and pollution of the environment.

(3) Pollution and ecological destruction as an issue arises from success in doing exactly what our economic system has always told us to do — pursue self-interest in competition with others. Spewing wastes into the atmosphere and streams is a means of reducing production costs. The automobile, solid wastes, and undue crowding of public recreation facilities are a few of the consequences of private consumption which does not consider social cost. The developer of tract housing that destroys and clutters an irreplaceable landscape is following the same urge which built the nation. Perhaps Americans have one additional ecological sin not elsewhere present — a frontier psychology which assumes natural resources to be inexhaustible. "Use it up and move on" has been a national heritage. Now appears a shattering blow to national ego: The affluent society reneges on its own promises. After celebrating for a generation the advent of superabundance, we suddenly face shortages of seemingly everything — particularly the energy sources upon which the output of abundance depends. We are still immensely rich by any available comparison in time and space. But having thought we could have everything — and behaving as if we could — we collide against constraints and suddenly feel poor.

(4) Modern economic knowledge is now such that any sophomore enrolled in an elementary course knows how to reduce unem-

ployment; but the most knowledgeable scholar or economic policy maker does not know how to do so without accelerating inflation.

(5) Most difficult is a subtle but insidious challenge to the traditional basis of society. Consider just two examples: (a) It is not enough that scientific knowledge appears to challenge many of the taboos which guarded such values as sexual morality and the sanctity of marriage and home. The consciousness of a divine presence which explained mysterious phenomena to superstitious primitive man did not keep him from personal combat with his enemies. However, it must require at least a subconscious rejection of the concept of divinity to justify raining mass technological destruction and death in pursuit of political objectives. (b) Throughout man's long history of near subsistence living, a condition which still prevails for most of the world's population, just staying alive was reason enough for being alive. Now for the first time, the majority in a whole society has been able to stand erect from unending toil and near starvation, look life in the face, seeking for its meanings, and conclude that it has none. Mind-expanding drugs, "copping out," dropping out, hedonism, radically changing life-styles, and altered commitments cannot completely blot out that terrifying blankness.

(6) At a more mundane but no less important level, a new sense of unrest is noted in the workplace. Much of it may be exaggerated by industrial sociologists, psychologists, and consultants pleased at an opportunity to expand their own roles. Disenchantment with the assembly line is no new phenomenon, and that type of employment is declining as a proportion of the total. Confusion is evident in the Labor Department's *Manpower Magazine* lamenting:

> . . . pay is at an all time high, but worker dissatisfaction is metamorphosing . . . into a fire-breathing dragon as workers begin translating their dissatisfactions into alienated behavior. Turnover rates are climbing, despite rising wage levels. Absenteeism has increased as much as 100 percent in the past 10 years in the automobile

industry. Workers talk back to their bosses. They no
longer accept the old authoritarian ways . . . (Herrick,
1972).

Yet the *Monthly Labor Review* rebuts Herrick's claims. Available statistics do not support much of the scare talk about worker discontent. Labor turnover is not experiencing a secular rise; absenteeism is up about 10 percent over a five-year period. Strike activity can be explained by a variety of circumstances, and little of it is related to working condition issues. Productivity has been down and up cyclically, following its familiar pattern. Labor force participation has not declined for men during their out-of-school, pre-retirement years and has risen for women (Wool, p. 41). As one might expect, the young are more dissatisfied with their jobs than the middle-aged, the black than the white, the lower paid than the higher paid. Dissatisfaction rises with education levels. Women are more dissatisfied with their jobs than men. The higher absenteeism is an international phenomenon. Older workers appear more satisfied with their jobs than younger ones, and the retired reflect great dissatisfaction with their lives. Employers report that they are dealing with a new breed of worker, one less easily satisfied by pay and caring more about the meaningfulness of work. However, they also report a reduced commitment to work. Many are reversing the long-term trends toward job simplification and are experimenting with job enrichment as an answer. There appears to be among employers a suspicion that the schools are at least partly at fault for not stressing the values of work.

Labor Market Trends

These developments are long run, but they have reached the level of consciousness within the last generation. All are penalties of success and sources of frustration. None were primarily caused by education's shortcomings. In fact, problems often arose because the school system taught us exactly what it was told to teach us. It responded no more and no less readily to new imperatives than the rest of society. Trends which are labor market oriented and of most relevance here were accelerated by World War II. To feed and arm ourselves and our allies along with the demands of our civilian population, while sending more than eleven million of our prime-age, male labor force off to war, required exigencies that turned out to be irreversible. Excess rural labor was transferred to urban production, and the process of capitalization in agriculture was speeded to free still more. The rate of increase of output per man-hour in agriculture leaped from 1 to 6 percent a year and has averaged around 5 percent for the past quarter-century. The pace of technological change throughout the economy was speeded, and that process continued at the new pace during the postwar period. Women entered the labor force in unprecedented numbers and never went back exclusively to the kitchen.

Then in the postwar period, the GI Bill sent unprecedented numbers to college, and an education cycle began in which, since educated people were available, all others needed education to compete. A new technology was created which assumed a well-educated labor force and therefore demanded it.

Important shifts occurred in the patterns of migration and the structure of cities. Throughout industrialization, the movement had been from farm to city, but the migrants were Europeans arriving in industrialized American cities. As poor people, they sought the cheapest housing. But the tenements were in the central cities, and so were the unskilled and semiskilled jobs. After World War II, the migration was internal from farm to city. But by now, many of the immigrants were black and, later, of Spanish-speaking background. They still sought the oldest and cheapest housing in the central cities; but the new technology demanded single-floor, continuous-process factories. And the necessary land at reasonable prices and acceptable taxes was in the suburbs, as were the skilled and technically trained workers. Public policy — agricultural price supports at one end and federally insured housing at the other — stimulated the trends. The new immigrants could not afford housing where the jobs were, and all too often were denied, through prejudice, the opportunity to rent or purchase what they could afford. Transportation systems were designed to bring the white suburbanites to downtown white-collar jobs, rather than distribute central city dwellers to suburban employment opportunities. Schools which had contributed to Americanization of European immigrants did not successfully industrialize and postindustrialize the American minority poor.

All these trends seemed to converge during the 1960s. A more rapidly growing labor force and rising productivity required — if unemployment was not to rise from unabsorbed new entrants and displaced workers — economic growth rates 50 percent above the traditional norm. A growing proportion of teenagers and women made the labor force more volatile, leaving the labor market when jobs declined and returning with a rush as jobs became available, seeking jobs in June and abandoning them in September, and often preferring and seeking part-time jobs and those with odd hours. The combination of increasingly sophisticated technology, the growth of white-collar jobs, and the competition of rising educational attainment created a demand for remedial manpower programs. The objective was to improve the employability of those experiencing a variety of disadvantages in the competition for jobs. But the remedial emphasis was largely unaccompanied by preventive measures. The effort was to siphon off the disadvantaged from the labor market pool without staunching the flow of underprepared people into it.

It was never clear what proportion of the unemployment and low incomes was attributable to the worker's own lack of employability skills, motivation, or other shortcomings and what was the fault of labor market institutions biased against the various groups among whom unemployment and poverty were concentrated. At any rate, blacks consistently had double the unemployment rate of the average, with youth experiencing triple the average rates and black youth suffering six times the average. Among the 5,200,000 poor families, more than two out of five were in that situation because they had no employable family head, over one-third because unemployment reduced their annual incomes, while one out of five had family heads working full time, full year who could not earn their way out of poverty. All these were labor market phenomena. Education might or might not share blame and might or might not supply remedies, but there was no doubt that society expected the schools to do more than they in reality could.

Then after being blamed for the unemployment of the underprepared, education seemed to fail in its promises to those who had hearkened most. A college diploma had come to be assumed a guarantee of employment opportunities. Suddenly the unemployment rates of college graduates began to rise, not to the 7 percent the total labor force suffered in the early 1970s, but an unprecedented doubling to roughly 2 percent. Starting from behind and pursuing a moving target, suppliers of highly educated manpower had pursued rising demand for a quarter-century. In retrospect, overshooting even a rising trend line is not surprising. It was largely coincidence that the convergence of the supply and demand trend occurred just as an economic recession coincided with a cutback in federal research and development expenditures, and more than a decade of declining birthrates reduced the demand for schoolteachers. But no matter who's to blame for faulty foresight, the schools were victims of further disenchantment.

All of this is a stereotyped oversimplification as any generalization is likely to be, but it is sufficiently representative to give understanding to what happened. It was in this same period and from these same forces that unprecedented growth and prosperity were failing to challenge the spiritual needs of the more affluent majority of the society.

None of these social ills is the fault of education. Yet we expect education to make major contributions to solving them all. We have been experiencing both overexpectation and underachievement. Education cannot solve all of these problems, but it can make greater contributions than it has. Before moving on to an inventory of education's specific shortcomings, it is useful for perspective to note a few of its preeminent achievements.

ACHIEVEMENTS OF EDUCATION IN THE UNITED STATES

It is only in the past few years that education has been seen by the general public as a means of solving most of the problems outlined above. At the turn of the century three generations ago, only a small majority of wild-eyed reformers believed that schools could or should teach much more than the elements of reading, writing, and arithmetic. As education has been assigned the solution of more and more problems, it has experienced its own revolution of rising expectations. As more and more has been accomplished, the public expects still more, and expects the "still more" to happen faster and better. Our rising expectations for education tend too often to obscure our view of the very real achievements.

The achievement which is the easiest to document is the enormous increase in the amount of education. Currently sixty million are enrolled in some portion of our education system. The average member of the

U.S. labor force has 12.3 years' education, putting even those who go no farther than high school in a minority position. Two-thirds of American workers are now high school graduates, compared to one-half a little over a decade ago. In 1953 only 48 percent of the high school students finishing in the top quarter of their classes entered college. As long ago as 1960 that figure had reached 80 percent. Whereas in 1955 only 58 percent of those who started high school graduated, by 1970 that figure was approaching 80 percent. Higher education enrollments more than doubled in less than a decade, growing from one-third to 45 percent of the 18 to 21 age population in that period. The result of all these factors has been that the total cost of education has risen enormously, from $3 billion to an estimated $85 billion per year over a thirty-year period. The proportion of the gross national product devoted to education has more than doubled, from 3.4 to 7.1 percent, in the last twenty years. No other nation can even approach this record.

The rapid increase of man's knowledge has imposed burdens on the schools which they appear to have met rather well. Elementary school children often have a far better working knowledge of ecology, science, mathematics, philosophy, nutrition, and economics than their parents. One of the major causes of communications problems between youth and adults lies in the different language and values held by youth as a result of the school's success in teaching independent thinking. It may even be that part of youth's unwillingness to accept the moral values of the parent stems from repeated demonstration that the parent's factual and scientific knowledge is too fallible to be a dependable guide. Why accept a father's dictum on the "thou shalt nots" when it is obvious that he cannot answer a simple question about primary arithmetic or chemical values?

Not only have we expected the school to teach more about each of the traditional school subjects, but we frequently add subjects to the school curriculum. The school is a better teacher of driving than parents; the reduction of automobile accidents has important social and economic effects, and a new subject is added to the school curriculum. Society expects similar benefits from such new subjects as sex education, drug education, and consumer education. Subjects taught traditionally in colleges, such as economics, sociology, psychology, statistics, and calculus, are taught now in high schools and even in elementary schools, and the results generally have been excellent. Colleges report that students are better prepared than they have ever been, and introductory college courses gradually are being dropped in recognition of these qualifications. In 1950 for example, calculus was offered as an intermediate or advanced course by most college math departments. By 1970 it became an introductory course. It is no accident that great scientific breakthroughs and their engineering applications have occurred in the nation where the commitment to education has been the greatest. Where nations have pursued a narrow range of scientific endeavor through production of a limited number of specialists, their achievements, though impressive, have been narrowly constricted. In the United States they have been widely pervasive.

One of the early successes of the schools was the education of immigrants and the children of immigrants who quickly learned a new language and perhaps too quickly accepted new values and discarded their own. One can argue whether this sudden change in language and values was desirable, but there is no doubt that the school was able to do largely what society expected it to do.

Similar successes have been recorded within the limited range of vocational programs which have been taught in school. Graduates of the vocational curriculum in high schools have unemployment rates that are about one-third as high as those of nonvocational graduates. When graduates from equal socioeconomic backgrounds are compared, the vocational graduates also have higher job satisfaction and higher annual earnings. These advantages are not short-lived but persist throughout the period covered by thorough longitudinal studies which have now continued for ten years.

DEFICIENCIES IN AMERICAN EDUCATION

Despite the very real accomplishments of schools in this country, serious weaknesses remain, particularly in the contributions they are expected to make to a work-oriented society. Federal legislation, viewed as solutions to these difficulties during the decade of the 1960s, has been ameliorative, but being primarily remedial in emphasis, has not achieved basic reform. Promises of the 1960s demand performance in the 1970s. In particular, the fifty million American families for whom work is necessary, but college unlikely or inappropriate, demand alternatives that will offer them status, security, satisfaction, and success. They should not wait much longer.

At the heart of their problems is societal worship of a college degree as the surest and most respectable route to occupational success. This attitude is as dangerous as it is false. When less than 20 percent of the population have been able to attain what nearly 100 percent of the population have been led to believe is desirable, it is inevitable that the majority must be dissatisfied with their lot. A viable democracy cannot afford to lead four-fifths of its emerging population to consider themselves as second-class citizens. Unrest is sure to exist when only one-third can try and less than one-fifth attain what more than nine-tenths regard as the optimal pattern of education as preparation for work. Yet this is what is occurring: A little more than three-fourths of youth complete high school, one-half of those enter college, and one-half, in turn, graduate — a proportion surprisingly close to the 20 percent of current jobs which are held by college graduates. Even many of the one-sixth who graduate from college are disappointed when they discover the irrelevance of much of what seemed to have had such great promise.

At a deeper level, this attitude has resulted from the erroneous application of a generally sound educational principle; namely, that more education can lead one to be better prepared to work. The principle is sound only if one recognizes that the optimal amount of education required as preparation for work will vary widely from occupation to occupation, and from person to person within an occupation. Furthermore, the worth of an occupation, and hence of its workers, is more properly judged by its societal contributions than by the amount of formal education required for entry into that occupation. Failure to recognize that expertise can be attained and should be rewarded in any occupation is an essential accompaniment of this misapplication. Education has other values and contributions than career preparation, and they should not be denied to any who want them. But the objectives should be clearly differentiated with no overpromise or false expectations.

The American system of formal education, in its basic structure, philosophy, and methodology, has been a major contributor to this societal attitude and must accept a major share of the blame for the unfavorable personal and social impacts. If American education can and will change, it can become a major contributor toward the goal of eradicating this attitude in our society.

To charge that college education has been overemphasized in work preparation to the extent that those youth who do not pursue it are often considered "second class" is not a denigration of the values of a college education for those who want it. Nor is it an intimation that a college education's only worth is its job preparation role. It is a plea for acceptance of a greater variety in life-styles and in types of career preparation. It also represents a conviction that college itself would be more meaningful if it were not considered a hurdle to be reached and overcome as soon as possible.

The basic directional change needed at the present time is the insertion of successful preparation for work as a major objective of education at every level and in every kind of setting. In terms of educational purposes, that objective simply means emphasizing education as preparation for making a living. There is nothing new about the goal. Historically, the two basic purposes of education have been: (a) preparation for living and (b) preparation for making a living. What is new is the relative emphasis placed on these goals as basic purposes of American education. In practice, the first has vastly overshadowed the second. No suggestion is being made here that the first be replaced by the second. Rather, we are pleading for changes that will recognize and implement their mutual importance.

Operationally, the problem is even bigger. If, in terms of educational philosophy, the prime purpose of American education has been preparation for living rather than preparation for making a living, in practice, education's prime purpose has seemed simply to be education. That is, in the eyes of the typical classroom teacher, the prime operational purpose of education has seemed to be readying students for more education. To halt this "school for schooling's sake" emphasis in American education, it will be necessary that the purpose of education in every classroom be clearly seen as preparation for living, as preparation for making a living, or, in most cases, as some combination of these two basic purposes.

The positive promise of career education can be translated into concrete attainment only if one first recognizes and corrects certain basic roadblocks in the current structure of American education.

The Roadblocks

The first roadblock lies in the fact that the organizational, administrative, and fiscal policies of public education are rooted in acceptance of the false attitude regarding the value of a college education that we have said must be overcome. Status among professional colleagues, salary differentials, and professional advancement possibilities are influenced to a very large extent among educators by the number of degrees held and the number of college credits accumulated. Further status among teachers is acquired by those whose academic specialties require the greatest amount of scholastic aptitude to master. Teachers, educational specialists, and school administrators are certificated and employed based to a considerable extent upon the college degrees they hold or the number of hours of college credit they have accumulated.

This deficiency is especially serious in that it is most evident in the professional preparation route one must take to become a prime decision maker in the education system; e.g., a school superintendent. Little wonder that superintendents favor the college preparatory over the vocational aspects of the curriculum. When one recognizes that in community after community, the local board of education to whom the superintendent reports is loaded with adults who have sought the college preparatory curriculum for their children and expect them to pursue careers that will require it, it is even less a wonder. Public educational policy on the local level has for years been dominated by a small minority of the public to whom the college preparatory curriculum seems most appropriate.

No sensible person would suggest correcting this deficiency by eliminating academic requirements for those who work as professionals in public education. Certainly, this represents an occupational area for which college preparation is appropriate for most workers. Three needed directions for change, however, would seem to be obvious. First, we must eliminate the absolute necessity for college degrees and college credits as a requirement for progress as an educator. Alternative routes to the acquisition of competence must be recognized, utilized, and rewarded. Second, control of public education must be returned to the real majority of our citizens. The national landslide of defeats for local school board issues in the last few years clearly indicates dissatisfaction with the system as it now exists. A more positive way of expressing citizens' views must be found. Third, conscious and conscientious efforts must be aimed at helping educators rid themselves of the attitude that a college degree represents an ultimately desirable goal for all.

The second roadblock lies in the overutilization of time, and an underutilization of performance, as a criterion for accomplishment. This deficiency can be seen everywhere in American education. For example, operationally, the prime way of identifying youngsters who "belong" in the fourth grade is by specifying those who have spent nine months in the third grade. High school diplomas typically are awarded on an accumulation of sixteen Carnegie units, each of which is defined in terms of the amount of time devoted to a particular subject. The entire apprenticeship system in the United States is rooted in devotion to a concept that counts the time an individual has devoted to a particular task or set of tasks. College degrees, like high school diplomas, are awarded, based on counting a form of Carnegie units that are operationally defined in terms of a time dimension.

Educational accomplishment must come to represent more than perseverance. Students cannot be expected to remain as disinterested parties while others determine their educational goals and assess their educational accomplishments. The establishment of differing educational goals having differing standards of attainment and differing times required for completion for different individuals must become a reality. Performance goals, jointly established by student and teacher, are badly needed as a routine part of all education. Only through establishment of such performance goals and application of realistic approaches to assessing their accomplishment can American education make sense to its students, its teachers, and to the general public. The technology for this change is already present. It is time that it be applied.

If the importance of time could be minimized and the importance of performance maximized, the way would be clear for extending the concept of the ungraded school, now present primarily only in elementary education, to all American education. In turn, this would make available ways of operationally implementing an open-entry/open-exit system that would allow multiple opportunities for combining education, work experience, part-time jobs, and full-time employment in a meaningful way. It would open the way to the creation and implementation of shorter units of educational performance that would be more meaningful and more acceptable to the "now" generation that seems to value immediate reward above delayed need gratification. It would do much to eliminate both the concept and the stigma attached to what must soon become an

WHAT IT IS AND HOW TO DO IT   63

obsolete term in American education — the "school dropout." It would allow a meaningful integration of vocational skills into the total school curriculum in such a fashion that they could become a possible choice for all students. It would eliminate the necessity for some colleges and universities to specify and impose upon the high school so much time in certain college preparatory courses that those who wish to attend college after high school are deprived of an opportunity for choosing vocational subjects. All this is possible if the roadblock of time can be eliminated.

The third roadblock is continuing acceptance of the assumption that elementary and secondary education must take place, for most students, during only nine months in any given calendar year and only in a school building. American elementary and secondary education must become a twelve-month operation and must take place in the occupational world as well as in the school. This of course is not to say that all students should be required to attend school for twelve months a year. If the time deficiency mentioned above could be corrected, there is no reason why, with an open-entry/open-exit system, any given student could not be in and out of formal education at various times in any given year. To eliminate this deficiency would provide, for those students desiring it, ample opportunity to combine education as preparation for employment with employment itself. It would not dump all students upon the labor market simultaneously at the close of the school year. It would make possible a system whereby classroom teachers could spend part of their time employed in other occupations without imposing an impossible summertime load on employers. Business, service, labor, and industrial personnel could spend part of their time instructing in the schools. It would make possible an exchange system between school administrators and those from business and industry that would hold positive potential for helping all concerned. The possibilities of devising these and a host of other means of bridging the gap between education and work are very great indeed. This roadblock too must be removed.

The fourth deficiency is the fact that public education now exists primarily for the benefit of youth. In these times of rapid technological and occupational change, public education must provide continuing opportunity for the public. Adult education — including general, recreational, and occupational education — must become an integral part and a major responsibility of public education. For this to happen, the doors of our elementary and secondary schools, as well as the doors of all post-high school institutions, must be open to the public eighteen hours a day, six days a week. If the concept of the ungraded school could be implemented, there is no reason why people of differing ages could not learn together. If the false worship of degrees as necessary qualifications for all instructors could be eliminated, there is no reason why our schools could not be staffed, in part, by persons who have acquired competencies outside the colleges. If the schools devote themselves to the task of readying youth for today's occupational world, there is no reason why they should not be simultaneously involved in retraining adults for that same world.

We cannot, in these times, afford to retain the outmoded concept that at some magical point in time a person "finishes" his education. Elimination of this fourth roadblock could help us quickly eradicate this concept. The current three separate systems of public education for those preparing for work, manpower retraining for those seeking new work, and welfare for those who cannot work must be combined in a single system for all the people. The system needed is one that provides a continuing cycle that will drastically reduce the operational validity of concepts of long-term unemployment and families on welfare in the United States. To the extent that education, welfare, and manpower programs in effect compete among themselves, they each fail to serve the public. Elimination of such competition can come only through a single, unified system built around the continuing, lifelong career development needs of the individual. Substantive programs of career education can make effective impact on the societal conditions noted earlier only if they are accompanied by correction of each of these four major roadblocks currently existing in American education.

Needed Basic Changes

The schools have done quite well what we have told them to do, but we have not insisted that they do a number of things which are important to society. Career education is a means for remedying some of these deficiencies, but it may also be that introducing career education without remedying those weaknesses which remain could foreordain its failure. Some of the more pressing of these weaknesses should be noted and discussed.

Individualized Instruction

As the schools have enrolled a larger and larger proportion of the school-age population, it has been inevitable that the range of student interests and abilities has increased markedly. Even in the elementary school, the inclusion of migrants, handicapped, and poor has widened the range of student abilities. The amount of individualized instruction required to cope with this increased range of need has not increased correspondingly.

In the elementary school the average class size is more than thirty, and a high school teacher may work with 150 students each day. Ideally, each of these students should be proceeding at different rates, learning material which has been adapted to meet his special interests and abilities; but we have not developed economical ways to let this occur. In contrast, college football often has ten coaches to work with a fifty-man team, and factory-operated automobile repair schools have six trainees per instructor.

One way of individualizing instruction is to provide a variety of instructional programs in which students can enroll. In 1900, 80 percent of high school graduates went to college; almost all of these received bachelor's degrees. There was only one curriculum in high school. It prepared everyone for college. Today 50 percent are prepared for college, but only 20 percent get a bachelor's degree. Around the time of World War I a limited amount of vocational training began to be included in the high school. This was gradually increased in breadth, but at no time has there been room for more than 25 percent of the students. The third addition to the high school was the general curriculum. Having no real goals, it enrolls about 25 percent of the high school graduates, but it also produces, according to limited evidence, 70 percent of the high school dropouts, 88 percent of the Manpower Development and Training Act trainees, and over 78 percent of the inmates of correctional institutions (Pucel, p. 29; Galloway, 1971; and Combs and Cooley, 1970).

In the elementary school and junior high school there is still only one curriculum. It is essentially designed to prepare students to enter college. It is a system of "school of schooling's sake," with each level of schooling preparing primarily for the next stage until graduate school ends the process. When the junior high school principals in a large state were asked to indicate the major goal of their schools, well over half said that the goal was to prepare students for college, not for success in either high school or work. In effect, then, the first eight to ten years of school are designed to prepare everyone for a goal which will be achieved by less than a fifth of them. One way of looking at this is to say that there has been an 80 percent failure rate. It is probably more factual to report that young people recognize the reality that only 20 percent of the existing and foreseeable jobs require a baccalaureate degree. It is the education system, prodded by the parents, which has not recognized labor market realities. Of course, higher education has other objectives than the ones which lead to employment, but there is little conclusive evidence that these are better achieved.

The Nature of the Learning Environment

It is difficult to imagine a more sterile learning environment that involves fewer stimuli than the formal classroom. It is expensive to construct and maintain, yet can serve little purpose other than a convenient location to impart abstract or rote learning. Yet the world outside the classroom is replete with learning situations, most of which are without cost to the learner.

Like many social institutions, education has been organized and structured with deep roots in the past. There has been a tendency to view education as something apart from the rest of life — as a process that only occurs in classrooms from 8:00 a.m. to 3:00 p.m., nine months of the year. While we recognize individual differences in interests, maturity, and learning styles, education continues to be organized according to age and specific grade levels, subject matter is structured into neat little packages pretentiously labeled as disciplines, and learning is divided into a set of uniform forty- to fifty-minute time blocks that begin and end in response to a bell. So long as we view education as taking place primarily in a classroom or in a school at a specific time in a single subject area and grade level, the traditional structure may be adequate. But when nonschool interests suggest that the schools provide instruction in drug dangers, environmental management, or consumer education, there is an understandable reluctance to add another subject to an already overcrowded curriculum.

This reluctance on the part of educators will persist so long as schools continue to be structured so that they impose artificial constraints of time and space and a limited body of knowledge. So long as this structure prevails, the educator will hold himself or herself responsible for covering a fixed amount of material over a set period of time. The goal for third grade teachers will be preparing students for the fourth grade, and senior high school English teachers will measure their effectiveness according to the number of their students who successfully pass freshman English in college. Achievement of academic credentials is accepted as proof of education's worth without demonstrating its contribution to economic, social, and personal performance. Thus, so long as one perceives of education within the framework of fixed time, limited space, and specialized subject matter, changes in curriculum will be difficult to introduce because every new community need will not be viewed as an opportunity to relate specialized subjects to a topical and relevant issue. Conversely, contemporary problems will be viewed as another effort to overload the curriculum and shorten the time of instruction for what is and has been taught in the past. New problem areas and new information will be seen as fads and not as opportunities to provide relevance. This is the principal reason for the brief longevity of new educational slogans and the programs which were supposed to accompany them.

The needs of students and adults in today's world are much too expensive and complex for schools to continue to function as they have in the past. Unfortunately, over time, and particularly over the past few decades, some local and state education systems have become so big and contain so many parts that it is not uncommon to get lost before one can focus on what is the most essential part of education: the learning environment. Federal aid to education, state boards of education, school administrators, facilities, and teacher certification may all be necessary to a well-run school system, but they are still paraphernalia in relation to what counts most; that is, what happens between students and teachers. It has been noted that minority parents are no more anxious than others to send their children to school outside their own neighborhoods. They consent to the practice because they hope that at the end of the bus ride there is a quality learning environment, something too often not available in their own schools.

It is the learning environment that stimulates discovery and encourages curiosity. That is where the lights go on or where they get turned off. Unfortunately, and too often, some environments demand of the learner a conformity and set of responses to a specific code of behavior and performance invented in an earlier society and useful only in an era long past.

Public institutions are supposed to serve the public interest — if not all the public, at least the majority interests. If this is so, why are schools structured and instruction organized in such a way that they emphasize the college bound at the expense of the vast majority who do not plan a university education? The only alternative in most school systems is either to postpone any sort of career decision and enroll in the college preparatory or general curricula or to make a decision to specialize in a vocational field at age thirteen or fifteen, though the school has provided little knowledge or information upon which to base choice of a vocational field. No matter how high the quality of instruction available in either college preparatory or specialized programs in vocational education, if the needs of the great majority of students are not being met, then the schools and the students they serve are both failing to meet their potential.

Segregation

It is now generally accepted that racial segregation interferes in a major way with learning, especially in metropolitan areas. But of equal importance are socioeconomic segregation and segregation based on sex.

The college preparatory curriculum ordinarily enrolls students of higher socioeconomic status than does the vocational curriculum, while the general curriculum students are more likely to be from an intermediate range of economic backgrounds. Whenever this distribution of students occurs, separate vocational high schools tend to segregate students socioeconomically. The Coleman report suggests that such segregation has a greater effect in retarding learning than does racial segregation or the quality of facilities and instruction. The reasonably good results achieved by separate vocational high schools may mean that the absence of a general curriculum from such schools and the presence of unusually capable vocational administrators nearly offset the disadvantages created by socioeconomic segregation. Even in "comprehensive" high schools, socioeconomic segregation can be created by keeping vocational and college preparatory students in separate wings of the school and refusing to allow them to enroll in common courses.

Segregation based on sex tends to reflect in vocational education the segregation which exists on jobs. Most business, distributive, health occupations, and home economics students are female. Most industry and agriculture students are male. Where this segregation is based on student choice, it can perhaps be tolerated. But in far too many cases it is based on rigid exclusion of one sex by teachers and counselors.

Failure to Explore Work Ethics

Teaching values in public education programs is a difficult task. Because values are by nature controversial, most schools have stopped teaching them, except for a few academic values which relate to cheating on tests, giving incorrect information for school records, plagiarism, and the like. A major casualty has been consideration of work ethics and work values and emphasis on quality of work, promptness, diligence, and similar characteristics of the "good" worker.

Preceding stages of economic history have produced value systems to provide needed incentives. An economy based on land, the original source of ownership of which was usually conquest, could be justified only by some form of divine right. A work ethic which explained social status as the will of God and promised rewards in the hereafter to the peasant, serf, or slave most docile in the present served nicely. Early capitalism needed incentives for frugality, self-denial, investment, and productivity — it needed what we came to know as the Protestant work ethic.

To teach a work ethic appropriate to an early stage of capitalism in its original form might cause problems for society and for the school. The present system is better described as consumerism than capitalism, and old-style frugality could wreck it. A part of the youth culture rejects every type of work ethic. The industrial work ethic is eroding, and a postindustrial work ethic has yet to develop. But it seems indefensible to fail to teach youth that employers do value the traditional work ethic and that major violations of it will lead to discharge. The failure of the school becomes more serious as the home and the peer group seem less and less able to teach the needed lessons. The high rate of job changing and unemployment which characterize dropouts and nonvocational graduates prior to about age 25 may be largely explained by this failure.

Evidence is strong that attitudes are formed most efficiently early in life. Therefore, a work ethic must at least be introduced in early childhood and in elementary education programs. However, before an appropriate work ethic can be taught, one must be developed. Because frugality is not so vital and there is now less sweat on fewer brows does not mean that productivity and achievement have less critical roles. Leisure time is not increasing as rapidly as many people assume it is, but that which is available provides more time for volunteer services that can be challenging over a period of time. It is paradoxical that an aging society encourages early retirement and a service society gives low status to personal services. At least four elements must appear in the new work ethic which philosophers must develop and teachers must teach: the values of volunteer activity, the dignity of all workers, the satisfactions of human service, and the necessity of careers based upon multiple occupations. Above all, it will emphasize that we are what we achieve, whether in service or in character development.

Early Childhood Education

It is not clear just why children traditionally have begun school at age six. It may be related to the age at which they were mature enough to walk several miles to school. We now know that children can profit immensely from formal instruction at a much earlier age, and that if this instruction has not been provided, ability to learn is impaired. Much of this early learning involves development of attitudes, including attitudes toward learning and toward work.

Most early childhood education now takes place in the home. In middle-class homes, where there is a great deal of individual attention from members of the family (supplemented by a wealth of instructional materials such as toys and books), it is usually effective. In many economically deprived homes the father may be absent, books and toys are less available, and the attitudes which are taught may be disfunctional in the broader society.

Most formal instruction for very young children is provided by privately supported nursery schools — which exclude lower class children whose parents cannot afford the costs involved. The probable widespread advent of day-care centers supported by government or by large employers offers a new opportunity for early childhood education for lower class children. The type of education to be provided in these day-care centers is in dispute. Some argue that day-care centers should be primarily custodial because, for a given amount of money, more children could be accommodated in custodial centers than in education centers, and thus more mothers would be available for employment. Public schools have had their financial resources strained by lowering their entry level to age five. In contrast, day-care centers emphasize service to children of ages three and four. Early childhood educators view the first two years of life as equally critical to the development of cognitive powers (Bell, 1972).

A major problem which remains to be resolved is the transition from day-care centers to kindergarten. The two types of education are operated by different agencies, and only a few children receive early childhood education. Yet the overworked public schoolteacher is likely to treat all of her 34 children alike.

An increasing number of experts are committed to early childhood education but reluctant to "institutionalize" the child at an earlier age. They believe the parents to be the appropriate purveyors of that education and the home to be the proper site for it to occur (Bell, pp. 13–14). They are also aware of the lack of preparation for the parental role and the handicaps under which many families function. In response to their urging, some school districts offer parent training seminars to teach early childhood development techniques to parents, as well as sending support personnel into disadvantaged homes.*

Education in the Prisons

Few of those in our prisons have succeeded in getting beyond high school. In addition, the most opprobrious are often from the lowest socioeconomic levels. Prisons are expensive because inmates must be housed, fed, and guarded, and there is little money left over to educate them. Partly because of their lack of occupational skills, some 70 percent of released prisoners return to crime and therefore once more to prison, thus furthering the costs to taxpayers.

Two methods have traditionally been used to attempt to reduce expenses: First, keep the prisoners in their cells for as much time as possible (this reduces the need for guards and for recreation and education facilities). Second, have prisoners produce goods and services

---

* Because of the interest induced by publication of T. H. Bell's *Your Child's Intellect*, at least two school districts — one in Utah and the other in California — have instituted such a program.

needed in the prison or in parts of the public sector (this provides opportunities for learning useful skills and attitudes). But there are two major problems: (a) the activities are designed for production rather than for learning; and (b) many of the activities have no significant relationship to the employment market. The result is that prisoners are "trained" in ladling soup, cutting hair, stamping license plates, or weaving denim cloth. Since there is an abundance of labor, there is no incentive to use modern equipment or methods. The result is that if a prisoner learns a skill which he can "sell" in the outside labor market, it is almost by accident. Prisoners are eligible for federal funds to give them genuine vocational training, but regular state school funds seldom are made available, and local school funds almost never are provided.

Adult Education

The supply of adult education varies enormously from state to state and from city to city. In some rural counties in a few states such as Wisconsin, Iowa, and Washington, the annual adult education enrollment exceeds the total population, due to multiple enrollments. In several cities the adult class enrollment is three to four times the full-time school enrollment in all schools combined. These are the exceptions, however. In most parts of the country adult education has the lowest priority among educational programs. If financial problems occur, adult education is the first program to be closed. Even if it is allowed to continue on a self-sustaining basis, it is typical for enrollments to be restricted to less than 1 percent of the adult population.

The growth of community colleges provides an opportunity to increase the variety of adult education that can be provided. The actual effect, however, is often for adult education programs offered by secondary schools to be closed out, and for the total amount of adult education to remain the same or actually decline. Where high-quality adult education is provided in reasonable quantity on a convenient schedule and at a modest price, the demand is nearly insatiable. One impetus in this demand is the need for education to cope with new materials, processes, and methods in jobs; another is the desire for vertical or lateral job mobility.

Birthrates persist on a historically low plateau. The number of youth to be schooled has been on a declining trend. Meanwhile, the adult population lives longer, has more time, and functions in a continually more complex world. The expanding potential for education and educators is adult and continuing education. But this is a different and more demanding clientele. It pursues learning out of desire, not compulsion. It knows what it wants and is in a position to directly test and challenge the usefulness and applicability of what it learns. Nontraditional education for the nonstandard student is a growing challenge providing both a market and a service opportunity for the schools.

Compulsory Education

In most parts of the United States students are required to attend school from the age of about seven to sixteen. A few southern states have repealed their compulsory attendance laws in reaction to demands for the end of racial segregation, but compulsory attendance laws have remained essentially unchanged for the past fifty years. During this period the actual average age of leaving school has increased more than two years. When further increases in the age of compulsory attendance has been proposed, the principal opposition has come from school superintendents. They maintain that keeping unwilling students in school longer would increase discipline problems, and that no change in compulsory attendance laws should be made until schools have a chance to develop courses which could meet the needs of such students. Similar arguments were advanced fifty years ago when the age of compulsory attendance was increased from fourteen to sixteen.

More than two-thirds of school dropouts are either in or expect to be in the general curriculum. Most school dropouts are sixteen, but with the exception of programs in agirculture and home economics, almost all vocational education begins at age sixteen. This may indicate either that the prospect of being able to enroll in vocational education is not sufficiently attractive to keep students in school, or that the student realistically expects that he will not be allowed to join the 25 percent of high school students who can be accommodated in vocational education programs. In any case, having dropped out before most vocational education begins, the student is highly unlikely to acquire any salable skills before leaving school.

Despite this lack of salable skills, many dropouts succeed reasonably well, particularly if they are white males. One reason may be that drop-

ping out occurs throughout the school year, and the competition for
entry-level jobs is lowest while school is in session. If schools were to
spread the time of graduation throughout the year, this advantage to the
dropout would disappear, and the problems facing the unskilled dropout would become even more severe.

Simply increasing the age of compulsory attendance would not result
in more students being graduated from the general curriculum. This is
the curriculum in which they are enrolled at the time of dropping out,
and it is the only curriculum in which most of them would be allowed to
continue. If increased opportunities were available in vocational curricula or if the general curriculum were made more meaningful, increasing
the age of compulsory schooling might be more attractive and feasible. If
the school encompassed within its scope alternative external learning
experiences, through work experiences, travel, and so forth, returning to
the classroom when appropriate, the incidence of the dropout and the
need for compulsion might both be relieved. The choices are clear:
Either provide salable skills to potential dropouts before they turn sixteen, or increase the attractiveness of continued enrollment.

Graduation Once per Year

Jobs become available at all times of the year, as workers retire, die,
or change occupations, and as new jobs are created by business expan-
sions and the like. Employers desire to fill vacant jobs quickly because a
needed worker improves profits.

The supply of new full-time workers appears once each year, in late
spring when the school year ends. Along with the graduates comes an
even greater supply of students who want jobs only for the summer. If
the supply and demand for the year are in balance, then some of the new
supply of workers will need to wait almost a year before jobs will become
available for them. Because the supply of vacation workers comes at one
time, fewer will get jobs than would be the case if school vacations were
scheduled at various times of the year.

The single graduation each year aids school dropouts, but it hurts
employers and graduates. A system which allowed students to leave
school for full-time employment or for cooperative work-education programs at any time of the year in which they were ready for jobs would be
far superior.

The Demand for Accountability

In complex ways, education in the United States manages to be both whipping boy and sacred cow. Its current "bad press" is probably more attributable to its failure to fulfill unrealistic expectations than to its actual weaknesses. Nevertheless, criticism and demand for reform and experiment are at peak intensity. Career education is a key concept in this ferment.

The dramatic postwar expansion in educational enrollments in the United States could have been expected to have eventual repercussions. Most radical social changes tend to follow a pendulum path, eventually swinging back then forward in search of balance. Such is the reaction that causes local voters to reject school bond issues, legislators to cut back on university budgets, and authors to give their books titles such as *Education and Jobs: The Great Training Robbery* (Berg, 1970) and *The Great School Legend* (Greer, 1972).

Education has become a sacred cow that constantly demands more feed from the public manger. Schoolteachers descended from their lofty professional perches into the marketplace to strike for and win substantial pay increases. Then students, instead of expressing their gratitude for better paid teachers and modern buildings, seemed to reject the establishment which provided their support. Taxpayers and legislators decided the sacred cow was no longer sacred. To some degree it may be traditional anti-intellectualism, to some degree resentment and jealousy, or to some degree the emergence of other priorities that appears to be "turning off" the public supporters.

Employers are also beginning to feel "had." They had accepted the premise that education credentials were evidences of competence. A high school diploma was the minimum employment threshold acceptable to many of them. Since high school and college graduates were available, why accept dropouts from either level? Even the postwar technology was structured around the assumption of a well-educated work force. Those without education were thus doubly burdened in competition, so those lacking it were well advised to pursue it.

Much of the growing educational demand from employers was real. The most rapidly growing occupations involved those clerical, technical, and professional tasks which required intellectual training as much or more than manual training. To some extent, the diploma was a useful

screening device for a lazy personnel man. It proved that the individual
had been reasonably regular in attendance and reasonably docile in relation to his superior. But to a substantial extent it was a false standard.
For many occupations, the relationship between job content and school
course content was minimal. Overtrained employees quit in frustration
and turnover costs were high. Employers were paying for the individual's
education costs and his expectations in addition to his performance.

Another major source of dissatisfaction was the failure of education
to eliminate in one generation the disadvantages which kept many of the
poor and minority from "making it" in the school, on the job, and in
society. The schools of rural depressed areas and central city ghettos
were notoriously ineffective, and few of the others could achieve to
expectation. It has been charged that the major reason for vastly expanding educational expenditures in recent years was to promote social
and economic equality, and that the schools have utterly failed to do so
(Jencks, 1973). How that could have been brought about — with the
higher socioeconomic groups spending and winning multiplied amounts
on the education of their children, even as more modest amounts became
available for compensatory education for others — is somewhat of a
mystery.

It is useful for perspective to recognize that the dissatisfactions which
produced the demand for career education were the same as those
undergirding other demanded educational reforms. All involved the
demand for accountability. "If we are to entrust to you educators our
resources and our kids, we want you to produce, and we want some objective measure of whether or not you did!"

Examples of this demand for accountability are performance contracting and the proposed voucher demonstration projects. Though
aimed at the same goal, the two are based on divergent philosophies.
Performance contracting involves identification of specific, short-run,
and measurable goals, contracting out the education task to a profit-
seeking contractor and rewarding him according to the degree to which
the objective is attained. It is a "father knows best" approach, assuming
that the authorities know what learnings are needed, can define them,
and can measure their achievement. Its early results appear to be that
the contractors are no more or less effective than the public schools they
were expected to reform or replace. The voucher approach applies

traditional private enterprise consumer sovereignty to the education market. Give each child and his parents a voucher good for so much education, and let public and private schools compete in their attractiveness to the consumer. It assumes that the student and his parents know what is best for him, can find it, and will choose it.

The demand for career education should be read in an accountability context. Employment is a key element in social welfare, and employment stability, earnings, and job satisfaction are measurable employment indicators.

In part, education has been blamed for the consequences of postwar fertility. Had there been fewer new entrants to the labor force, employers would have no choice but to hire them, and youth unemployment would not have been so high. This does not mean that these youth would have been well prepared — only for the relatively few who were vocational students or were trained for professions, had there been any serious effort to prepare youth for work.

Youth, whether dropout or graduate, at secondary or post-secondary level, have been inadequately prepared to earn a living and to meet the needs of the labor market. The deficiency has not been just job skills. In fact, those are often the easiest to supply through alternative routes such as on-the-job training. It is those attitudes toward work, those human relations skills, the knowledge of alternative career choices and their implications, the ability to manipulate the labor market, and so forth — which are the essence of career education — that were the major lack.

Career education promises to supply these attributes along with the job skills. It also provides a specific objective and measurable criteria for evaluation. Whereas education has traditionally been evaluated by the input — How many pupils per teacher? Were the teachers certified? Were the appropriate pedagogical techniques used? — an output criterion would then be supplied: Did they get jobs? Were they retained and promoted? How much did they earn? Equally important and harder to measure would be: Did they find their work fulfilling? Perhaps ultimately even the relationships between inputs and outputs can be measured. What expenditures and what services and instruction for which students resulted in how much job success?

Career education is but one proposed educational reform. It will require some radical restructuring of philosophy, objectives, and techniques. Its current popularity in concept, if not yet in practice, is attributable to the hope that it might be responsive to the vague misgivings of society and to the objective shortcomings of current education.

Conflicts in Goals

Anyone who has tried to allocate time or energy to several activities quickly becomes aware that goals frequently are in conflict. In such a case, evaluation which focuses on only one goal can lead to distortion of programs aimed at others. Evaluation of vocational education has tended to be in terms of the proportion of graduates who are placed in the occupation for which they were trained. This is entirely consistent with the goal of meeting the immediate needs of employers, but it often conflicts with the goal of increasing the options of students. For example, if a program seeks the greatest short-term placement of graduates in the occupation for which trained, it should:

(1) Prepare them for employment in a particular establishment

(2) Concentrate on special skills needed for employment at that time

(3) Shield the student from considering alternative occupations

(4) Emphasize only the desirable aspects of employment in the occupation for which he is becoming prepared

(5) Reject all students who would not be accepted enthusiastically by employers and labor organizations

(6) Encourage students not to enter higher education

(7) Encourage each student to stay in the field originally selected, even if he feels he no longer is interested in it

(8) Fail to graduate students who plan to enter an occupation different from that for which they were prepared

Such a course of action would be repugnant to any teacher in this country, in part because it obviously limits rather than increases the options open to the student. Some of these actions also do not help to meet the long-term manpower needs of society. But it seems clear that there may be considerable conflict between these two goals of vocational education. Moreover, the larger the proportion of the work force we prepare through vocational education, the greater the conflict. If we are expected to prepare nearly all of the entrants to a vitally needed occupation, and if we attempt to increase student options by passing on to them new information about undesirable aspects of that occupation, the manpower needs of the nation may be unmet. Even more dramatic, if we are successful in convincing a large number of students that their options will be decreased if they enter an occupation which has a declining need for entrants, we may succeed in ensuring that this need is completely unmet (and that the options of some students might have been increased if they had not been steered away from it). Occupational instruction which increases the intelligibility of general education and general education which increases the intelligibility of occupational education are closely related to the increasing of student options, but probably also have considerable value in meeting manpower needs more effectively.

Whenever organized labor has expressed itself on education, it has insisted that a major goal should be to increase the options open to individuals. This point of view also has been held by most educators, but there has been much disagreement as to the best way it could be achieved. Vocational educators generally held that the best way to increase options for students was to provide them with skills which met the needs of employers, while general educators felt that postponement of any consideration of career goals gave students maximum flexibility.

The extremely poor results of the general curriculum as compared to the vocational curriculum appear to invalidate this latter claim, but these results are not widely known, and general educators are still sure that they are right. At the same time, too many vocational instructors are convinced that most general education instructors are impractical theorists who are unconcerned with the real world. Students have been known to capitalize on these feelings of distrust between general and vocational teachers by telling each what they want to hear about the other's programs. One of the principal advantages of the career education program will be to encourage working relationships between the two groups of teachers, and to convince each that the other has something important to contribute to the education of students.

Employers face a similar conflict. Some occupational education programs are conducted in part or in whole by an employer in order to meet a manpower need of his organization. If the program costs must be paid in whole or in part from his operating budget, he wants to be sure that the workers he trains remain with him at least long enough so that they will repay the training expenses he incurs. If the training is designed in such a way that it not only meets his manpower needs but also increases the options of the trainees, they may leave his employment immediately after they are trained. If this occurs too frequently, the employer is apt to redesign the training program to eliminate some elements which increase trainee options, or seek full funding of training costs from some governmental or employer association to spread the costs of training.

The objectives of the teacher may not be at all the same as those of the student. The auto mechanics teacher who is trying to prepare all his students for gainful employment often has half or more of his class intent on learning how to repair or modify their own cars, or even how to enter and start a car without a key.

Teachers from different departments face conflicting objectives as well. The "fundamental processes" which should be taught may mean the three Rs to a fourth grade teacher, blocking and tackling to the football coach, and Ohm's law to the electronics instructor. "Economic efficiency" may mean salable skills to the practical nurse teacher, consumer knowledge to the homemaking teacher, and the law of supply and demand to the social studies teacher.

The use of vocational education to increase the intelligibility of general education and the use of general education to increase its own intelligibility through career education examples cause few conflicts with other objectives except in the allocation of time. The most common reason given for teachers from grade four and higher for not devoting time to career education is: "I don't have time." They agree with the concept of career education, but are so busy preparing students for the next level of schooling that they have no time to add anything. They have yet to recognize in career education, not an addition to the total curriculum, but an approach by which all subject matter can be taught with greater motivation and effectiveness. Thus one of the major gains from career education may come from a clear restatement of goals which allows and encourages an appropriate ordering of priorities throughout the whole of education, and at the same time convinces teachers that the added motivation provided by career education actually increases rather than decreases the flexible time available to the teacher.

3 Career Education: How It Developed

It is crucial to the implementation of career education that educators and the community at large be assured that career education is not a fad, and that its implementation is but a stage in the development of a concept with the strength of long discussion and experimentation behind it. The enthusiasm with which the drive for career education was launched can be largely attributed to the energy and commitment of Dr. Sidney P. Marland, Jr. The ready response can be attributed to the widely felt need for new and practicable approaches. The continued intensity of interest can be credited to the persistent promotion by staff members of the U.S. Office of Education, to professional educators and economists who see in it a potential for improvement in the social welfare, and to consultants and publishers sparked by an honest hope for profit. However, it would be an underestimate of the power of the concept to attribute it to one man or agency, and it in no way diminishes that contribution to recognize that the proponents are helping to channel and focus diverse forces which for many years have been moving in the direction they are encouraging. All of the sources, forces, and directions from which the emerging concepts have been drawn cannot be inventoried here. One who has need for a detailed tracing of career education's development is referred to Bailey and Stadt's carefully documented work. It is sufficient to our purposes here to supply a few examples of the years of thought, experiment, and experience which undergird the decision to push career education as a high-priority policy and to demonstrate the continuity and likely durability of current developments.

CHANGING OBJECTIVES IN CAREER PREPARATION

The goals of public school education in the nineteenth century paid little attention to occupational preparation. The emphasis was on training the mind, because it was assumed that once trained, it could respond appropriately to every type of problem. The major goals of school were avocational (not antivocational), but the vocational uses of the mind were assumed to be less important than its moral or recreational uses. Secondary and higher education had as an important goal the teaching of a style of speaking and writing English, embellished with bits of dead languages, which clearly separated a vocational elite from the rank and file.

Most vocational skills, knowledge, and attitudes were taught in the home and on the job, though private schools and colleges provided vocational skills for a few occupations. It was generally assumed that women and men would follow the careers of their mothers and fathers, respectively. Women were expected to have no career aspirations outside the home, though men whose fathers were derelicts could be expected to be able to "rise" somewhat through strict application of the work ethic. Inculcation of this ethic was an important task of elementary schools, especially in schools for children of the lower classes.

In the early twentieth century it became clear that the old system of career education was inadequate. Job content was changing more rapidly, work sites were accessible for observation, and employees were less likely to remain with an employer long enough to repay a substantial investment in his training. Even the increasing division of work tasks into smaller and smaller jobs which required less training could not keep up with the rapidity of changes in job content.

One result was the federal subsidy to vocational education which lead to the inclusion of two to four years of specific job preparation in secondary schools. In its early years, vocational education for boys was limited to agricultural education in rural schools and to a few industrial occupations in urban schools. Girls were taught home economics. In the period from 1917 to the mid-1930s, there was only one principal goal — to meet the manpower needs of local communities. The agricultural needs were clear: More and better trained farmers were needed to increase the production of foods and fibers. The home economics needs were similarly agreed upon — to enable housewives to better feed and clothe their families. Industrial needs were not so clear, and community surveys were made to determine the occupations in which there were shortages of qualified persons willing to work under prevailing conditions. In a few communities, this lead to the training of strike breakers. But as organized labor became more powerful, vocational-industrial education emphasized theoretical training for unionized apprentices and entry-level skills training for occupations in which unions were not strong. Increased mobility led to planning, which took into account the region to which students might migrate. Career education for professionals expanded rapidly in colleges and universities, but secondary school preparation, for those who planned to enter career training and for those who planned to enter the traditional liberal arts program, was identical.

The War Production Training programs of the early 1940s convinced some vocational educators that a far higher proportion of the population could be prepared for useful work than they had ever felt possible, and that the goals of vocational education should be expanded to include the development of skills for all students, not just those who were most employable. The attitude of most general educators toward increased options for students did not change dramatically until the 1960s, when results of "Project TALENT" showed clearly that two-thirds of the students in the high school general curriculum dropped out, and that among those who did graduate, employment and college-going rates were very low.

Vocational education has had three basic objectives, and these are being transferred to career education: to meet the manpower and economic needs of the nation, to increase the options available to individual students, and to increase the intelligibility of both general and occupational education. The third came about as vocational educators noticed that many of their students increased rapidly in reading and computational skills after making a tentative career choice and learning something of the requirements of that career. Gains in comprehension of other school content often occurred as well. A typical student statement was: "For the first time, some of this school stuff makes sense." Usually this change in student awareness was not the result of planning on the part of the school. If it occurred frequently by accident, wouldn't it occur much more frequently if the vocational teacher encouraged it through planned activity? It is from that experience that career education resolved to go one step farther and ask all teachers to plan instruction so that its career implications became obvious.

Thus, although few schools changed their stated objectives between 1940 and 1970, actual emphases have changed markedly. For example, during World War II, school vocational programs ran 24 hours a day, training war workers, while in regular classes boys received pre-induction training, girls studied first aid, and all were involved in physical conditioning programs. After Sputnik, some schools deemphasized vocational education and markedly increased enrollments in physical science and mathematics. Since the mid-1960s, vocational education is being reemphasized, but in new contexts contributing to the concepts of career education.

A landmark, so far as the objectives of career preparation was conceived, was the Vocational Education Act of 1963. It changed the assignment of vocational educators from an emphasis on meeting the skill needs of the labor market to greater concern for the employability of people. It also began broadening the definition of vocational education and, perhaps more importantly, supplied sufficient federal funds that a demand for evaluation followed.

However, career education probably has a greater debt to career development theory than to vocational education legislation and practice. For decades it was thought that if only the skill requirements of jobs could be analyzed and the essential traits of potential workers could be identified and measured, happy occupational marriages would be almost assured. The search proved fruitless; neither job factors nor individual traits were fixed and immutable. Vocational interests upon which career decisions are based develop from lifelong experiences. There are certain generalizable patterns through childhood, youth, and adulthood, but decisions for no individual are predictable. Family background, personality, and the accidents of experience, acquaintance, and exposure are at least as important as any inherent abilities. Career development theory is a disorderly array with as many prophets, dogmas, and disciples as organized religion, but the developmental concept is a central thesis. For vocational guidance, its implication is exploration in search of self-concept: In what occupational roles can I visualize myself? For career preparation, the implication is that attitudes, work values, maturity, emotional stability, human relations skills, and so forth, are prerequisites of and at least as important to success as job skills. That recognition, of course, is a key contributor to the drive for career education.

PRECURSORS OF CAREER EDUCATION

The dissatisfaction with a system which ignored career preparation and development, except for a limited number of vocational and graduate students, is deep seated and long term. Numerous experimental projects have explored and developed concepts and components which are now recognizable as integral parts of career education, though none of them alone ever comprised a comprehensive career education system. Commissions and advisory councils have recommended principles, practices, and legislation with the same impact.

To mention examples risks criticism for neglecting even more influential examples, but a few are noteworthy. The Ford Foundation during the 1960s funded a number of projects which experimented with important elements of what is now known as career education. The "Technology for Children" project sponsored by the New Jersey State Department of Education, the Nova schools in Florida, and the "American Industries" project sponsored by Stout State University in Wisconsin are examples of programs which exposed children to the vocational choices they will eventually have to make. The New Jersey program was not designed originally for career education, but rather served as a counter to the post-Sputnik emphasis on pure science and mathematics, with all traces of technology removed from the instructional program. "Technology for Children" encouraged elementary school students and teachers to experiment with tools, materials, and processes in an effort to strengthen a neglected part of general education. The program rightly criticized the elementary school for emphasizing vicarious rather than direct experiences and for telling students about the world rather than doing something about and with it.

Later, as the need for career education in the elementary school became better recognized, it became evident that many of the activities of the "Technology for Children" program could serve as education for certain types of careers. Though not originally designed as a career education program, it now consists of a systematic kindergarten through grade twelve exposure to the nature of technology and some of the occupations connected with it. As a bonus, in addition to increasing the realism of vocational choice, the students are expected to gain a general understanding of scientific and engineering realities and to find all learning more relevant.

In grades one through six, the Nova children were introduced to a wide range of employment-related experiences through tools, mechanical devices, and games. In grades seven through twelve, the program became more directive. In grades seven and eight, the students were exposed to fundamental concepts of technology, and a variety of introductory experiences was provided to help them become more aware of vocational alternatives and career requirements. Specialization increased in grades nine through twelve, with encouragement constantly offered to remain in school as long as the student could profit from further education. All experiences and decisions were structured not to pose obstacles to continuation. The objective was to develop confidence, knowledge, and skills within a family of occupations, enhancing the immediate employability of the student, yet holding the door open to continued education and training. Learning experiences were individualized, with the teaching of concepts and reliance upon problem solving as a teaching technique emphasized. The intent was to measure progress by achievement of competency rather than time in any particular phase of the program.

The "American Industries" project began at the eighth grade rather than in elementary school, but has equally broad objectives. From a general understanding of the major concepts of industry and technology and simple problem-solving techniques, the student was to progress to the ability to recognize and solve complex industrial problems within broad concept areas or clusters of concepts appropriate to the individual's interest and abilities. Economics, finance, and marketing received more emphasis than in similar programs of the same general type.

The Nova schools and the "American Industries" project are also examples of efforts to offer a broad academic education but to give it relevance, increase motivation, and provide salable skills by structuring the academic offering around a core of manual or technical occupational skills. A number of other programs have shared similar objectives.

The Nova preemployment program required every student to elect one technical science course each year. In addition he enrolled in science, social studies, English, mathematics, and foreign language courses, each with units and activities directly related to the student's interest field. Vocationally certified teachers were teamed with other certified personnel for curriculum development and presentation of related disciplines. By learning the concepts and processes of the world of work and by using problem-solving techniques, the student was to be prepared for current employment, yet be able to cope with change. Despite preparation for immediate employment in a broad occupational area, students were prepared for and encouraged to continue their education at college.

The "American Industries" project was also interdisciplinary, combining academic and vocational education. Its basic philosophy was that American industry provides a body of knowledge that can be analyzed in terms of identifiable concepts and that a structure could be developed to provide order to the body of knowledge. As the structure was formulated, it was prepared for instructional purposes and tested in cooperating schools. The courses drew heavily from the disciplines of psychology and sociology and also relied to a great extent upon the natural curiosity and motivation of students.

The San Mateo Unified School District in California developed a "zero-reject" concept for curriculum planning. The assumption was that with proper teaching techniques, every student could earn a high school diploma with significant standards and a broad liberal and vocational education. The schools accepted the responsibility for seeing that students were employable whenever they chose to leave school, whether as a dropout from grade ten or with a doctorate. Occupations were grouped by clusters and by levels which formed ladders of progression throughout the educational experience. Academic disciplines, it was urged, should be established for the convenience of teaching and understanding rather than the standard "watertight compartments" adopted largely for convenience in administration. The intent was to state performance objectives clearly and mix discipline components to fit the student's own individualized learning strategy.

The principal rival to the "American Industries" project has been the Industrial Arts Curriculum Project. In part because it was more self-contained (and hence required cooperation from fewer teachers), and because it was presented in an attractive publications package, it is the largest and most rapidly growing career education program. The project concentrated on the world of construction and the world of manufacturing, each designed for one year of the junior high school. The picture of the industry is presented so cogently, however, that it is being used in the instruction of apprentices and architects as well. Emphasis is placed upon the roles of various types of workers and their interdependence. Career ladders are clearly identified. The importance of academic subjects is presented largely by the Industrial Arts Curriculum Project teacher, though other teachers have become involved in the instructional program in some schools. Clever use of games, simulated production activities, and visual aids keeps student interest high. The project pays little attention to finance, marketing, and service activities, but what it does, it does well.

The "Partnership Vocational Education Project" at Central Michigan University, Mount Pleasant, was a joint effort between the university and the secondary schools, community colleges, and industry of the area. The project employed a teaching team from mathematics, science, English, and industrial education. The program began at the ninth or tenth grade of the secondary school and continued through the university, serving all individuals who had industrial-technical aptitudes and interests. It was structured on three levels: (1) a college-bound upper ability group, (2) an intermediate-level group who might choose to enter the labor force after high school or advance to the community college or university, and (3) a lower ability group of students likely to enter the labor force after or even before graduation from high school.

No student was permanently locked into any one of the three levels; each might shift to another level according to his interests and aptitudes. The program at each level used the vocational interest of the student as the motivating force for a sound educational program, but the vocational interest was not to result in a vocational dead-end. Occupational and personal guidance was emphasized to familiarize youngsters with the industrial-technical occupations and higher educational opportunities open to them, including the building of realistic aspirational levels. A basic premise was that the motivation, particularly related to the immediacy of the economic levels, was directly related to the immediacy of the reward and the relationship of the task to its achievement. Therefore formal education was to be related as directly as possible to the personal goals of the individual. A problem-solving approach attempted to give meaning to formal education. The students developed capability in the identification of meaningful tasks, in the selection of appropriate knowledge and skills, and in applying them to the solutions or problems.

The "Pre-engineering Technology Program," also known as the "Richmond Plan" or "Pre-tech Program," now used widely throughout the San Francisco Bay area, was initiated by the Richmond High School District and Cogswell Polytechnical College, California. Its target population was the average, capable, but undermotivated student who was achieving below his ability. The program was especially structured for a geographic area in which the majority of students attain some education beyond high school. The immediate occupational goal was that of engineering technician. However, care was taken in curriculum planning and through cooperative relationships with the junior college and baccalaureate college systems to assure that the graduates were qualified for the latter if their motivation was revived. Though broadly rather than narrowly prepared, the program turned out students who were in high demand from employers in the area. Curriculum units were planned by the industrial arts instructor. Each instructor from mathematics, science, English, and other subject matter areas then structured his or her offering around that project, stressing their interrelatedness.

The project proved the effectiveness of the interdisciplinary, employment-oriented approach in achieving a variety of occupational goals. Approximately forty schools in the San Francisco Bay area adopted the approach, applying it to twelve different occupational goals. One of the more successful was "Project FEAST" (food, education, and service technology) which prepared the students for jobs in commercial food services. Though it enrolled students with all levels of ability, it was particularly effective and appropriate for those with less than average ability. The disciplines drawn upon were home economics, science,

English, and mathematics. Close ties with the Hotel and Restaurant Foundation at San Francisco City College assured both employment and further educational opportunities to the students involved.

The state of Maryland for a number of years has been supporting a statewide "career development" effort. The Maryland program is especially concerned with work attitudes and the freedom and appropriateness of career choice. It emphasizes orientation to the world of work, followed by exploratory experiences which aid a child to perceive herself or himself in many work settings, the provision of experiences as well as data for choice making, and the maintenance of options in personal career decisions.

Each of these examples represents nearly a decade of experience with parts of what is now called career education. Other innovative programs of the same vintage could be cited. The Junior Achievement program and the Explorer program of the Boy Scouts of America follow a similar philosophy. Their concepts of the interrelatedness of career development, academic and vocational education, and all levels of the educational process, and the need for adaptability throughout a working life, are all precursors of present advocacy of even broader programs. Even the traditional business-industry-labor-education days are forerunners of some of the career education components.

Remedial manpower programs for the disadvantaged were another source of career education thinking. The Manpower Development and Training Act of 1962 recognized the need for retraining adults as technological and economic change threatened their means of livelihood. Then the Act later shifted to providing competitive skills to disadvantaged people. Several components of the Economic Opportunity Act were also remedial in nature, designed to provide work attitudes and job skills to those leaving the school system without having acquired them. From the Skills Centers which evolved under the Manpower Development and Training Act and the Job Corps of the Economic Opportunity Act emerged important insights into the needs of underprepared adults and ways of remedying their lack of occupational skills and training. Examples are:

(1) Remedial adult basic education

(2) Prevocational training to offer those with limited labor market exposure an opportunity to try a number of skills before choosing one for training

(3) Open-entry/open-exit practices designed to remove all entry requirements and to allow the student to leave when employability was attained without being labeled a dropout

(4) The structuring of all training according to a ladder concept, assuring that even if the individual could not complete a full course of training, he or she could always leave with some salable skills

These programs have simultaneously demonstrated the need for better career preparation to prevent youth from entering the labor market unprepared and the need for adult opportunities for remedial education, retraining, and upgrading their working lives.

Another precursor of career education was a decade of change in the thinking of many opinion and decision makers in vocational education. The 1963 Vocational Education Act's basic shift in philosophy from the skill needs of the labor market to the employment needs of various groups within the present and potential labor force made little difference in fact. The Act was too permissive in allowing but not requiring change, and too nonspecific in failing to define the changes which were needed.

The Advisory Council on Vocational Education involving both general and vocational educators and a number of noneducators ranged far beyond traditional skills training and clearly presaged career education when its 1967 report advocated five operational principles for vocational education (Evans, Mangum, and Pragan, pp. 63–64):

(1) Vocational education cannot be meaningfully limited to the skills necessary for a particular occupation. It is more appropriately defined as all of those aspects of educational experience which help a person to discover his talents, to relate them to the world of work, to choose an occupation, and to refine his talents and use them successfully in employment. In fact, orientation and assistance in vocational choice may often be more valid determinants of employment success, and therefore more profitable uses of educational funds, than specific skills training.

(2) . . . Where complex instructions and sophisticated decisions mark the boundary between the realm of man and the role of the machine, there is no longer room for any dichotomy between intellectual competence and manipulative skills and, therefore, between academic and vocational education.

(3) . . . Education cannot shed its responsibilities to the student (and to society in his behalf) just because he has chosen to reject the system or because it has handed him a diploma. In a world where the distance between the experiences of childhood, adolescence, and adulthood and between school and work continually widens, the school must reach forward to assist the student across the gaps just as labor market institutions must reach back to assist in the transition . . . .

(4) Some type of formal occupational preparation must be a part of every educational experience. . . . In addition, given the rapidity of change and the competition from generally rising educational attainment, upgrading and remedial education opportunities are a continual necessity.

(5) The objective of vocational education should be the development of the individual, not the needs of the labor market. . . . The system for occupational preparation should supply a salable skill at any terminal point chosen by the individual, yet no doors should be closed to future progress and development.

Based upon these principles it recommended a "unified system of vocational education," some of the key components of which were (Evans, Mangum, and Pragan, pp. 65–68):

(1) Occupational preparation should begin in the elementary schools with a realistic picture of the world of work. Its fundamental purposes should be to familiarize the student with his world and to provide him the intellectual tools and rational habits of thought to play a satisfying role in it.

(2) In junior high school, economic orientation and occupational preparation should reach a more sophisticated stage with study by all students of the economic and industrial system by which goods and services are produced and distributed. The objectives should be exposure to the full range of occupational choices which will be available at a later point and full knowledge of the relative advantages and the requirements of each.

(3) Occupational preparation should become more specific in the high school, though preparation should not be limited to a spe-

cific occupation. Given the uncertainties of a changing economy and the limited experiences upon which vocational choices must be made, instruction should not be overly narrow but should be built around significant families of occupations or industries which promise expanding opportunities. . . . All students outside the college preparatory curriculum should acquire an entry-level job skill, but they should also be prepared for post-high school vocational and technical education. Even those in the college preparatory curriculum might profit from the techniques of learning by doing. On the other hand, care should be taken that pursuit of a vocationally oriented curriculum in the high school does not block the upward progress of the competent student who later decides to pursue a college degree.

(4) Occupational education should be based on a spiral curriculum which treats concepts at higher and higher levels of complexity as the student moves through the program. Vocational preparation should be used to make general education concrete and understandable; general education should point up the vocational implications of all education. Curriculum materials should be prepared for both general and vocational education to emphasize these relationships.

(5) Beyond initial preparation for employment, many, out of choice or necessity, will want to bolster an upward occupational climb with part-time, and sometimes full-time, courses and programs as adults. These should be available as part of the regular public school system. They should not be limited to a few high-demand and low-cost trades, but should provide a range of occupational choice as wide as those available to students preparing for initial entry.

(6) Occupational preparation need not and should not be limited to the classroom, to the school shop, or to the laboratory. Many arguments favor training on the job. Expensive equipment need not be duplicated. Familiarization with the environment and discipline of the workplace are important parts of occupational preparation yet are hard to simulate in a classroom.

Supervisors and other employees can double as instructors. And the trainee learns by earning. On the other hand, the employer and his supervisors may be more productive and training oriented. The operations and equipment of a particular employer may cover only part of a needed range of skills, necessitating transfer among employers for adequate training. The ideal is to meld the advantages of institutional and on-the-job training in formal cooperative work-study programs.

(7) Effective occupational preparation is impossible if the school feels that its obligation ends when the student graduates. The school, therefore, must work with employers to build a bridge between school and work. Placing the student on a job and following up his successes and failures provide the best possible information to the school on its own strengths and weaknesses.

The 1968 amendments to the Vocational Education Act were based to a large extent upon the council's recommendations, and though they did not give legislative sanction to the concepts, they removed a number of legal obstacles and made their implementation possible. The amendments did earmark certain amounts and proportions of vocational education funds for the disadvantaged, the handicapped, post-secondary vocational training, cooperative education, and consumer and homemaker education. They broadened the vocational education definition to include all general education incident to occupational preparation, opened it to emerging as well as recognized occupations requiring less than four years of college, and allowed experimentation in the elementary and junior high schools. They did not accomplish the crucial task of merging the academic and vocational in education and of generalizing career awareness into the total education scheme. A gradual warming to vocational education by national education associations, a broadening of concepts within the American Vocational Association, and the probing and prodding of the National Advisory Council in Vocational Education authorized by the 1968 amendments were all important contributors to the emergence of career education.

IMPLEMENTATION EFFORTS OF THE OFFICE OF EDUCATION

The continuity which marked career education's development is well illustrated by the fact that Commissioner of Education James B.

Allen, predecessor to Marland in that office, used the term "career education" in a 1970 speech advocating some of the now familiar concepts,
even though the emphasis of his own administration was on the "right
to read."

Career education's official date of birth is January 23, 1971, when
Commissioner Marland delivered a speech before the National Association of Secondary School Principals (Bailey and Stadt, p. 278). However, the speed with which the U.S. Office of Education was able to
move to disseminate career education concepts, once the public announcement had been made, demonstrates the depth of dedication the
staff had given to the task over previous years, going back at least to
1968. Exemplary vocational education projects, funded by the Office
of Education after the 1968 amendments, were the leading edge of
those developments, and they incorporated in their totality most of the
presently organized career education concepts. Conferences involving
observers and participants in these projects had popularized the notion
among professionals. Work had already begun on a classification system
to subsume all occupations into fifteen career clusters as a convenient
device for analyzing and studying the world of work.

From this base, staff of the Bureau of Adult Vocational and Technical Education in the Office of Education were able to move quickly to
additionally popularize the newly announced priority and to start its
implementation. Concept papers soon emerged. Models were designed
for school, employer, home, community, and rural/residential-based
career education programs. Contractors were recruited to develop materials and bring the concepts before the public. The Center for Occupational Education at North Carolina State University, the Center for
Study of Vocational-Technical Education at Ohio State University,
and regional education laboratories (all launched and subsidized by the
Office of Education) were available for assignments in materials development, research, and supervision of model undertakings. Since the
concepts were not entirely new but were familiar, many school districts
had had experience with exemplary and foundation-funded projects,
as well as some they had created on their own initiatives.

Response was immediate and spontaneous. For example, as early
as the summer of 1970, New Jersey had appropriated funds to begin
experimental career education programs in three cities. Because of the

success of the programs, the governor called a meeting of the mayors of 24 cities to review the results of the experimental projects and to discuss further spread of the program on a statewide basis. By the end of 1971, five states had passed legislation promoting and implementing career education. Such legislation was pending in two states and had been proposed in twelve others.

In the spring of 1971, Arizona's legislature enacted a bill providing $2 million to launch career education in a selected number of public schools in that state. Fifteen school districts are converting their programs into a comprehensive kindergarten through twelfth grade career education system. Much of the material which the Arizona State Department of Education used for launching the effort was derived from experience and documentation which grew out of the vocational exemplary projects.

During the summer of 1971, with the help of a grant from the Office of Education, the state of Delaware began a one-year planning effort for statewide conversion to a kindergarten through twelfth grade career education program. In Mississippi, Jones County schools served as the focal point for a model career education program in this state. School personnel from neighboring counties were sent to observe the Jones County model and to adopt its techniques.

North Dakota used the Bismarck public school district as the demonstration site for a kindergarten through fourteenth grade career education program. The Bismarck program featured broad occupational orientation at the elementary and secondary school levels to increase the students' awareness of options open to them in the world of work. There was concentration on cooperative work experience and intensive occupational guidance and counseling for students during their final years of school. The program assisted initial placement of all students either in a job or in post-secondary education.

Georgia and Wyoming were also states which followed the same pattern of early implementation, each developing a kindergarten through twelfth grade career education system in a local school district (with the aid of federal funds) and then spreading the model to other districts within their states later on.

The Dallas Independent School District in Texas spent more than $21 million on constructing facilities, procuring equipment, and developing curriculum for its massive career education effort. In May 1971 the San Diego School Board passed a resolution promulgating the development of a comprehensive kindergarten through twelfth grade career education program for its schools in California.

These are but a few examples. Throughout the country, spontaneous program designs by local educators and administrators were leaning in what is now clear was the career education direction. When personnel at the Center for Occupational Education at North Carolina State University were assigned by the Office of Education to identify locations and programs that could be described as career education systems, they found 41 such programs operating which could be studied and described for dissemination. In these and other instances, concepts of the interrelatedness of career development and personal and social development, of academic and vocational education, of all levels of the educational process, and of the need for adaptability throughout a working life were precursors of present advocacy.

Building on some of this background and providing most of the spark for the recent acceleration of career education interest, the U.S. Office of Education is clearly giving high priority to career education as a policy. In actual allocation of dollars — the real measure of priorities — the commitment has been limited largely to the vocational education component of the agency's budget.

In the summer of 1971, with the help of outside consultants, the Office of Education selected six sites from many nominees for the development of large-scale demonstration models of career education in public school systems. Two million dollars of Office of Education funds are being spent to help implementers in these six sites in their development efforts. The six are: Atlanta, Georgia; Hackensack, New Jersey; Pontiac, Michigan; Jefferson County, Colorado; Mesa, Arizona; and Los Angeles, California.

In the meantime, 52 "mini-models" of career education, funded as "exemplary programs" under the Vocational Education Act, were activated in local school districts in all fifty states and in Puerto Rico and the District of Columbia. Most of these responses — which occurred within one year after the Office of Education's formal announcement of the career education emphasis — emerged from locations already treading along the same road. But their response and the speed with which others are "getting on the bandwagon" are support for the view that the idea was one whose time had come.

The Office of Education was reorganized in accordance with 1972 legislation, with all research on education being directed by the National Institute of Education, which gave research priority to limited but important aspects of career education. However, the Office of Education, as an operational arm, established a "deputy commissioner for occupational education" within whose jurisdiction was placed a "national center for career education" assigned to coordinate efforts throughout all branches of the Office of Education. Without expansion of education budgets, the career education effort had to depend upon reallocation of funding from other sources, always a difficult assignment.

By 1973, documentation of all of the career education applications around the country would be an impossibility. More than two hundred exemplary programs had been established with federal funds, in addition to those using the funds of local education agencies. More than forty states had held statewide career education conferences. Over twenty state boards of education had issued official policy statements endorsing career education. National conferences had been held on career education in relation to the elementary school teacher, the middle/junior high school, minorities, exceptional children, and the gifted and talented, among others. The U.S. Chamber of Commerce had sponsored a national conference on the subject for businessmen. Ohio State University had held three similar conferences for different groups of higher education administrators. Other national organizations had added acclaim, and career education had been a leading item in the convention programs of almost every major education association. The outflow of books and materials to implement the concepts was swelling from a trickle to a substantial stream. No major voices seemed raised against it, and its few academic critics expressed views that suggest they have little understanding of what career education is all about. It seems reasonable now to conclude that regardless of changing Office of Education leadership, and even of changing titles and rhetoric, career education can now be called "a movement" and has taken on a durable life of its own.

The best evidence that career education is a new name for a long-term trend may simply be that such an immense amount of nationwide and grass-roots interest and activity has emerged, although the Office of Education has allocated only a few million dollars of vocational education discretionary monies from its $8 billion education budget. If such a conflagration can be ignited with so small a flame, spontaneous combustion must have been near. Career education is an idea whose time has indeed come. Apparently, what is now most needed is guidance in how to do it.

4 Career Education: How to Do It

Chapter 1 supplied two definitions, seven concepts, five components, and three stages for career education. This chapter gets at the "nuts and bolts" of how to do career education by expanding upon the definitions and by exploring the ways in which the components can be and have been implemented in practice in the home, school, and community.

EXPLORING THE DEFINITION OF CAREER EDUCATION

Chapter 1 of this book defines career education as:

> . . . the total effort of public education and the community to help all individuals become familiar with the values of a work-oriented society, to integrate these values into their personal value systems, and to implement these values into their lives in such a way that work becomes possible, meaningful, and satisfying to each individual.

It is around this definition that chapter 4 structures the concepts and components of career education. The emphasis is on the values of a work-oriented society. The advocacy is on major changes in the education system to develop and inculcate these values.

This definition of career education will appear relevant only to those who accept the basic propositions upon which it is based. The propositions are as follows:

(1) Given equal natural resources and ingenuity among its people, the expected productivity per unit of population associated with any society bears a direct relationship to that nation's commitment to work.

(2) The classical version of the Protestant work ethic in American society is currently being eroded by a variety of forces and is no longer a viable concept for many members of our society.

(3) No great civilization in history has continued to prosper after it abandoned its basic commitment to work. There is no reason to believe the United States is exempt from this historical pattern.

(4) The basic goal of career education is the restoration of various forms of work values adapted to reflect new social and economics realities as a strong and viable force throughout our society.

The classical societal commitment to work includes such concepts as the following: All honest work possesses innate dignity and worth. Excellence can be attained and is rewarded in any occupation. One should strive to do his best in whatever work he does. The worker who is satisfied with doing less than his best is, to some extent, dissatisfied with himself. The contributions one can make to society stem, to a large extent, from the work one does. Work is seen as possessing personal as well as financial rewards for the worker and the saying "A task well done is its own reward" has real meaning. Persons to whom work is personally meaningful want to work, prepare themselves for work, and actively seek to work; they are, most of the time, happier when they are working than when they are not. A significant portion of the pride individuals have in themselves is seen as the best and surest route to the highest level of occupational success possible for the individual.

The extent to which the classical societal commitment to work has been eroded is illustrated by the old-fashioned sound of these statements. It is likely that this description of work values is simply not considered applicable to large segments of the American work force today. Those very changes that have increased our potential for work productivity — mass production, automation, cybernation, and occupational technology — have ironically resulted in making a societal commitment to work, in its classic form, less meaningful and seemingly less appropriate for the individual worker.

In part, the erosion has occurred because the so-called Protestant work ethic was also a savings and investment ethic. Since frugality is no longer emphasized, the "work to save in order to invest" continuum is broken. Retaining the work ethic by itself requires emphasis on other values growing out of productivity and achievement. For one thing, the traditional emphasis tended to be individualistic and selfish — "work to get ahead and to achieve financial independence and wealth." It said little of "work to serve and take satisfaction from that service." Social insurance may have reduced the need for the former but not for the latter.

The rapidity of occupational change brought about by the invention and creation of new products and services is another factor in the erosion. Relatively few youth can or should now aspire to follow their parents' occupations. The increased complexity of occupational technology and the resultant need to break occupations into smaller components have also played a role. It is hard for the assembly line worker to find great personal pride and innate dignity in his work. Industrial psychologists are recognizing the need to reverse the trend toward job simplification and replace it with job enrichment. Technology cooperates also, since the ultimate goal of technological trends is to simplify repetitive tasks until no human labor is involved, leaving people the more challenging tasks that only they can do.

The movement toward a "throwaway" economy, based more on a replacement of components that fail to work than on their repair, has also contributed. How is a worker expected to develop a sense of craftsmanship in producing a product that is planned to last only a limited period of time? Satisfaction must come from a knowledge of the use to which the product is put and how it contributes to social well-being. Finally, increases in the geographic fluidity of the sources of employment have resulted in a degree of personal and family instability among members of the work force that has also contributed to erosion of a classical societal commitment to work.

Our formal education system, too, has contributed greatly to erosion of this commitment. Education as preparation for making a living never has been a basic and pervasive goal of our system of elementary, secondary, and higher education. A "school for schooling's sake" emphasis is far too common. In our secondary schools, over 70 percent of our students are enrolled in nonvocational programs. Hundreds of thousands of college and university students pursue their studies with no clear-cut vocational goals. Our education system has contributed to the false and dangerous worship of the baccalaureate degree as the best and surest route to occupational success. This false value has been transmitted to and is now a part of the personal value system of both parents and children throughout the United States. Our public education system has been a prime transmitter of this false value.

Our education system must become dedicated to helping all individuals acquire a personal meaning of work that holds value for them. Where the classical societal commitment to work can be used as a basis for such meaning, it should be fully utilized. Where, in its classic form, this commitment cannot be applied, then alternative ways of bringing meaning to work must be developed and used. Thus career education is perceived as dedicated to helping all individuals in all occupations in all settings acquire a personal meaning of work that holds value for them.

The Process of Career Education: A Three-Pronged Approach

Our definition of career education presented in chapter 1 envisions a three-pronged approach. First, all individuals must be helped to become *familiar* with the values of a work-oriented society. The aim is not to impose any particular set of work values on any individual, but to see that each is exposed to a variety of forms of work values so that he or she will know and understand those that exist. An essential prerequisite for the adoption of work values on the part of any individual is to know about their existence and to understand their basic nature. It is an element of awareness.

The second phase is to help individuals *integrate* work values into their personal value systems. In this step, the individual thinks both about himself and about work values, decides the meaning various work values have for him, accepts those in accord with his total personal value system, and rejects those that are not. It is a step of exploration and personal decision making. Included in this step are all those activities and procedures designed to help individuals explore the personal meaning various forms of work values hold for them.

The third phase is to help individuals *implement* work values in their lives. This is essentially an occupational preparation and job place-ment step. It consists of all those activities and procedures required for an individual to become proficient in vocational skills and to enter into employment. Again, the concept must be viewed broadly enough to in-clude those individuals who choose not to work.

Most individuals will experience this three-step process more than once in their lives. Indeed, it must occur whenever the individual is faced with choosing or changing his occupation. The process is tied as intimately to why an individual chooses to work as it is to why he chooses one form of work over another. It cannot be assigned to any one part of the educational establishment, but must involve all educators at all levels in all kinds of educational settings. Education, as part of the total society, cannot accomplish the process by itself. Rather, the process demands the active involvement of the total community of which the school sys-tem is a part.

Implementing Career Education's Components

With this general background, we turn now to a discussion of the five components of career education specified in the general definitional statement. It will be important as each component is considered to keep clearly in mind that career education represents a concept considered appropriate for all students at all educational levels and in almost all kinds of educational settings.

Component A: Career Implications of the Substantive Content of Education

Career education, like any other educational concept, will succeed or fail largely because of the efforts, know-how, and dedication of class-room teachers. Helping students learn the career implications of all educational subject matter is the major goal of this component. If this goal can be attained, the teacher will have added to the educational motivations now in use a new and powerful way of helping school make sense to students; namely, a view of education as preparation for making a living.

This is not to argue that education as preparation for work should be substituted for other legitimate sources of educational motivation currently being used by classroom teachers. Rather, career education offers the classroom teacher an additional source of educational motivation — one which should appeal to all students some of the time and to some of the students most of the time. There are many students who will seek to learn whatever the teacher tries to teach. They want to learn simply because they do not know. Other students will find themselves particularly interested in a given subject matter area. They want to learn basically because of their deep interest in the content being taught. For many students, to see some relationship between the substantive content they are being asked to master and their eventual qualifications for work will prove to be a powerful motivational force. Even if they do not eventually follow that particular line of work, the knowledge that the material they study is useful in the "real world" outside the classroom would have been motivating.

Thus a career education emphasis is in no way intended to minimize the importance of the substantive content teachers seek to help students learn. On the contrary, it is intended to serve, in part, as a way of helping students learn more of this substantive content. Similarly, a career education emphasis for the classroom teacher does not itself represent a vast body of new knowledge to be added to an already overcrowded curriculum. Rather, it is more accurately pictured as a new and different basis for organizing and presenting educational content.

The effectiveness of career education depends upon the skills of the teacher who is using it, the background knowledge that the teacher possesses, and the enthusiasm of the teacher for the approach. There is no special magic to this form of educational motivation that makes it superior to others that good teachers have always used. Any classroom device which helps students express themselves has potential for helping teachers understand their students. Any device which can excite the students or make the subject matter appear to be of positive value can motivate their efforts and spark their intellectual responses. But the career emphasis has the value that nearly every child has a built-in interest in *What am I going to be when I grow up?*

To ask students, even those in lower elementary grades, about their career aspirations does not introduce a question most have never been asked before. Well-meaning parents, relatives, and friends will have asked the same question of the student frequently throughout his life, and he will have play-acted career roles in his childhood fantasies. For the teacher to express such interest should, if done properly, carry no implications that the student is being asked to make a firm commitment to a particular occupational choice. Rather, the teacher is simply inquiring about the student's current view of himself as a potential member of the work force. There are few other questions more effective in helping the teacher gain some understanding of self-concepts. When a person expresses a preference for a particular kind of work, he or she is really saying in part, "This is the kind of person I see myself as becoming." From student answers, good classroom teachers receive many clues regarding specific ways in which school may make sense to that student.

Career Education for Young Children

The recent push for career education appears to have generated a more ready response in the elementary and junior high school setting than in the senior high schools. Elementary school teachers probably have grasped the concepts better than those at any other level, with college faculty apparently the most unaware or disinterested. The elementary school response is an appropriate one which, it is hoped, will be introduced even earlier with the growth of early childhood education.

The old proverb "As the twig is bent, the tree is formed" is based on sound psychology, but only recently has the theory begun to catch up with the practice. "Bending" a child in some preconceived direction in school, or even in the home, is abhorrent to many people. Nevertheless, recent research in the education of young children has shown two facts conclusively: (a) if children are taught early in life, they learn better and faster than if they are kept in an environment where learning is difficult, and (b) many, if not most, basic personal values are learned very early in life, and once learned, are difficult to change. The new emphasis on the importance of early childhood development and greater clarity about career education should eliminate this gap.

For those who define "career" as synonymous with occupations, it has seemed that career education should begin in the secondary school years as students begin to approach full-time entry into the labor market. However, though "career" is defined as the totality of *work* one does in his or her lifetime, it is obvious that the career of most people begins considerably before starting elementary school. That is, we define work as conscious effort aimed at producing benefits for one's self or for others. Most children exert such efforts very early in life. The argument that career preparation should be postponed until high school or later has permeated education during this century, but it has been based on a misconception of the importance of early childhood experiences on later life and on a misunderstanding of what career education attempts to do for young children.

Career education is concerned with what is learned about meaningful work and with the attitudes toward work which people acquire. In the home, the nursery school, the kindergarten, and the elementary school many children are taught that most work is dirty, boring, confining, exhausting, menial, repetitive, and noncreative. Work is used as punishment ("All right, for that, young lady, you can stay home and wash the dishes"). It is described as something to be avoided ("Learn your multiplication tables so you can go to college instead of going to work"). All of this teaching, whether at home or at school, form attitudes toward work. And attitudes formed early are hard to change. Millions of dollars are spent on vocational education or remedial manpower training to unteach and reteach these attitudes so essential for society and for the individual. So long as preparation for employment emphasized specific job skills, it seemed appropriate to leave it to the later high school years. As soon as work values are seen as a vital element, it becomes obvious that an earlier start is necessary. Day-care centers, nursery schools, and other early childhood education programs are obvious beginning points. Parents need guidance in providing home-based career education. But in the present state of flux, the elementary school is the logical place for action to begin.

Two ingrained policies that are being forced to give way before career education are beliefs about the desirability of prolonging childhood and the assumption that the best way to increase children's options in life is to start as early as possible to prepare them for college and for white-collar employment. The desire to prolong childhood led to a school program which sought to postpone even the most tentative of occupational choices for as long a time as possible. The unstated assumptions about the desirability of a particular type of white-collar employment led to a "general" education program, even in the elementary school, which is not general at all but emphasizes the skills, knowledges, and attitudes associated with pursuit of further education ending in middle-class, white-collar jobs.

Career education in early childhood education and in the elementary school seeks a more balanced view of work and its relationships to life. It accepts and promulgates the assumptions already stated that:

(1) At least some people must work if society is to survive.

(2) All work needed by society is honorable.

(3) Any worker who performs such work well is honorable.

(4) Work that is enjoyed by some people is disliked by other people.

(5) No one has the right to impose his work likes and dislikes on others.

(6) A career is the totality of work done by a person over his lifetime, including, in addition to paid work, that which is done for the benefit of self and others without pay. Thus even children are already engaged to some extent in their careers.

(7) Generally, those workers who are trained, experienced, and productive find their work satisfying, and they will always be more in demand than their opposites.

(8) Almost everything the school teaches can be helpful in at least one type of career.

(9) Going through school with no consideration of the types of careers in which one might be interested causes one to miss much of the value in school.

(10) Postponing consideration of personal career plans until one is out of school virtually guarantees that the individual will begin work with no training and no experience and will be nonproductive, even in an "unskilled" job.

(11) Work values should be taught and become personally meaningful to students. Both societal and personal consequences of each type of choice should be taught. Students, even kindergarten students, should think of themselves as actual as well as potential workers and should not be discouraged from making tentative career choices but should be helping to modify or reaffirm their career commitments periodically throughout the school years.

All programs of career education for young children at this level place major dependence upon the classroom teacher for carrying out the instructional program. This is a different instructional scheme from that used in the junior high school, high school, technical institute, community college, four-year college, and adult education program. In each of these latter levels of career education it is assumed that major responsibilities will be undertaken by specialist teachers who are trained for one phase of career education.

Ideally each day-care teacher and elementary school instructor would receive some preservice training in career education, but such training has barely begun to be offered in a small fraction of teacher training institutions. In an effort to cope with the needs of teachers now employed, three types of aid are provided:

(1) Instructional materials

(2) In-service training

(3) Assistance from specialists who work with the classroom teachers

Career education materials which can be put in the hands of teachers of young children take a variety of forms. The most common is a series of suggestions for class activities — e.g., take your class on a field trip to see people at work; have a worker come to school to describe his work and answer questions; wire light bulbs and switches to get the feel of what an electrician does. More useful is a set of suggestions for ways in which material now taught can be related to careers — when you teach students the sequence of letters in the alphabet, point out that file clerks use this skill, and have students alphabetize the names of their classmates. Less common, and perhaps most useful, are suggested lesson plans and kits of materials for specific instruction, such as OCCUPACS produced by Eastern Illinois University.

Instructional materials for use by teachers in career education efforts are currently being developed by a wide variety of commercial publishers. Most of those now in use, however, have been developed at the local level. Perhaps the best examples are found in materials developed in 52 "mini-models" funded by the U.S. Office of Education, whose Exemplary Programs branch, in addition, funded a number of other projects in which teacher career education materials are being developed. Some local school systems (e.g., Cobb County, Georgia, and Anne Arundel County, Maryland) have expended considerable amounts of local school funds in the development and demonstration of instructional materials for use by classroom teachers in career education.

An ERIC clearinghouse center for career education is being established under auspices of and funding by the Office of Education. When this becomes fully operational, it should be of significant help to those interested in discovering examples of practices, procedures, recommendations, and research in career education. The Center for Occupational Education at North Carolina State University has identified 41 school systems throughout the United States which supposedly have innovative kindergarten through twelfth grade career education programs. From these 41 school systems a wide variety of teacher-made materials has been collected and has been accumulated at North Carolina State University and is available in capsule form.

It is apparent that at present, most development of career education instructional materials goes on in isolation from similar efforts in other school systems. It is also apparent that the most innovative materials, at present, are being developed at the local school system level and not in the college and university settings.

Instructional materials are often developed by teams of teachers working with consultants from universities and sometimes from the world of work. This type of material development obviously has in-service training implications. It is assumed that if teachers play an active role in developing the career instructional program, they will learn of its values and will use it more effectively and enthusiastically. It is also assumed that they will be more likely to continue the program after the removal of outside stimuli. What is really needed, however, is the availability of reasonable effective materials which can be *revised* by classroom teachers. Involvement of teachers in revision of effective materials should produce as much acceptance as involvement in creation of materials which are less effective. Certainly revision requires far less time than creation *de novo*. Creation of materials requires that teachers be freed from their usual employment for substantial periods of time. Summer employment on curriculum development serves as one way of rewarding teachers who are unusually effective during the nine-month school year, and can result in the production of materials which will be used. A number of universities are providing summer school workshops in career education for employed teachers. Those in which each school is represented by one teacher have had little impact. Those involving teams of teachers and counselors from the same school have been more effective in bringing about change in that school during the following school year. Those in which the team included the school principal have, according to our observations, been by far the most effective.

A great deal of what passes for in-service education amounts to bringing in an outside expert who lectures to a group of teachers about career education. Usually, when the expert leaves, little or nothing remains behind.

Large school systems, or consortia of smaller school districts, can employ career education specialists who can work with individual classroom teachers or with groups of teachers. This assistance may be outside the classroom, as in the development of instructional materials or the leadership of in-service teacher training, or it may occur inside the classroom, with the specialist actually conducting lessons. This type of assistance to the classroom teacher is common in school subjects such as art, music, and physical education. Too often the classroom teacher sees no need to be involved in instruction which is produced by an outside specialist. Since career education should involve all aspects of the school curriculum, it may be best to have the outside specialists work through classroom teachers, rather than replace them.

With all our enthusiasm that career education begin as early as possible for the very young, a word of warning is in order. Little has yet been done to build an appropriate rationale to relate and integrate all that might be done through career education at this stage with what is known of the cognitive and maturation processes of children. This is no excuse for not doing something now. It is a challenge to those in education and psychology concerned with these ages and processes to get the needed hard intellectual work under way.

Approaches to a Career Education Emphasis in the Classroom

Thousands of classroom teachers in the last several years have tried literally hundreds of specific activities designed to provide a career education emphasis in their classrooms. Here, rather than attempt any comprehensive listing of such activities, a few general categories will be described, along with one or more specific examples of each in action.

At the elementary school level, several school systems have concentrated primary attention on helping all students become aware of the values of a work-oriented society while acquiring a general awareness of the occupational world. This has been done by developing teaching resource guides for teachers at various levels with respect to various basic work concepts and differing subject matter emphasis. Figure 2 is an example of one page from a set of guidelines for fourth, fifth, and sixth grade teachers.

By viewing systematically the basic values of a work-oriented society and then suggesting specific learning activities designed to acquaint students with those values for each subject matter area, an elementary school can plan a meaningful, total school program designed to attain these objectives without having every teacher repeat what previous teachers have already done. This approach represents, in a generic sense, an attempt to impart work values to students through specific learning activities associated with routine classroom instruction. The approach is being placed increasingly in learning packages organized around specific subject matter content. The example given in Figure 2, for instance, was used in the fifth grade as an integral part of a learning package on uranium. Students learned a great deal about uranium in carrying out the activities contained in the learning package. They also talked about workers associated with the uranium industry in ways that furthered the career education objectives as outlined above.

A second general approach is the schoolwide activity project designed to involve as many teachers and as many students as possible in a career education activity. Again, examples are as numerous as the imagination and enthusiasm which exist in a local community. One elementary school designed its entire project on an ecology basis. A teacher decided to have her students clean up a polluted stream near the school as a science activity. English assignments involved writing about the project, social studies examined its social causes and history, and the art class designed a new landscape, including park facilities that could be constructed once the stream was cleaned up. The principal secured cooperation of local employers in donating men and machines to the project. The students learned by close observation about many unfamiliar occupations. In order to raise funds for their project, the students undertook several small business enterprises calling for the production,

Concept: 2. Persons have to be recognized as having dignity and worth.

Objective: a. Accept that people bring dignity and worth to their job.
b. Appreciate the manner in which work may provide the opportunity for the individual to enhance his dignity and worth.

Learning Outcome	Learning Activities	Resources	Evaluation
a, b. Through his actions, the child will show that he values the dignity and worth of others.	1. The children will list or discuss persons who affected their lives that day. 2. The child will interview some member of his household to find: (a) where he works, (b) how his job contributes to the well-being of others, (c) why he is proud of what he does, etc.	Every person with whom the child comes in contact	The teacher will observe the children.

FIGURE 2. One Page from a Set of Guidelines for Middle/Junior High School Teachers

the distribution, and the marketing of goods, along with all clerical and accounting work that accompanies such projects. In short, the entire school was involved, as well as large parts of the community, in a project that produced a tangible end result and allowed students to learn about many occupations, to gain actual work experience, and to use their academic skills in solving real problems in science, mathematics, language, arts, and social studies. A positive learning atmosphere pervaded the school.

A second example of a schoolwide project occurred in a junior high school where the science teacher expressed an interest in constructing a radio tower. There was no local radio station in the remote, rural area. Teachers and students became involved in raising funds, constructing a station, selecting public service announcements to read over their station, rehearsing musical groups and drama groups to perform on the radio, selling ads to local businessmen to help support the ongoing operation, and conducting many other activities that helped to make school more meaningful to both the students and the community. The fact that their radio transmitter is limited to less than a ten-mile radius did not dampen enthusiasm.

Other elementary, junior high, and senior high schools have designed, built, operated, and maintained one or more businesses calling for many of the skills being taught in the school. In some schools, this has been carried through to the point of forming stock companies, declaring profits and losses, and even going through "bankruptcy" proceedings on a simulated basis. Where products are made, assembly lines have been set up, with students taking turns working on the line. It doesn't take long for the student to learn about the true meaning of such concepts as boring routine, dependability, cooperation, success, and quality control. By conscious efforts to expand the scope of activities to cover as many community occupations as possible, students learn much about occupations and about themselves as prospective workers, as well as the fact that the subjects they are studying in school represent important skills to be mastered.

Individual classrooms as well as entire schools can undertake such projects. Those cited are intended to illustrate several points:

(1) Career education activities can be designed by *all* teachers for *all* students.

(2) Career education activities can be designed to teach basic work values, to provide occupational examples of utility for academic content, and to provide real or simulated opportunities to use academic skills in occupational endeavors.

(3) Career education activities for classroom teachers almost always involve programs of school-community participation, involving community resources, both personal and economic, in their accomplishment.

The Junior Achievement program is an example of an industry-supported organization which helps to plan school and industry cooperation in establishing student-operated companies.

There exists no academic discipline that is devoid of career implications for some students. Most subjects taught by most teachers at most levels of education have multiple career implications for most students. Good teachers have been emphasizing career implications of their subject matter for years. It is now time to make this a common practice in all schools, at all levels, in all parts of the country, and for all students. To understand why such practices have not been common, we must review some of the obstacles facing the classroom teacher.

Operational Problems for Classroom Teachers in Career Education

There exist many good reasons why most classroom teachers have not been extremely active in career education. Teachers will need the sympathetic understanding, support, and active assistance of educational administrators, boards of education, business and industry, parents, and the general public if operational problems are to be resolved.

First, many classroom teachers simply do not know the career implications of their subjects. They are not unwilling to include such activities in their teaching procedures, but they cannot communicate to students what they themselves do not know. The need for instructional materials in this area is very real but of relatively minor importance when contrasted with the need for teachers to acquire personal knowledge and experience concerning the world of work. Far too many teachers have never held any job outside formal education itself. For many, their adult social contacts are largely limited to others who, like themselves, work within the formal structure of education. Perhaps in another generation, teachers will themselves emerge from a career education system and understand the world of work. Until then, solving the problem will mean providing classroom teachers with work experience outside education. This, in turn, may mean twelve-month contracts for teachers, exchange programs between teachers and other workers in the community, the insertion of formal work-study programs as routine parts of undergraduate teacher education programs, sabbatical leaves for teachers to work in occupations outside formal education, or giving summer work experiences the same credit for salary increases as now given for taking additional university courses during the summer. There will be no easy or inexpensive way of providing typical classroom teachers with the knowledge they need in this area. It will represent a sizable educational investment that will have obvious financial implications for local school districts. Teachers cannot be expected to shoulder the entire responsibility for securing the knowledge they need simply on their own or in an incidental way.

Second, for the classroom teacher to reorganize his or her presentations to include a clear career education emphasis, it will be necessary to find time to accumulate new materials, make new contacts, and devise new lesson plans. Again, this is not something the teacher can do with limited effort. Classroom teachers must be provided with the needed time and materials, again suggesting summer employment of teachers working either alone or on curriculum committees to construct materials that can be tried out and evaluated during the school year. National projects can also develop curriculum materials which can be revised and adapted by local teachers.

Third, teachers in a particular school, when instilling a career education emphasis, are faced with the need to coordinate their efforts and activities in ways that complement rather than duplicate each other. Some school systems — such as Anne Arundel County, Maryland — have released a number of teachers for an entire school year simply for purposes of planning and developing coordinated curricular approaches to career education. Other school systems have made this a prime topic of an extended preschool workshop. In those schools where this is not done, the potential for confusion, repetition, and student ridicule exists. We have seen schools, for example, where in four successive classes, students were asked to complete the same vocational interest inventory just because their teachers had all learned about that inventory in a preschool workshop.

Fourth, in schools actively engaged in schoolwide, coordinated career education programs of the project type, there are always some teachers who have difficulty incorporating career education concepts into the particular substantive content they are trying to help students learn. We have seen schools where such teachers have been severely criticized and accused of being uncooperative. In the enthusiasm for career education, it is imperative that all education officials keep clearly in mind that this represents only one of many sound educational goals. It is unreasonable to expect that all teachers will at any given time be able to incorporate a career education emphasis into their classroom activities. Career education, as a concept, recognizes this and does not request teachers to do so. All it asks is for teachers to examine, try out, and attempt to capitalize on the multitude of ways in which a career education emphasis can help make school a more meaningful learning experience.

Finally, one of the most serious operational difficulties facing the classroom teacher in career education is the temptation to concentrate career education emphasis on those students who are having difficulty mastering the academic content while failing to provide a career education emphasis for those who are mastering the academic content with little or no apparent difficulty. This merely serves to reinforce some of the false attitudes career education is trying to overcome — particularly those associated with the usually unspoken but powerful attitude that work is for those who cannot make it in the academic arena. Career education holds as much promise for the valedictorian as it does for any student in a special education class. Those school systems now operating special career education programs for what they like to call the "hard to reach" students in the system may be harming, rather than helping, the goals of career education.

Component B: Vocational Skills Training in Formal Education

In the absence of vocational skills training, individuals who are thoroughly familiar with and accepting of the values of a work-oriented society are likely to be frustrated. Possession of good attitudes toward work, the presence of good work habits, and the sincere desire to become a productive worker are of minimal value to the individual until he has acquired the job skills that will enable him to perform productive work in an increasingly complex occupational society. The acquisition of such skills represents a major part of that portion of our definition of career education that seeks to help students implement those work values that have become a part of their personal value structure.

The term "vocational skills training in formal education," rather than the term "vocational education," is used here for two reasons. First, it is intended to emphasize the concept that whenever one is acquiring skills related to a proposed area of occupational choice, he is in effect engaged in vocational skills training. In this sense, student purpose becomes a more important definitional criterion than the subject content itself. That is, a high school art course for the prospective artist represents vocational skills training. So, too, does a high school course in auto mechanics for the prospective auto mechanic. Yet in each of these classes, some students may be found whose interest in pursuing the subject may be much more avocational than vocational in nature. Ordinarily, a class is designated as vocational education because federal funds appropriated to that purpose are used in its support. It is more meaningful that those classes where the teacher believes most students are striving to acquire skills at a level which would enable the graduate to enter directly into employment be labeled as "vocational education." The point is, for some content in most classes at the junior high, senior high, and post-secondary levels, there are likely to be some students for whom the class is really vocational skills training — and some such classes are known as "vocational education." Perhaps this concept will help integrate vocational education into the total education program in ways that will bring both meaning and dignity to education as preparation for making a living.

The second reason for the use of the term "vocational skills training in formal education" is simply to recognize that more such training occurs outside than within the structure of formal education. For purposes of organizational convenience, such training is later discussed as part of Component D. The scope of the present component has been purposely limited to vocational skills training taking place within the structure of educational institutions. The term does not imply that manipulative skills are the only learning of vocational value. Knowledge, computational skills, communicative skills, work attitudes, and many other learnings are included within vocational skills.

At the elementary school level, the prime purpose of career education is to help students become aware of the occupational world, helping them to become familiar with the values of a work-oriented society and to incorporate such values into their personal value structures. Vocational skills training, at this level, exists primarily for motivational purposes and is best included within Components A and C. The present discussion is limited to the concept of vocational skills training at the junior high, senior high, and post-secondary school levels.

The three major motivations for engaging in vocational skills training are: (a) to explore the meaningfulness that various vocational skills hold for individuals, (b) to discover relative aptitudes and abilities for various vocational skills, and (c) to acquire specific vocational skills that will enable the individual to enter and work successfully in a particular occupational field. While the degree of emphasis on each of these three purposes will vary at the junior high, senior high, and post-high school and adult levels, some students at each level will be found for whom one of these three purposes represents their primary educational motivation.

Vocational Skills Training at the Junior High School Level

For most students, the junior high school serves as a period of occupational exploration. Vocational skills training provided at this level has as its prime purpose teaching students those basic vocational skills which have applicability to broad families of occupations and helping students decide, from among such broad families, those that they may want to study further during the senior high school years.

The Office of Education occupational clusters for consideration by students at the junior high school level are listed in chapter 1. The Office of Education concept calls for the student to gain initial knowledge regarding all fifteen and then to select three as areas in which basic vocational skills are to be acquired on an exploratory basis. According to this scheme, the student, by the end of grade nine, will have selected one of these occupational clusters for further intensive study.

There are several implications of this cluster arrangement that deserve serious thought. First, it can be seen that the clusters do not represent equal (even approximately equal) numbers of employed workers —

health occupations, for example, employ millions of workers, while only relatively few thousands are presently employed in environmental control occupations. Second, these clusters are considerably more inclusive in scope than most vocational education programs now readily available to most students either at the senior high or post-high school level. Third, some of the occupational clusters are completely foreign to those which until now have been labeled as "vocational education" (e.g., fine arts and humanities occupations). Fourth, the occupations within each of these clusters appear to have more in common among the working conditions of the workers than among job skills or geographic locations. Fifth, each of the fifteen clusters includes occupations ranging from the unskilled level through those in the traditional college preparatory curriculum. Sixth, the cluster concept can provide the thread of continuity for at least four of the five components of career education. This comment is sufficiently important to be expanded upon later.

Under the Office of Education cluster model, it would be possible for a student to select one occupational cluster for study in sufficient depth so that he *could* acquire an entry-level vocational skill prior to reaching the tenth grade. This illustrates a general principle of career education; namely, that at whatever level a person chooses to leave the formal education system, he should be equipped with a salable job skill. It also illustrates the extreme degree of flexibility envisioned under this concept. Since most will not leave school before the completion of high school and a growing number continue to some post-secondary education, choice should not be too rigid too early. It is perfectly feasible to assure the acquisition of a salable skill upon leaving school before graduation, yet not require a definite occupational choice before adequate exposure to available alternatives.

Within each occupational cluster, the Office of Education envisions the inclusion of "on-site observation, work experience, hands-on laboratory experience, role playing, and other appropriate activities." Other cluster plans are under development outside the Office of Education and may also provide useful structures for career education. Its cluster proposal is only suggestive and is not binding on schools. Were anything like it to be adopted, it's obvious that major changes would result in the junior high school curriculum. In fact the entire curriculum at that level could be structured around these fifteen occupational clusters, a choice which we believe would be a mistake.

Present junior high school career education programs are considerably less sophisticated than the Office of Education model. It is more typical to identify pieces of a career education program rather than the complete program itself. For example, the Indianapolis schools are offering a summer vocational exploration program for seventh grade students in which, during a period of six to eight weeks, students can spend one week in each of up to eight vocational education programs normally offered at the senior high school level. In Norfolk, Virginia, the local vocational-technical education center, which normally serves primarily eleventh and twelfth grade students, has been opened to junior high school students for summer programs of vocational exploration.

In Racine, Wisconsin, curriculum guidelines for grades seven through nine that attempt to emphasize career implications of all subjects have been prepared, but the curriculum itself has not been reorganized around occupational clusters. A similar approach exists in Anne Arundel County, Maryland. In other cities, such as Bridgeport, Michigan, a career exploration course has been added to the curriculum for all seventh through ninth grade students, but once again, the more traditional subjects of English, mathematics, science, and social studies remain as separately identified parts of the total curricular structure.

In still other cities, such as Clearwater, Florida, at least one junior high school concentrates on offering exploratory occupational education in a variety of typical vocational education areas during the seventh and eighth grades, with basic vocational skill acquisition in one area being emphasized in grade nine. Some of these areas are available for study in greater depth during the senior high school years, while in that community, others have no counterpart in the senior high school offerings.

The problem of finding bona fide work experience opportunities for junior high school students as part of a career exploration program is complicated by child labor laws and the reluctance of employers to hire students at this age level. Some experimental programs are trying to find ways around this. For example, in one junior high school in Baltimore, 21 "high risk" students were selected for a work experience program under which one instructor assumed responsibility not only for finding them jobs for half a day, but also for teaching them related academic subject matter for the remaining half day.

In Hazelton, Pennsylvania, video tapes, showing junior high school students interviewing workers on their jobs, have been prepared. Sonoma County, California, encourages junior high students to make slide-tape presentations from their own photographs of people at work. Where this kind of localized educational-occupational information is being prepared as part of junior high school career exploration programs, it is usually the product of social studies classes, although we have seen such developments in almost every kind of classroom at this level.

The junior high school programs which do not use their community resources to provide students with basic vocational skills often use a combination of coeducational industrial arts and home economics classes to accomplish this objective. Simulation techniques are sometimes used, with "line production" being a fairly common practice. Most often industrial arts is an exercise in learning the handicrafts by which our grandfathers made their living. A few schools use it to familiarize youth with modern service and production processes, materials, and tools. However, few junior high schools include even half of the clusters suggested by the Office of Education.

Many operational problems remain to be solved in order to make the concept of comprehensive programs of career exploration a viable part of the junior high school in American education. Perhaps foremost among these is the question of whether career exploration should be integrated within the traditional subject-oriented curriculum, or whether the traditional academic content of the junior high school should be integrated around a career exploration model such as that outlined by the Office of Education. If all junior high school students are expected to choose one or more from a number of occupational clusters, what is the school to do with the student who appears unready to choose any of them? If students select one occupational cluster and concentrate on developing basic vocational skills related to that cluster, what is the student to do if opportunities for further vocational skills development in that area are not available in the senior high school to which he transfers? How can work experience programs be expanded to be readily available to all, or even to a simple majority, of junior high school students? If the basic vocational skills needed, say, by the prospective lawyer consist simply of academic subject matter content, and if his academic teachers refuse to allow him to read or write about law, how can his program be viewed, both by himself and by others, as carrying a career education emphasis? How can a sufficient variety of vocational tools and materials be made available in the typical junior high school so that those students who seek salable vocational skills at this level can be given a comprehensive set of vocational choices to consider? Is an occupational cluster for marine science occupations *really* appropriate for junior high school students in Liberal, Kansas? Could it *really* be provided?

The above questions are raised here not to discourage communities from engaging in junior high school career exploration programs, but rather to illustrate the fact that the installation and successful operation of complete programs will be no easy matter. While it can be said that no one yet knows how best to organize or to operate these programs, it must also be said that there is growing agreement on objectives for the junior high school level. Included among these objectives are the following:

(1) Every junior high school student should be able to explore his occupational interests and aptitudes from among the broadest possible range of occupational areas.

(2) Every junior high school student should see clearly the relationships between the academic content he is being asked to master and his tentative occupational choices.

(3) As many junior high school students as possible should acquire some real work experience.

(4) Junior high school students should be provided with some basic vocational skills which they can use as building blocks in their later career education development.

(5) Occupational choice options should be kept open for all junior high school students, while each should be simultaneously encouraged to make tentative personal commitments to one or more broad occupational areas at some broad level of competence.

(6) Junior high school students should be provided with sufficient knowledge about and experience in the various vocational education areas open to them at the senior high and post-high

school levels so that these students can really *choose* among them.

(7) Those students who express an intention to leave the formal educational structure, at least for a while, near the end of the junior high school years, should be provided with a set of salable vocational skills that they can use in obtaining employment.

(8) Vocational exploratory programs should be provided in such a way that academic learnings in traditional junior high school areas will be enhanced rather than de-emphasized.

Within this broad framework of objectives, there is room for a wide variety of approaches. As with most other educational concepts, specific methods that appear ideal in one setting are likely to appear completely unworkable in another. Yet the objectives can remain consistent for all.

Clusters as Linkages

The cluster concept has particular advantage in providing linkages among Component A (emphasis on the career implications of all subject matter), Component B (vocational skills training), Component C (career development), and Component D (employer, employee, and labor union involvement). Any academic subject matter area at any grade level can make use of broad industry/occupation clusters in giving realism to its content. The same clusters can provide the structure for orientation to the world of work and career development exposure to alternative occupational choices. General work experiences ranging from field trips, interviews, and visits to the school by workers through cooperative part-time school, part-time work experiences, and on to summer and longer term employment can all be structured within these same clusters.

Use of any clustering approach as a career education focus increases with age and with school level. For adding realism to academic subjects, all fifteen of the occupational clusters can be used universally. For direct observation of the world of work, any school is limited to those activities within reasonable field trip range. For actual exploration, access becomes increasingly important; for "hands-on" skills training, there must be at least simulated workplaces; and for work experience, there must be jobs available.

The major difficulty for the curriculum developer is knowing which of the many cluster arrangements now available or under development will come to be most widely accepted. Occupations can be clustered by industry, by product, by the physical and psychological characteristics of those who engage in them, by job content and skill transferability, and by numerous other criteria. The occupational clusters, being developed along industry lines, are particularly useful at the awareness and orientation stages as the youth views the linkages between the products and services produced and his classroom learning. They are not as well designed for skills training as would be some alternative which clusters around transferable skills. There is added difficulty because Department of Labor publications on occupational information and manpower statistics are more often structured on occupational and skill rather than industry lines. Here is an area where national guidance and decisions will be necessary.

Closely aligned with the cluster concept are three other familiar concepts of vocational education and manpower training which can be adapted to the career education framework. The ladder concept involves moving the trainee up through related jobs in a broad occupational area from the simple to the complex in such a fashion that he has mastered and can always obtain a job in a specialized skill if he does not continue on to the full range of skills involved. In the simplest of examples, an auto mechanic trainee learns first to be a service station attendant, then a brake specialist, then onward, component by component, until he masters the full range of skills of the journeyman mechanic or quits to accept a lesser but related job. The lattice concept is similar but allows lateral as well as vertical movements. The open-entry/open-exit concept insists that everyone at any age must have an opportunity to enter wherever he is and move ahead as far as he can or chooses. Exit must not be final and reentry should remain available, with minimum or even zero penalty to the student.

These concepts are most easily implementable for adults seeking remedial assistance in specific occupational skills. However, there is no reason that, with imagination, they cannot be applied throughout the career education experience.

Vocational Skills Training at the Senior High School Level

Given a successful career exploration program at the junior high school level that has been built upon a comprehensive career awareness program at the elementary school level, we should expect to find three groupings of students at the senior high school level: (a) those preparing for careers that will require a minimum of a baccalaureate degree for entry, (b) those preparing for careers that will require occupational education at the post-high school level but at less than the baccalaureate level, and (c) those preparing for careers that can be entered at the time the student leaves the senior high school setting.

Ideally, every senior high student will be seen and, more importantly, will see himself or herself as fitting one of these three categories. If we can envision a situation where the degree of commitment of any given student to any of these broad options is permitted to range from a very tentative to a clear and definite choice, then this ideal can be closely approximated in practice.

If this is to come about, a number of basic changes in the organizational and operational structure of the American senior high school must first take place. While such changes are essential for the successful operation of career education programs, their implications extend to the total pattern of goals and purposes of American education. Such changes include the following:

(1) The initiation of an open-entry/open-exit system of education that allows education as preparation for work to be combined with work itself and thus makes the concept of the "school dropout" obsolete and without practical meaning

(2) The substitution of performance evaluation for time as the prime criterion in assessing educational accomplishment, allowing a student credit for a particular educational task whenever he has demonstrated its mastery

(3) An educational accounting system that allows students to gain credit for skills mastered outside the four walls of the school as well as for those things learned within the school itself

(4) A twelve months' school operation running eighteen hours a day, six days a week under arrangements whereby youth and adults can and do learn together

(5) A curricular structure whose modules are of a sufficiently varied nature that all students are able to elect a wide variety of learning experiences

To adequately discuss such far-reaching changes in American education is obviously beyond our scope here. (They are discussed to some limited extent in the last chapter of this book.) At the same time, it must be made clear that without these kinds of changes, there is little hope of implementing complete programs of career education.

If such changes can be brought about, goals can be derived for the vocational skills training of each of these three major student groupings: the prospective high school graduate school leaver; the post-secondary, less than baccalaureate enrollee; and the person who expects to be a college graduate. It is realistic to assume that for the majority of students in any of the three groupings, occupational choices will still be a tentative nature; that is, changes in membership from one group to another must be expected and their possibility assured by the organizational and administrative structure of the school system. The career choices of each student should be viewed as ranging from very tentative to very firm, with the student himself being the prime decision maker.

The most tentative career choices can be expected to be found within that group of students preparing themselves for college. This is true not only because of the great amount of flexibility remaining for them, but also because definite career choices cannot, in many instances, be made until the student has had considerable academic exposure to alternatives presented at the college or university level. In spite of this, the career education philosophy would encourage each student to think in terms of some type of career goal, both when he makes the decision to embark on the college preparatory curriculum and as he progresses through that curriculum. This is as important for girls as it is for boys. One of the prime problems of today's college students is the small proportion who have thought about either college or themselves in terms of career goals. A career education emphasis at the senior high school level for this group of students as well as the early school leaver can do much to correct this situation.

Since approximately half of all students who enter four-year colleges and universities remain to graduate, it is especially important that students in the college preparatory curriculum have opportunities for career exploration in areas that will not require the baccalaureate degree. Ideally, every student in the college preparatory program, somewhere during his high school career, will acquire one or more salable skills which he could use to help work his way through college or use for a career beginning, should he not go on to or complete college. The assistance such training would give him in choosing his college major would be an additional bonus.

It is particularly important, in a career education program for college preparatory students, that some opportunities for observational *and* work experience programs be available. Opportunities for systematic observations by college preparatory students of professionals working in areas of their expressed career choices are present in almost every community. Some of these contacts, made through observational programs, may result in opportunities for bona fide work experience, in a paraprofessional capacity, for such students. Where this is not possible, college preparatory students should be encouraged to participate in the broad, comprehensive work experience program that every secondary school must establish as part of the career education covenant.

Technical occupations that require education at less than the baccalaureate but beyond the high school level are a rapidly growing segment of America's occupational structure. Such occupations typically require a combination of strong preparation in science and mathematics with some kind of mental or manipulative skill. The science and mathematics courses appropriate for students in this program may well be at a similar level and nature as those pursued by students in the college preparatory curriculum; all such courses should emphasize their utility to practitioners in and outside disciplines being taught. The specific vocational skills preparation offered such students should cover a wide variety of possible occupational skills. Three purposes of manual or manipulative skills training should be: (a) the acquisition of those basic skills common among large families of technical occupations, (b) the opportunity to continue career exploration with a view toward selecting a particular technical area for study at the post-high school level, and (c) appreciation of the work of others.

As with students in the college preparatory curriculum, extensive provision should be made for pretechnical students to engage in both observational and work experience programs in the occupational world. By the end of his or her senior high school year, each should have acquired a sufficient degree of competence in at least one occupational area to be employed at a paraprofessional level. At the same time, most such students should be moving toward post-high school occupational education in either a technical institute or in a community college setting, and programs should be planned in cooperation with post-secondary schools to ensure that this movement is accomplished by collegiate recognition of skills mastered in high school.

While the proportion will vary greatly from school to school, depending on student goals, it is estimated that approximately half of all senior high school students should be enrolled in vocational education programs for purposes of acquiring vocational skills training. Some of these students will have selected a specific occupational area prior to beginning grade ten, and by the end of grade twelve they will be equipped with fairly high degrees of vocational skills, enabling them to enter their chosen occupations immediately. Others may have selected one broad occupational cluster and, having acquired basic skills relevant to a number of related occupations, will be prepared to start work at one of the entry levels in that cluster. Still others may enroll in vocational education, continue the vocational exploration process throughout the senior high school, and, if they want specific skills in one occupation, pursue post-high school occupational education in another kind of institution. Even the most unsure of these students should receive sufficient basic vocational skills training that he or she would be able to gain entry at some level in the occupational world.

All vocational education curricula should be constructed around a "success" mode; that is, within any given area of occupational study, every student should be encouraged to identify those skills which, in fact, he or she can and will acquire. Too many of these students have seen, at many times in their school careers, how they can fail, but too few have seen how they can succeed. To attain this objective, vocational education curricula must be built in fairly short units with frequent opportunity for completing a learning assignment at some level that represents marketable job skills. These skills should be tabulated along with a list of some of the places in which they may be useful.

Such finite learning assignments, in addition, provide multiple opportunities for students in the college preparatory and the pretechnical programs to equip themselves with skills in vocational education without taking too much time away from their primary curricular objectives. In addition, these assignments serve as a natural means by which students can change training objectives at any time during their school career that it seems appropriate to do so.

The variety of course offerings available to vocational education students should be based on a combination of expressed student interests, local labor market conditions, and national-regional-state statistics reflecting projected occupational demand for workers. The range of offerings should be broad enough not to deny the individual any reasonable choice. Curricula should change as rapidly as any one of these three variables changes. This rate of change will demand frequent replacement of one kind of training equipment with another, changes in physical space arrangements, and instructor changes. It will be expensive.

Some school systems will find it feasible to provide such vocational education within the confines of a single large comprehensive senior high school. Many others will find it necessary to combine forces with other school districts to form a larger, more comprehensive high school or an area vocational school with a comprehensive set of vocational offerings available, on a part-day basis, to students from each of the operating high schools. In sparsely settled portions of rural America and in the crowded inner city areas of our large cities, residential comprehensive schools are badly needed. In such residential schools, vocational curricula should be offered that reflect state-regional-national labor market demands, rather than only those jobs available to students in the immediate geographic area in which their families happen to live.

Students enrolled in vocational education programs at the senior high school level should have multiple opportunities for actual work experience integrated with the school study program. No student should leave school without the chance to benefit from such work opportunities. Throughout the secondary school vocational programs, these objectives should be emphasized: education which is salable in terms of labor market needs, education which increases student options, and education which contributes to the intelligibility of nonvocational learning.

Post-secondary, Less Than Baccalaureate

Post-secondary occupational education, which extends and expands on vocational education offerings at the high school level, is available in community colleges, in area vocational schools in several states, in private trade and business schools, and in residential vocational schools in four states at the post-high school level. In addition, many high schools and area vocational schools serving primarily a high school population by day offer post-high school occupational education programs for out-of-school youth and adults in evening classes. Manpower training Skills Centers and Job Corps centers offer skills training, accompanied with remedial education, for out-of-school youth and adults. These programs also provide stipends for financial support while the recipients are in training. Another significant source of skills training for many out-of-school youth is the military.

Few post-high school, vocational education, or college students intend to use their education simply to learn how to lead the "good life." They seek to learn something that will give them a return on their investment and to attain the "good life" through gainful employment. The same principle should hold for them as for earlier school leavers — some capability upon exit from the school system which makes them attractive to employers. There is room for each of these institutions within a concept of a comprehensive program of career education. Since each appeals to different students for differing reasons, all these forms of post-high school occupational education should be assisted to grow.

Whatever their basic nature, all forms of post-high school occupational education concentrate on preparing students with vocational skills required for successful entry into specific occupations. In addition, most do, and all should, provide opportunities for occupational upgrading. It is important from a career education standpoint that the student be able to differentiate each type of institution from the others in terms of its unique strengths and weaknesses. While no comprehensive picture can be presented here, thumbnail generalizations illustrating this concept of uniqueness may point up the desirable pluralism of career education.

The community college, because it offers both college transfer and terminal occupational education programs, represents an ideal setting for technician training. Many students aspiring to such training want to keep options open for baccalaureate-type programs if they decide to go on, and the programs in the community college offer this option. The basic science and mathematics departments of the community college contribute efficiently to the need for technician training. Most community colleges now offer vocational programs in occupations which do not require post-secondary education for entry. These are particularly useful to the student who has changed occupational goals after leaving high school. The liberal arts offerings, as well as the opportunity to live at home while going to school, appeal to many students and make the community college the best of places for them.

The separate technical institute typically offers more specialized training for technicians with a greater variety of equipment and greater instructor resources in particular occupational areas than could be afforded by most community colleges. For the student who has made a firm career decision to become a particular kind of technician, the separate technical institute may be ideal.

The private vocational or business school appeals to students who want to acquire specific vocational skills in the shortest possible time with the least emphasis on liberal arts offerings. The typical short units of instruction, each of which results in a salable skill, the pressure for successful placement of graduates as a criterion for staying in business, and the opportunity to enroll at any time during the year rather than only at specified intervals add to the attractiveness of these private proprietary schools. The major problem is separating the reasonably priced, highly competent schools from the overpriced or even incompetent private vocational schools.

Adult education programs in nearby vocational schools offer many employed youths and adults their only real opportunity for post-high school occupational education without leaving either home or job. However, the limited range of occupational offerings may not include those of interest to particular individuals.

The public residential vocational school operating at the post-high school level offers sufficient unique advantages to justify at least one in every state. Yet because of political pressures, academic snobbishness, and a general lack of understanding on the part of both educational decision makers and the general public, this concept has been implemented in only four states to date. Among the advantages of the residential vocational school are:

(1) Access for students from every location within the state

(2) A wide variety of occupational offerings (especially in fields for which there is infrequent student demand), better quality of training equipment, and more expert instructors than could be afforded for institutions catering only to students in a particular community

(3) Opportunities to integrate the disadvantaged and the more advantaged members of the general population in a residential living situation

(4) Provision of the status of a college campus

(5) Service to broad labor markets and knowledge of jobs available at the state, regional, and national levels

Skills Centers, established under the Manpower Development and Training Act, have the added advantage of: (a) gathering at one site all of the supportive services required to make skills training viable for persons of limited backgrounds; (b) offering a range of occupations in an open-entry/open-exit, ladder, and cluster setting; and (c) providing stipends to those who could not undertake training without that support. Individual referral programs under MDTA refer elligible individuals from less disadvantaged backgrounds to regular vocational programs and pay them stipends during their training. The Job Corps offers a broad range of both basic education and skills training, along with financial support (in a residential setting), to those recipients whose limited home and neighborhood environments would interfere with their successful training. The military offers, along with training, financial support, discipline, and travel.

All post-high school occupational education institutions face common problems: (1) giving appropriate credit to students who have acquired vocational skills in high school vocational education or on-the-job training, (2) serving both as a postgraduate institution for graduates of secondary school vocational education programs and as the beginning points for those with no previous vocational education or for those who have changed occupational goals radically, (3) providing multiple exit levels at varying degrees of job competency from each occupational training program, (4) enabling students to assess their interest in and potential for particular skills prior to beginning training, (5) overcoming the social stigma of inferiority to four-year colleges or universities, and (6) developing and maintaining a capacity to place competent graduates in training-related jobs. A comprehensive career education program demands that each of these problems be faced and solved within the pluralistic approach to post-high school occupational education envisioned here.

Baccalaureate and Graduate Degree Career Education

It is part of the conventional wisdom that the more education one has, the more one earns and the happier one is. These beliefs have contributed markedly to the growth of college enrollments in recent years. One can argue as to the reasons for the positive correlation between education and earnings, but there can be little argument that the American people have chosen to invest more heavily in higher education than any other people in history. Nor can there be much argument that a belief that education is a quick route to the good life has been a major factor in this investment.

Increasingly, college education has become career oriented. Approximately a third of our college graduates are prepared to teach in the elementary and secondary schools. Undergraduate departments and colleges of nursing, business administration, accounting, agriculture, engineering, journalism, and the like have expanded rapidly. Even in colleges of liberal arts and sciences, half or more of the graduates are prepared for specific careers or are receiving education to become a better practitioner in an existing career.

Career counseling and placement offices exist on almost every college campus. Interviews with prospective employers are arranged. Feedback from employers and former students helps to shape curricula. Scholarships and research funds from employers help to support students in school. Indeed, one can argue that our colleges are more oriented to career education than any other part of our education system. There are signs, however, that all is not well with college-level career education. Dropout rates and transfer rates are high, in part due to misconceptions about the duties and qualifications required for certain careers. Emphasis is placed on admitting students with the best test scores and high school grades, rather than those who can profit most from instruction. Markedly more people are prepared for certain careers than can be employed. Indeed, some legislators are now suggesting that "too many" people are going to college.

Employers require a baccalaureate or graduate degree for approximately 20 percent of the jobs in the United States. However, this percentage has been rising steadily as more college graduates have become available for employment, causing one to question whether demand or supply has been the dynamic factor. Elementary school teaching, for example, now usually requires a baccalaureate for entrance, though only a generation ago graduates of two-year "normal" schools were employable in many states.

The consequences of awarding substantially more college degrees than there are "college-type" jobs can be severe. In some underdeveloped lands, for example, college graduates compete for minor clerical jobs, and clerical jobs, especially in government service, are created just to keep them occupied. These clerical jobs often bear no relationship to the field of study of the college graduate, and considerable dissatisfaction exists because the college graduate feels his talents are not being employed suitably. Political instability has been a consequence as these frustrated intellects hope for more challenging assignments in new revolutionary governments.

A distinction must be made between college degrees which are designed for specific careers and college programs and degrees which, though not designed for careers, create an expectation in the degree recipient that a professional or managerial career will be provided automatically. Both types of programs obviously have involved career education, though in the latter type it is neither formal nor planned. Indeed, some proponents of liberal arts education seriously advocate that no one should think about a career until after the baccalaureate has been completed. The results of this philosophy are powerfully evident in the complete frustration of many college graduates who are forced into jobs they do not enjoy because they lack preparation for careers which would give them satisfaction.

Component C: Career Development as Part of Career Education

Our definition of career education has been formulated in terms of helping individuals take actions. The effectiveness of career education will ultimately be evaluated by the degree to which the recipients of career education assume responsibility for their own decisions. The individual recipient of career education, not the society in which the individual lives, is the prime focus of concern. The term "career development" refers to the total constellation of events, circumstances, and experiences of the individual as he makes decisions about himself as a prospective and as an actual member of the work force. Thus in basic, underlying justification for initiation of career education programs, the component of career development is of pivotal importance and of central concern.

It would be easy to conceive, and relatively simple to operate, a career education program that in effect "brainwashes" individuals into choosing the occupations we want them to fill. Given sufficient resources and dedication of effort, this society could probably produce conditions that would control and direct the occupational aspirations of individuals, their attitudes toward work, their choices of occupations, the vocational training that they would enter, and even the specific jobs in which they are employed. There are, of course, countries in the world today that in effect operate from such a set of objectives.

To control the lives of others is diametrically opposed to the basic nature of a democratic society. Individual freedom of choice, the worth and dignity of each individual, and individual responsibility for actions taken are basic cornerstones of our society. Programs of career education must recognize the fundamental importance of these concepts in both their philosophical formulation and in their operational practices.

Basic Understandings Regarding Career Development

In order to discuss ways in which career development operates as a component in career education, a clear understanding of its basic nature is essential. First, career development is essentially a lifelong process, beginning early in the preschool years and continuing, for most individuals, through retirement. As a process, it includes the view one has of himself as a worker, the view he has of work itself, the knowledge he acquires about himself and his possible work opportunities, the choices

he makes related to himself as a worker, and the ways in which he imple-
ments those choices. Programs of career development concern themselves with each of these facets of the total process.

Second, personal choices involved in career development are taking place on a continuing basis throughout the life of the individual.
Choices involving personal life-styles, personal values, and leisure time
preferences are as much a part of career development as are occupational choices.

Third, occupational choices made as part of career development are
expressed in many forms and with many degrees of firmness and insight
at various times in the life of the individual. In very young children, we
expect these choices to have large degrees of fantasy associated with
them. Occupational choices, in a typical developmental pattern, move
from a fantasy to a tentative to a firm decision and then to an implementation stage. The process of making occupational choices will, for
almost all individuals in today's society, occur more than once during
their working lives. It is certainly not a matter of making an occupational choice and then being asked to live with it for the rest of one's life.

Fourth, choices are, in various stages of career development, made
on the basis of what the individual would enjoy doing, on the basis of
what appears possible for him to do, given his personal and societal
limitations and strengths, on the basis of what seems most important for
the individual to do, and, when made in what we call a "mature" way,
on the basis of the interaction of all these kinds of factors.

Fifth, in terms of career choices, the prime goal of career development lies in its process, not in its end result. It is not *what* the individual
chooses that is of primary concern. Rather, it is *that* he chooses which
is important. It is the reality of *choice* rather than the *realism* of the
choice that is our primary concern. The wisdom of the basis on which
individual choices are made is much more germane to evaluating
effectiveness of career development than are any judgments regarding
the supposed "wisdom" of the choices that are made.

In career development, the right to change is held to be as sacred as
the right to choose. Career development aims to help individuals learn
how to make decisions in a wise manner. While with each succeeding
career decision the individual's effective opportunities to make other
career decisions are affected, no career choice can or should be regarded

as truly irreversible. What may be nearly irreversible are the effects of reaching adulthood without ever having considered a career choice. If every time the child asks "How can I decide what I want to be?" the parent or teacher says "Don't worry about that until you get through college," the effect in loss of self-esteem may be disastrous.

Finally, the wisdom of career choice lies in the extent to which and the basis on which it is a *reasoned* choice, not in the degree to which it seems *reasonable* to others. Given bona fide choices and adequate assistance in the decision-making process, most individuals will choose in ways beneficial both to themselves and to society in general.

The Nature of Career Development Programs in Career Education

Career development operates at every level and in every setting represented in career education. In the elementary school, the prime focus of career development lies in helping the student become aware of the work, the values of a work-oriented society, and of himself to a degree that will enable him to think of himself in terms of his role as a prospective worker. The elementary school student is encouraged to express occupational choices, not out of any illusions that most such choices will be effectively implemented in adulthood, but rather because of the value of the process in helping the student think about himself as a person. Student expressions of occupational choice, at this level, are highly influenced by perceived interest in an activity rather than by such factors as aptitude, availability, educational requirements, and economic implications of the choices that are made.

At the junior high school level, where the question of elective subjects typically first arises, most students are led to consider occupational choices, at least in part, in terms of their educational requirements for entry. In this connection, an important responsibility of career education is to make sure that alternatives are presented as being different in kind rather than in innate quality. Unless this can be successfully accomplished, no real *choice* is present. That is, if alternatives are pictured as being on some universally accepted hierarchy running from "best" to "worst," students do not "choose" from among them. Rather, they "settle" for an alternative that is the most favorable available to them. Career development programs operate under an assumption that the "best" choice is something to be determined individually by each student — the best choice for one will be the worst choice for another.

At this level, the student can typically be expected to be engaged in a process of occupational exploration. Such exploration will help each student narrow the range of occupations he is considering from the more than thirty thousand occupations listed in the *Dictionary of Occupational Titles*. To do this, it is convenient to group occupations, in some fashion, around broad occupational families. The Office of Education grouping, which uses fifteen occupational clusters, represents one of several alternatives available for doing so. Its particular advantage lies in the ease with which the subject matter content of the junior and senior high schools can be integrated within this classification system.

Other occupational classification systems include those based on the *Dictionary of Occupational Titles* (oriented around similarity in job skills and duties), on Roe's occupational classification system (based primarily on similarity in personality types), and on the U.S. Bureau of the Census system (based primarily on a sociological-economic rationale). The particular model which will best help a particular group of junior high school students explore the total world of work in terms of their tentative occupational choices can be expected to vary widely. Eventually, however, a few of these models will be found to be far more useful than the rest.

No matter what classification scheme is adopted, students should be helped to explore differences and similarities among occupations from several dimensions. One dimension is the nature of the job skills employed. A second is the educational level required for entry. Environmental conditions — both physical and geographic — associated with the work is a third dimension. Finally, a fourth dimension is differences existing in life-styles among workers in various occupations. Each of these dimensions must be considered by the student in terms of his own currently available skills, his aptitudes, his interests, his work values, his environmental restrictions, and his motivations.

It is the blending of these dimensions of occupational differences coupled with personal considerations that represents the stuff from which occupational decisions are made. The process is both complicated and complex. When the dynamics associated with the current rapidity of occupational change are added to the progress, it becomes even more complex. It should therefore not be difficult to understand why, at the junior high school level, the goals of career education for most students are stated in terms of "tentative" occupational choices. Programs of career education must recognize that this tentativeness may, and for many students should, extend through the senior high school years and beyond. To insist on a goal of "firm" occupational decisions for all students at any level of secondary education would be both unfair and unrealistic. Care should also be taken that the firmness of decisions does not foreclose options by denying the student or the adult the opportunity to change his mind or pursue new interests.

To recognize the complexity of the occupational choice process in no way diminishes either the importance or the appropriateness of occupational exploration at the junior high school level. No matter how incomplete or inadequate the base, the individual, when expressing a tentative occupational choice, is also expressing a view of the kind of person he sees himself as being. He is also expressing a degree of motivation for learning. Occupational exploration programs in the junior high school offer the student a way in which he can see school as making sense to him. They also offer him an opportunity to experience the vocational decision-making process. The fact that, at this stage, he finds himself unready to make firm vocational decisions detracts not at all from the validity of engaging in the decision-making process.

Effective career development programs combine provisions for giving students information, with a wide array of opportunities for them to gain information for themselves through direct personal experiences. There is no way in which students, at any level, can be expected to acquire an adequate informational base for vocational decision making solely through unaided personal experiences. Thus both self-assessment and environmental information systems are important aspects of career development programs.

The self-assessment systems needed include paper and pencil methods, along with "hands-on" assessment devices that allow students to become better aware of their skills, their aptitudes, their interests, and their values. The environmental information systems needed involve a multiple-basis concept that includes one based on local information, one based on state and regional information, and one based on national information. At each base, the system requires the coordination of information regarding both educational and occupational requirements and opportunities.

No matter how complete or elaborate, to simply present information to students about themselves, their educational opportuntiies, or the world of work will be an insufficient basis for vocational decision making. Information presented *to* students must be combined with a wide variety of opportunities for students to discover information for themselves. Thus career development programs involve a heavy emphasis on helping students engage in experiences, both within and outside the school setting, that will help them acquire a firmer basis for making educational and vocational decisions. These activities should involve both observational and actual work experience for all students in the high school.

The provision of opportunities for educational and vocational choice in no way guarantees the quality of choices individuals make, or even that such choices will be made. Assistance in the actual decision-making process is a crucial aspect of the career development component of career education. Such assistance is, of necessity, a highly personalized matter. The prime vehicle utilized for rendering this assistance is professional counseling. Some of the necessary counseling can be carried on in groups, while at other times, individual counseling is necessary. Whether conducted on a group or on an individual basis, the goal is to help the individual make reasoned decisions based on the widest possible accumulation of both self and environmental knowledge in ways that fully protect individual freedom of choice. Such counseling is an action process where such action terms as "know," "reflect," "assimilate," "understand," and "decide" are appropriate parts of the total description of the process.

Counseling is a "reasoning out loud" process in which the individual is encouraged and assisted in expressing his thoughts, his knowledge and perceptions, and personal meaning that various bits of information have for him, the bases on which he is considering making decisions, and the actual making of decisions themselves. It represents a means by which the individual can validate for himself the bases on which his decisions are being made and the quality of such decisions. It also represents a means by which the skilled professional counselor can make sure that the student is basing his decisions on the widest possible array of information and that he has properly interpreted and integrated the information on which decisions are being based.

The need for counseling in career development is a relative matter that will vary greatly from individual to individual. It is true, of course, that almost all individuals are capable of making decisions if they are forced to do so. Counseling, then, is not viewed as helping individuals do something they would otherwise be incapable of doing. Rather, the goal of counseling is to improve the quality of the decisions that are made. Thus opportunities for professional counseling should be made available to all individuals. Some will need counseling more than others, but there is no individual who could not profit from good educational-vocational counseling. It is, thus, a crucial and essential part of career development.

Implementing Decisions

A career development program that stops at the point individuals have made decisions cannot be truly effective. In addition to helping individuals make decisions, assistance must be provided to individuals in implementing decisions they have made. This implementation function in career development includes such things as helping the individual locate specific training or work opportunities, helping him make contacts with prospective schools or employers, helping him proceed through the actual application process, and helping him make a successful transition from the setting in which he now finds himself to that setting where he has decided to move. Again, the extent to which such assistance is required will vary greatly from individual to individual. It will be particularly great among those individuals who are severely disadvantaged in terms of economic or social barriers. Such individuals are frequently painfully aware of such barriers and have little, if any, need to be told that they exist. Rather, they need systematic and effective help in overcoming such barriers so that they, too, can experience maximum freedom of choice in making and implementing educational and vocational decisions.

The implementation function should be ready to go into action whenever decisions are actually made. For some students, this means assistance in obtaining some specific vocational skills training while still in the junior high school. For others, it will mean assistance in selecting and entering into specific vocational skills training at the senior high school level. For still others, it will mean assistance in entering appropriate senior high school programs that will lead to post-high school occupational training in a community college, university, or elsewhere.

Much of what has been said regarding career development programs at the junior high school level apply equally well to the senior high school setting. The differences are in degree more than in kind. Decisions made at the senior high school level are typically more firm and relatively more irrevocable than those made in the junior high school. In this sense, they can be considered as more serious. Since many such decisions involve not only a change in the kind of activity in which the individual plans to engage, but also a change in residence and in home-family relationships, they are more crucial and have longer range implications.

Yet there are subtle but important differences expected on the basis of which vocational decisions are made at each level. In the elementary school, students tend to make decisions based largely on interest and liking for one activity as opposed to another. In the junior high school, students are likely to add to the interest base a dimension in which they consider their relative ability and aptitude to perform various kinds of work. Upon entering senior high school, most students will add personal values as a third dimension to those developed earlier, based on interest and aptitudes. Thus near the end of the senior high school years, we find many students asking "What is important to me?" as well as "What would I like to do?" as they engage in the vocational decision-making process.

As the time draws nearer for such students to actually leave the secondary school setting, two more questions must be considered: "What is possible for me?" and "What is probable for me?" While both should have been asked and answered to some extent earlier in career development, these two questions take on added significance at the point the student finally realizes that he does, in fact, have to decide *something*. After all, if he is not to be "required" to be back in school the following fall, he must decide what, in fact, he will do. At that point, even to decide not to decide is to decide something. For a sizable proportion of students, the answers to these questions are postponed until some time later in life, perhaps at the end of college, or upon marriage, or after the youngest child has entered school. For a few people, the questions are never answered or even asked. It should be easy to see why career development is emphasized here as something that should begin very early in the life of the individual and operate on a continuing developmental basis. It certainly should not be a topic that is raised, for the first time, at the point when the student is about to leave the secondary or post-secondary school.

Wide variation in problems of career development can be expected to exist among students from various portions of the senior high school population. At one extreme we find the severely disadvantaged student who, from a very early age, has been learning a very great deal about what appears to be impossible for him. For such students, career development programs are needed that greatly expand not only the possibilities the student sees for himself, but also the probabilities that he will be given an opportunity to try that which he eventually decides to do. At the other extreme, we might picture the exceptionally brilliant student from a highly affluent home who appears to be interested in everything he encounters. For such students, career development programs are needed that help the student learn enough about himself so that he can narrow his vocational considerations in ways that will provide him with the most meaningful personal life-style. For others, specific needs for career development, as part of career education, will fall between these extremes.

Personnel in Career Development Programs

The career development of any individual is influenced, to a considerable degree, by a wide variety of factors, including his home and family structure, his socioeconomic status, his peer relationships, his own personal characteristics and idiosyncrasies, and his school experiences. Without the systematic attention and efforts of persons specifically concerned about his career development, the individual's career decisions are much more apt to become a matter of chance than of wise and reasoned choices. It is imperative that specific responsibilities for assistance to individuals in career development be understood, accepted, and implemented.

Of the persons influencing career development of youth, none are more important or crucial than those in his home and family structure. These are discussed in Component E.

Within the formal educational setting, three distinct types of personnel are essential in comprehensive career development programs.

The first of these is the classroom teacher. As teachers emphasize the career implications of their subject matter, it is both natural and expected that students will seek to discuss career decisions with teachers. When this occurs, teachers should be both willing and able to listen to students as they try to wrestle with problems of career choice. However, the primary career development force of the academic teacher must be imparting to the students the career implications of his or her subject matter. Similarly, the primary focus of the vocational education teacher must be on the teaching of vocational knowledge, skills, and attitudes. Both academic and vocational education teachers are limited, in terms of time and formal training, in their ability to help students make and implement career decisions. To whatever extent classroom teachers possess such ability and can find time, they should be encouraged to enter into a counseling-like relationship with students. It must be recognized that in most schools and for most students, teacher efforts, by themselves, will not be sufficient to meet total career development needs of students.

The second type of personnel needed in career development programs is the professional counselor. In the school setting, such a counselor should possess a solid understanding of and commitment to education. In addition, his training should include competence in student assessment and in the psychology of learning, of individual differences, of personality development, and of career development. Added to this should be basic understandings of both economics and sociology as fields of study. He must be conversant with sources of data on present employment opportunities, further projections of manpower requirements, the demands of employers, and the workings of labor markets. Furthermore, he must have a heavy concentration in counseling theories, methods, and procedures, including supervised practice in counseling. To this the really qualified counselor will add substantial work experience outside the field of education. Finally, he must possess the kinds of personal qualities that lead students to confide in him, knowing that he is interested, concerned, and can be trusted to work in their best interests.

Just as career education is properly viewed only as a part of education, so is career development properly viewed only as part of personal development. Thus the professional counselor must be prepared to help students with a wide variety of problems they bring to him, in addition to those concerned specifically with educational and vocational decision making. Despite the diverse nature of such problems, the professional counselor in the school, more than any other professional on the school staff, sees his primary function as being in career development within a total program of career education. There is no way in which an adequate career development program can be expected to function in the absence of sufficient numbers of professionally prepared counselors.

The third essential kind of personnel needed in career development programs will be paraprofessional, support personnel specifically concerned with career education. A wide variety of such personnel is needed. Some will concentrate on helping classroom teachers assemble and disseminate career implications of their subject matter to students. Others will function as technicians assigned to the counselor's office, performing such functions as administering assessment devices, collecting, collating, and disseminating occupational and educational information, and conducting follow-up studies of former students. Still others will function as active agents of environmental change by seeking out job and work experience programs for students, working with employers in their efforts to help students make the transition from school to work, and working with community agencies in their efforts to help students overcome personal, social, and economic handicaps that are interfering with the student's career development opportunities. Such paraprofessionals are badly needed but in short supply at the present time.

Component D: Contributions of Employers, Employees, and Labor Organizations

No part of society is more likely to benefit from career education than the business, labor, and industrial community. For many years, employers and labor leaders have pleaded for the schools to prepare persons with the skills and work values to make them productive, successful, and satisfied members of the labor force. If career education is to become a partial answer to such pleas, it will be essential that employers and labor organizations become active participants. More is required than simple cooperation with the formal educational structure, leaving it the primary responsibility. Rather, business and labor must become an integral part of the program. The definition of career education used here refers to "the total effort of the school *and* the community."

Before the proposed involvement of employers, employees, and unions in career education is outlined, two points must be made: First, career education funds must be made available to support this effort. It is unrealistic to expect that the degree of involvement envisioned will occur supported only by good will and good intentions. Second, though the goals of such involvement are relatively clear, little is known at this point about how such goals can be attained. Few proved examples are available in current practice. The success of career education is dependent upon finding solutions to the problems posed here. This discussion is organized around a variety of goals whose attainment is directly dependent upon the active *participation* — not just the *cooperation* — of the business, labor, and industrial community in the total career education effort.

Problem 1: Serving as a Source of Information

The solution to most problems is a function of the accuracy, the adequacy, and the timeliness of the data brought to bear on the problem. Career education is no exception to this general rule. Several examples of needed data are discussed below.

There is need for the occupational community to serve as an answering service for specific questions that students, teachers, counselors, and others in education have about specific occupations, particularly as they exist in a given community. Currently available occupational information leaves much to be desired, but some communities are moving in appropriate directions. For example, in Albuquerque, New Mexico, the names, occupations, and telephone numbers of several hundred workers and employers who have agreed to answer questions from counselors, teachers, and students with respect to their work are being made available to the schools.

State employment services have found employer estimates of future employment of little use in projecting future occupational requirements. However, information on current employment by age, occupation, and industry is vital to conduct and plan vocational skills training. Whether such surveys are performed by the schools or by the employment service for the schools, cooperation of employing institutions is vital.

The occupational community should also cooperate in school projects to build occupational information libraries on a localized basis. In some communities, this is done by sending junior and senior high school students out to a work setting to take photographs, make video tapes, and secure tape recordings of interviews held with workers and employers. In others, employers are asked to fill out forms to be used by the school system as input into computer data banks. A variety of other equally time-consuming methods are in use in various parts of the country, but little is available nationally or even regionally.

There is continually a need for active involvement of the occupational community on advisory councils for career education in the schools. In addition to advising on the nature of training requirements, such councils are also needed to work with school officials on a host of school-community activities that are part of career education.

While other examples could be provided, these few will perhaps be sufficient to illustrate both the nature of the problem and its possible magnitude.

Problem 2: Serving as a Source of Observation for Career Education

An essential element of successful career education is actual observation of workers in the workplace. Such visits will involve elementary, junior high, and senior high school students. In addition, work observation will involve observation by teachers, counselors, and school administrators, not only when they accompany students, but when they seek to increase their own knowledge.

Baltimore operates a monthly seminar for school counselors throughout Maryland. Taking a different occupational area each month, large groups of counselors are given tours of business and industry, with oral explanations of the occupations involved and the technology and economies of the industry. The groups are encouraged to ask questions.

Student groups have been visiting business and industry settings for years. Under the career education approach envisioned here, many more such visits will take place. Furthermore, with career education occurring from the elementary school through the high school years, there will be a need for systematically planned approaches which are appropriate to the career development needs of the students involved and which will continue to hold student interest year after year, while not eliminating cooperation from those who control the places where work may be observed. Very little systematic work has been done to date in planning such coordinated programs of observation. This planning must be a joint product of schools, employers, and employee organizations, but becomes fairly complex in metropolitan areas served by several independent school districts. If the total amount of observational visits envisioned by career education ever comes to pass, business firms will be confronted with a serious logistical problem. It seems unlikely that in the long run, actual physical visitations will be as common as some are currently proposing. It will be too upsetting to business and industrial production were this to occur. It seems more likely that as more experiences are gained in this area, a variety of media — including films, video tapes, and slide tapes — will be used in schools as a partial substitute for regular visits of large numbers of students to the real work setting.

Problem 3: Work Experience and Work-Study Programs
   for Students

As in learning to swim, there is only so much that students can learn about work through studying books, listening to instructors, or observing others working. If students are going to acquire the work attitudes employers seek, they must have actual opportunities to work. Few youth find sufficient opportunities in their own homes. The schools cannot provide meaningful work opportunities for all who need them. The success of this effort will demand the active involvement of the occupational community.

Again, programs to gain work experience and to combine it with study have been in operation for years as part of high school vocational education. Two things serve to make the situation drastically different under the proposed model of career education. First, there will be many more students involved than ever before. Second, students from all ability levels at both the junior and senior high school levels will be involved. If jobs are limited, the natural tendency of the employer will be to choose the high-ability student from the college preparatory program, while the special education student who, in terms of immediate needs, has more to gain from the work experience will find no one willing to accommodate him.

It seems quite likely that considerable financial incentives will be required in order for business and industry to create sufficient work experience and work-study opportunities and to provide adequately for the wide individual differences in students needing such experiences. Such incentives may be particularly useful in time of economic recession when there is conflict with commitments to laid-off workers. Labor unions may oppose work experiences or work-study programs or other career education activities if these appear to threaten the jobs and welfare of union members. Such conflicts of interest must be considered and accommodated. Moreover, especially with junior high students, child labor laws pose problems which will have to be solved.

Problem 4: Work-Study Programs for Educators

The potential for educational upheaval involved in providing work experience programs for teachers, counselors, and school administrators is enormous, but the problems of providing this experience are severe. Yet if the goals of career education are to be attained, it is essential that work experience in noneducation occupations be provided for those who now work as educators. Without such experiences, few of today's educators will be fully capable of internalizing, for themselves, the true meaning of the goals of career education, let alone acquire the background knowledge required for their attainment.

Too few educators have work experience outside education. Many went from the public schools to a teacher education institution and immediately returned to the public schols. Too many such teachers have never had to keep up with an assembly line, to feel the vibrations of heavy equipment at work, or to cough at the odors of a heavy industrial operation. They have experienced neither the boredom of performing a routine job in a mechanical fashion nor the exhaustion that can come from physical labor. They know little more about the realities of low-level, white-collar, and clerical jobs or of technical and professional jobs outside the education industry. They have never met a payroll or missed a payday. They believe a college degree is the best and surest route to occupational success because that is the route they chose for themselves. Their perspective, knowledge, and attitudes must change if career education is to work.

With the active participation and support of the occupational community, this problem can be attacked from at least two broad approaches. The first consists of a massive program of summer work-study programs for educators. So long as the nine-month school year remains fashionable, this may be the best we can do. Assuming the twelve-month school year will shortly become a reality, a more workable system might consist of frequent sabbatical leaves for educators, allowing them to acquire work experience. Such leaves would surely be as justifiable as are rewards for many of the courses educators now pursue in summer school classes.

A second and, in the long run, more profitable approach would be exchange programs between education and the occupational community under which some educators would work on jobs outside education, while noneducators from the "school of hard knocks" rather than the "school of hard books" would take their place in the classroom. Too many changes are needed in the education system to make this procedure workable on more than a tiny scale at present. However, the fact that something is hard to do does not justify judging it to be wrong, impractical, or impossible to attain. As a start, this exchange approach could be undertaken for counselors.

More important than such in-service retraining in the long run is change in the teacher education institutions themselves — the vocational skills training sources for public school educators. The most practicable way to change teacher education institutions is to provide sizable amounts of federal funds to those initiators of work experience programs as part of the required curriculum for degrees and certification in education. Implementing such programs would require the active cooperation of the occupational community beyond the immediate geographic area in which the teacher education institution is situated. Teacher education institutions have already solved geographic problems in finding assignments for student teachers. The same practices could prevail in work experience assignments with the active cooperation of the occupational community.

Problem 5: Education and Training in the Occupational Community

Any employer knows that problems in the transition from school to work do not end the first day the worker is on the job. It is rare to find an individual who, having just finished an occupational education program, is ready to perform adequately in the specific position to which he is assigned by his employer. A considerable amount of occupational education — and thus of career education — must take place after the worker is on the job.

The principles of occupational education outlined earlier have as much applicability to on-the-job training, apprenticeship, and formal industrial training programs as they have to education in the schools. Career education is a lifelong process. With the right training in the occupational community itself, current needs to retrain and upgrade adults by formal education could be greatly lessened. Career education dollars could be wisely invested in these efforts.

Problem 6: Making Work Meaningful to Workers

Career education seeks to make work possible, meaningful, and satisfying for every individual. Because many jobs in our current occupational structure are organized, it is difficult for many workers to view themselves as performing meaningful and satisfying tasks. While such problems are probably beyond complete solution, much more could be done to make work meaningful and satisfying for the individual worker. There is no necessary virtue in choosing only goals that are capable of full attainment. Some goals are worthwhile, if only because people strive to reach them.

Effort invested in the study of work values and in the formulation, tryout, and evaluation of various approaches to bring work into accord with the work values held by workers would be well spent. This is a task that can best be done by the occupational society itself. However, job enlargement structured by the worker is often to be preferred to job enlargement structured by the process engineer.

Problem 7: Job-Placement Programs

If formal education is to devote a significant portion of its total efforts to readying students for work, better means must be found to aid students in the transition from school to work. The public employment service, despite its long years of effort, is not regarded by either schools or employers as an adequate solution. Whether, given vast increases in funds, the public employment service could do the job is at present a moot point. It would appear necessary for systematic, coordinated, and comprehensive job placement programs to be established through the joint efforts of formal education, the public employment service, and the occupational society itself.

Provisions are needed for local, state, regional, and national systems of communication between employers and educational institutions. Such communication networks must include current, accurate, and continuous data regarding areas of need for employees, the sources of trained employees who are ready for work, and the means by which those employers needing trained workers can communicate with the prospective employee seeking work — *and* with those who have assumed responsibility for preparing the prospective employee for his work.

The technology, the tools, and the know-how required for accomplishment of this task are already present. The funds required to use these in a workable job-placement program have not as yet been made available. The schools have thought their task completed upon handing out a diploma. In general, they have treated the labor market with disdain. Employers have made some use of both the schools and the employment services, but those two public institutions, with few exceptions, have held each other at arm's length. If career education is to attain its ultimate goals, follow-up must occur to provide continuing help and to gain feedback from the placement efforts to modify and improve school programs. Feedback is vital. Nothing changes a school program as rapidly or as radically as knowledge that students have been hurt by sins of omission or commission. Fear of obtaining such knowledge is a major factor inhibiting feedback.

Component E: The Role of Home and Family

The home and family structure in almost all societies serves as the most powerful influence on both the attitudes and the actions of youth. As with any other powerful community force, this structure can become a tremendous ally in furthering educational objectives, and conversely, it could become a formidable foe. In any event, it cannot be ignored. Whether, if ignored, the home and family structure would help or hinder the goals of career education is a moot question. It is, however, essential to recognize that these goals are too important to be left to chance.

At a conceptual level as treated thus far, most parents would support the basic concepts of career education. However, that support could easily turn to suspicion if some of the current plans for implementing programs of career education in the schools were not carefully explained to them. A good many parents, if ignored, would resist comprehensive programs of career education for their children unless such programs were extremely well run, though in the beginning, many will not be. In short, unless the home and family structure is made a major component of career education, many parents will regard it in the same way they currently view vocational education; i.e., as a program needed in the schools, but one that is for the children of other parents.

However, it is not simply fear of a possible negative parent reaction that requires inclusion of the home and family structure as a major component of career education. Rather, it is recognition of the tremendously powerful potential the home and family structure has for furthering or for defeating career education objectives. No major proposed change in American education has ever succeeded without parent support, and no major changes should take place in American education without the full knowledge and support of the parents of the children in the schools. Parents should have a special interest, since many of them were victims of the variety of societal forces that have combined to create the need for career education in the schools today.

There are three major thrusts involved in the home and family component of career education. One is concerned with increasing knowledge among parents concerning home and family living. A second is concerned with changing certain parent attitudes that currently hold negative implications for attaining the goals of career education. The third is concerned with active involvement of parents in the total career education program.

Teaching of Home and Family Living

No worker is unaffected by events taking place in his home. No home is immune from either the positive effects that come from what is regarded as a "successful" day's work or the negative effects that result from a "bad" day on the job. Thus to the extent that the goals of career education are pictured as making work possible, meaningful, and satisfying to each individual, the home and family structure stands as a potent force for attaining or defeating attempts to reach that goal.

The teaching of family relationships both to parents and to secondary school students represents one of three major aspects here. That such knowledge exists and can be transmitted to others has been well demonstrated for a good many years by persons in the vocational homemaking field. Unfortunately, vocational homemaking, viewed as part of vocational education, has been regarded as "second-class education for second-class citizens." It is seldom a required course in any high school perhaps because it too often limits itself to the skills of cooking and sewing rather than the skills of parenthood or fraternity. Rarely are boys exposed to the contents of home and family relationships, despite the fact that they are expected to become within a relatively few years significant influences in families of their own. Considering the current instability of the family structure, home and family living should clearly be included in the knowledge to be transmitted to all students.

A second important aspect is consumer education. Consumer purchases play a major role in home and family relationships. The wise use of consumer goods is being recognized as having at least equal value. Consumer education is rapidly acquiring the means of collecting and transmitting pertinent facts to the consumer in a wide variety of areas. For only a very small amount of what is currently being spent by business and industry in advertising their products, an effective nationwide consumer education program could be mounted and operated that would offset the negative effects of misleading advertising and help people everywhere gain more valuable knowledge from the good in advertising and from other consumer information.

A third essential aspect is the teaching of work values in the home itself. The home is a place of work in every sense of the word. The home, as a workplace, constitutes a viable laboratory for teaching children the basic concepts of work. There is no basic principle of work itself that cannot be easily demonstrated in the home. Such concepts as the interdependence of workers on each other for successful production, the importance of cooperation among those who work together, of following directions, of specialization of work roles, of punctuality if a task is to be completed on time, of accepting personal responsibility for performance of assigned tasks, of avoiding unnecessary waste, and of cleanliness in the work area are first introduced there. So, too, can such basic concepts as the boredom that comes from performance of an important but routine task, the rewards that come from successful completion of an assigned task, and the necessary reprimands that typically come when a worker fails to correctly perform an assigned task.

With the relatively large amounts of time most students spend in the home, multiple opportunities exist for such work concepts and work values to be transmitted within the home and family structure. For many thousands of students, there will be time in their adult lives when work, in the classic sense of something one does for money, will be un-

available to them. Work, as a means for meeting the normal achievement needs of individuals, will, at various times for many thousands of
people, increasingly have to be found within the home and family
structure.

Changing of Parent Attitudes

Whatever positive potential for career education exists through viewing the home as a place of work matters little if parents fail to capitalize
on this potential. It is apparent that few are doing so today. Thus if this
aspect of career education is to be made effective, a massive program
of parent education must be undertaken so that parents will be both
inclined and able to make this happen. This, then, is the first example of
parent attitudes to be changed.

A second example of needed changes in parent attitudes is illustrated
by the pervasiveness of the false worship of the baccalaureate degree
as the best and surest route to occupational success for their children.
This false attitude is much more prevalent among parents than among
their children. For the schools to attempt to present educational alternatives to students as differing in kind rather than in innate worth will be
only minimally successful so long as parents continue to believe that, for
their children, a college degree is necessarily a desirable goal. One does
not effectively counter one bias with another. If this false parental
attitude is to be changed, it will be necessary to collect and disseminate
clear evidence regarding the advantages of alternative forms of education. Economic, sociological, and psychological benefits possible from
alternative forms of education as preparation for work must be made
known and presented in an objective, honest fashion to both parents and
students. Such evidence can be accumulated, but it is not available in a
systematic, understandable form today.

A third example of parental attitude that must be changed lies in
helping parents accept and endorse the inevitability of some form of
work as an essential part of the lives of their children. Far too many
parents seem to believe that if they could only make things easier for
their children than they were for themselves, their children would somehow be better off. It is almost as if the ideal would be to create a condition under which their children would never have to work at all. This
of course is diametrically opposed to what we know and can predict
about work in society. The preservation and renovation of work values

serves as an underlying goal of career education because it is necessary for the success of our society. Parents who need to take pride in their children's aspirations for work and in their demonstrations of successful performance of work tasks, no matter how small, are teaching concepts that are vital to our future.

Finally, a fourth example of needed change in parent attitude is that toward vocational education programs offered at both the secondary and at the post-secondary school levels. Again, today's students appear far more receptive than their parents. Many parents are themselves working in occupations for which vocational education is needed. Far too many appear to be ashamed of the work they do and the education required for such work. This is part of the total societal erosion of the commitment to work. Somehow, parents must be convinced that there is nothing inherently bad or inferior about working with both one's hands and one's head rather than with one's head alone.

To date, effective programs designed to bring about such needed changes in parental attitudes have not been initiated on any national scale. Yet in a nation with the demonstrated merchandising potential of the United States, it should be a relatively simple matter to mount a national campaign designed to effect such attitudinal changes. Without such changes, it is doubtful if a national program of career education can succeed.

Participation of Parents in Career Education

Where better can students gain an appreciation for the dignity of all those engaged in honest work than through studying the diverse occupations in which their parents engage? Far too many students have no good idea regarding the specific nature of their father's or mother's occupation. For parents to cooperate in a school career education program by supplying information about their own jobs represents one sizable parental contribution to the goals of career education.

A second example of possible parental participation lies in the willingness of parents to share knowledge regarding their work (including both its nature and educational requirements) with teachers and counselors who are working toward the goals of career education. This could be easily done as part of both parent-teacher conferences and home visitations, both of which are already common parts of American education. We have seen communities where, in cooperation with local business and industrial personnel, parent-teacher conferences are held at the father's place of work under conditions whereby, in addition to visiting with the teacher about his child's progress in school, the father shows the teacher basic facts about his job.

A third example is the tremendous potential parents have in enlisting community support for career education emphasis in local schools. Career education will be more expensive than typical programs of classroom education that now exist. It will also, because of the needed involvement of the business and industrial community, make for changes in the length and content of the school day for many students. This, too, if it is to be effective, must receive parental support. It may even change the time of the day at which the student attends school and the months of the year he spends in the schoolbuilding. All such changes will require adjustment in current patterns of home and family living. If parents resist such changes simply because they represent *change*, career education will be in difficulty.

CHANGES REQUIRED

To adopt the basic concepts of career education will call for major changes in organizational, methodological, administrative, and fiscal policies of American education. While many of the needed changes have been referred to earlier, others have been omitted. It now seems appropriate to attempt a synthesis of these major changes.

We again emphasize that career education, as the concept has been presented here, refers to only a part of American education. No claim is made that necessarily represents the largest or the most important part. Rather, it represents the most neglected part and, as such, deserves concentrated effort at the present time. As with any other integrated whole, to bring about major changes related to career preparation will of necessity require major changes in other parts of our total system of education.

Career education, if it is to succeed, must be adopted as total concept. To select only certain portions for adoption while rejecting the rest is to sentence the entire movement to failure. The changes will be more expensive in terms of effort and the kind of internal anguish that always accompanies great personal change in individuals than in money. Yet the total price will be high. It is time to ask for commitment.

Changes for Academic Classroom Teachers

Career education does not ask the academic classroom teacher to simply add one or more units to an already overcrowded set of learning objectives. Rather, it asks the teacher to change and adapt current lesson plans to accommodate a career education emphasis. If the current Office of Education emphasis were to be adopted, it would amount to a major revision of the entire curriculum in the secondary school, along with significant adaptations in the current curriculum of the elementary school. Regardless of whether or not school systems adopt a view that requires complete curriculum revision, it is apparent that major changes in the daily lesson plans of the classroom teacher are called for. To accomplish such changes, teachers must be given time, knowledge, materials, and an opportunity for personal attitude change.

For today's practicing classroom teachers, *time* will be the first requirement. With the heavy teaching loads now common throughout the schools, the typical teacher does not have time to engage in major lesson-plan revision during the regular school year. Both the short-term and long-range goals of career education will require twelve-month contracts for teachers. In the next few years, the summer months will have to be devoted in part to helping teachers develop new lesson plans. As career education programs swing into full operation, schools will be open twelve months a year. While most teachers will probably not teach all twelve months, they will certainly need the full year to keep abreast of the rapid social and occupational changes that must be taken into account in effective career education programs.

Second, today's academic classroom teachers will need new knowledge and expertise if they are to become active participants in career education. Too many teachers have never had work experience outside the field of education. Too many are now lacking in knowledge regarding the career implications of the subject matter they try to help students learn. Systematic and continuing attempts to acquaint teachers with the career implications of their subject matter must be mounted and maintained. Many teachers are today quite unaware of good practices in career education that some teachers in some parts of the country have already developed. They need opportunity to study and think about such practices in terms of their own future teaching plans.

Third, there is great need for appropriate teaching materials for teachers to use in imparting a career education emphasis in the classroom. Textbooks, at both the elementary and at the secondary school levels, need revision.

Audio-visual materials — including films, slide tapes, film strips, audio tapes, and video tapes appropriate for use in career education — are currently in short supply. Many more such materials must be developed for purchase by local school systems. It will be at least as important to provide means by which teachers can develop such materials for themselves. Career education, more than most other parts of education, requires materials that reflect a local and a topical emphasis. Schools will need equipment to produce such materials.

Fourth, there will be great need for career education technicians working as support personnel for classroom teachers. Such technicians will be required to make and maintain contacts between the school and the business-industry-labor community, to assist in the gathering and processing of career education information and materials, and to actively assist in the increasing numbers of field trips that will be necessary.

Fifth, there will be need to consciously help academic classroom teachers change their current attitudes about work and about workers whose jobs do not require a baccalaureate degree for successful performance. Far too many still believe that the "best" jobs are those that require a college or university degree. Far too many still believe that it would be a mistake for any truly intellectually able or academically gifted student to consider occupations that do not require the baccalaureate degree as a minimal entrance requirement. Far too many still believe the profit motive in business and industry carries inherently evil connotations. The fact that most academic teachers in elementary and secondary schools today would vehemently deny that they hold such attitudes makes it even more imperative that some systematic attention be devoted to helping teachers understand and have an opportunity to embrace the attitudes and philosophical premises on which career education is based.

Changes in Vocational Educators and in Vocational Education

Many have pointed with great pride to the significant improvements made in both the quantity and quality of vocational education since passage of the Vocational Education Act of 1963, and especially since passage of the 1968 amendments to the Act. It should be clear that in terms of the goals and objectives of career education, such changes represent only a very small beginning.

Further changes will be demanded on the part of those who call themselves "vocational educators." Some such persons will have to develop both an interest and a competency in working at the elementary school level with elementary school children. At the junior high school level, the classic and traditional form of industrial arts and home economics will have to be broadened to embrace the concept of occupational clusters. Junior high school vocational educators must be found — in sufficient numbers, with sufficient interest, and with sufficient expertise — to teach the occupational cluster concept to *all* junior high school students. Some vocational education leading to entry-level job skills must be made a part of the junior high school. At the senior high school level, vocational education teachers must abandon the traditional three- or four-hour per day block-instruction approach in favor of shorter units that can be presented separately or in combination to allow for the flexibility in both kinds and levels of vocational skills training called for in career education.

Students in the college preparatory curriculum must be provided with opportunities to participate in vocational skills training programs. Work experience opportunities must be provided for all students, not just those enrolled in vocational education. Appropriate vocational education programs for girls as well as for boys must be developed and operated.

Every secondary school student must have multiple opportunities to choose from among the major areas of vocational skills training needed in the country. The equipment and materials in such training programs must be susceptible to a degree of change that reflects the rate of change in our occupational society. No student should be discriminated against in terms of his or her opportunities for choosing from a truly comprehensive set of vocational education programs because of the student's geographic place of residence.

Residential vocational schools, at both the secondary and postsecondary school levels, are badly needed. At the secondary school level, the needs are primarily those of severely disadvantaged, inner-city youth

and youth from sparsely settled rural areas. At least one residential vocational school for males and females, operating at the post-high school
level, is needed in every state. Such a post-high school institution should
offer quality occupational education in a wide variety of areas and at
a wide variety of levels. As with the concept of the state university, it
should be open to students from all over the state and should place its
graduates throughout the state and beyond. It should serve as an appropriate postgraduate institution for graduates of secondary school
vocational education programs and as a source of in-service education
for teachers in such programs.

Changes in the Business-Labor-Industrial Community

If the concept of the business-labor-industrial community as an
active participant in career education, rather than simply a cooperating
agent, is to become a reality, major changes must take place here too. As
in formal education itself, such changes will be expensive in many ways.

Some means must be found for persons from the business-labor-
industrial community to find time to actually work in the schools. Some
training in educational methods and philosophy must be provided such
individuals. Some means of compensating them for their time and providing for them to return to their regular jobs must also be found. The
procedures used in many states for certifying these individuals to work as
vocational educators (some states call them "instructors" rather than
"teachers") without insisting that they follow the traditional teacher
education route should be extended to other parts of education and to all
states. All of these problems will require time, money, and an immense
amount of creative thought if they are to be solved.

If work experience and work-study programs for junior and senior
high school youth are to be expanded as envisioned in career education,
places must be found for these youth to work within the employing community. Child labor laws in many states will have to be revised. New
jobs and new settings for work will have to be created and supervised
in ways that will provide instructional learnings for students as well as
productivity for employers. Both labor unions and joint apprenticeship
committees will have to reexamine and adjust some of their current policies if the massive kinds of work experience and work-study programs
envisioned for career education are to become a reality.

The provision of both work experience and work-study opportunities for teachers, counselors, and administrators regularly employed in formal education will also pose a major and costly problem for business, labor, and industry. It will be complicated to find means of carrying out such programs, preferably on an exchange basis, that will work to the positive benefit of all concerned.

The need for advisory assistance from employers and labor organizations will increase greatly. Major problems will result when field visits by students, observational visits by educators, and data collection visits by career education technicians begin to occur in great numbers. Again, significant expenses, both direct and indirect, will be involved.

Changes in School Counselors

The school counselor will become a person of pivotal importance in the career development component of career education. At present, neither the quality nor the quantity of school counselors in the United States comes close to meeting the needs and demands envisioned by career education.

Among the 47,000 school counselors now employed in the United States, there are significant numbers who are not only ready for but also actively engaged in career education activities. However, there are also significant numbers of currently employed school counselors to whom the concepts of career education are neither familiar nor have been of much professional interest. Even more important is the relatively minor interest in career education exhibited by those who train counselors in colleges. Extensive provisions must be made for school counselors and counselor educators who now lack work experience outside formal education to correct this deficiency. Extensive provisions must also be made for upgrading the professional preparation of today's school counselors through appropriate graduate-level university courses.

School counselors need much better occupational assessment devices for use in career counseling than those currently available to them. The need for performance assessment devices, rather than paper and pencil instruments, is especially great. The lack of current and comprehensive educational and occupational information systems is currently a major handicap.

Computer-assisted systems are certainly possible, and a few promising experiments are under way; but none currently exist that could be considered truly adequate for use in a comprehensive program of career education. Particularly great is the need for adequate information required for career counseling of students contemplating post-high school programs of occupational education in either a private or a public school setting. While systems exist for meeting this need, none have yet been made operational on a comprehensive scale.

The number of school counselors currently employed in the public schools of this country is woefully short of the number needed for implementation of the career education concept. At least twice as many professionally prepared school counselors are needed. Support personnel in the form of clerical assistants and career education technicians are much more scarce at present than are counselors. Great numbers of such support personnel must be trained and employed, and counselors must be taught how to work effectively with them.

The need for attitude change on the part of counselors is as great as it is for classroom teachers. Programs must be designed and undertaken to meet this need.

Changes in Home and Family Education

The home and family component of career education must grow basically out of the current structure of vocational homemaking education. This field, despite significant improvements resulting from the Vocational Education Act of 1963, finds itself today far short of the capability it will be called upon to provide in comprehensive programs of career education.

Provisions must be made for teaching of home and family living at the junior high, senior high, and adult education levels. Neither the curricula nor the teachers have yet been prepared for attainment of this goal.

The immediate needs for massive programs of parent education must be met. At the same time, these needs must not be allowed to take precedence over the equally great need to prepare boys and girls now in our schools for their roles as home and family members.

The vocation of homemaker must finally become a fully understood concept across the land. In spite of the valiant efforts of vocational

WHAT IT IS AND HOW TO DO IT 165

homemaking personnel, this concept has not been widely accepted. Career education cannot work until and unless this problem is solved.

Changes in the Organizational and Administrative
Structure of Education

Perhaps the biggest challenge facing our educational leaders is to make sure that as the concept of career education is implemented, no other sound educational objective suffers. If career education is to be properly implemented, large changes in the organizational and administrative structure of American education, each of which holds positive potential for *all* educational goals, must take place. Perhaps career education can serve as a stimulus and a catalyst for effecting such changes.

One such change consists of the creation of a truly open-entry/open-exit system of education extending from the junior high school years through all of adult education. Under such a system, students could combine school with work, sometimes as a joint enterprise each day, and sometimes with either work or school receiving full emphasis of the student. We must, in these times of need for continuing education on the part of all persons, eliminate the concept of the school dropout.

A second needed change is the substitution of demonstrated educational performance, rather than time, as a prime criterion for evaluation of educational accomplishment. The classic Carnegie unit must be replaced by the more viable concept of performance evaluation. We have known for a good many years that people learn at differing rates as well as to differing degrees. We must pay attention to this fact in the organizational and administrative structure of American education.

A third needed change is in the means used to evaluate the professional qualifications of educators who work in the schools. Again, some form of performance evaluation is needed as a replacement for the simple accumulation of college credits.

A fourth needed change is for a more effective community voice in the determination of educational policies. The nature of the total parent population and the total population of the community which houses a school district should be taken into account in providing representation on school boards. Too many local school boards are currently overloaded with physicians, lawyers, and other professional persons. The fact that individuals laudably seek election and try to serve the public has no bearing on the more important fact that the real majority of the people in many communities are not fairly represented on school boards. Some better system must be found and implemented to correct this inequity.

A fifth needed change is to recognize and provide in school budgets for the significantly greater per-pupil cost for vocational education as opposed to academic education. There is no longer room for the school with only a college preparatory curriculum. The equal worth of various kinds of educational opportunities must be recognized and implemented.

A sixth needed change is the expansion of adult education. Our schools need to be open at least eighteen hours a day at least six days a week and for twelve months each year. The public schools must serve the public — adults as well as youths. Provisions must be made for adults and youth to study together when this seems appropriate.

Needed Changes in Teacher Education

Career education will fail if in its teacher education component it seeks only to overcome the deficiencies of persons who have been or are currently being graduated from our teacher education institutions. In the long run, the teacher education institutions themselves must change in several significant ways.

The undergraduate teacher education programs must be invested with a career education emphasis. Such an emphasis is now almost completely lacking. Work experience and work-study programs for prospective teachers should become as important to their preparation as student teaching.

Counselor education programs are in need of great revision. Not only must such programs contain a much heavier emphasis on career development, but they must also provide prospective counselors with broader concepts of career education and the means by which counselors can interact effectively with teachers, parents, and the business-industrial-labor community in a total career education program.

Prospective school administrators today have almost no emphasis on career education as part of their formal preparation. It must be made an integral and important part of the preparation of such personnel.

Teacher education institutions must assume responsibility for solving the need for support personnel in career education. Perhaps an even bigger responsibility for teacher education is the preparation of teachers as teachers, especially personnel who will work in the community college setting in training support personnel for career education.

The need for research and evaluation in career education is an inescapable responsibility of teacher education institutions, particularly those in universities.

Teacher education personnel must join with state department of education personnel in assisting local school systems with the massive problems of in-service education that career education will bring. Faculty working in teacher education institutions must be given time to do this job.

A QUESTION OF COMMITMENT

There can be no doubt that widespread dissatisfaction exists with respect to our system of public education. Nor can there be any doubt that failure of our education system to prepare its students adequately for occupational success represents a major cause of this dissatisfaction. The concept of career education represents one attempt to improve our education system to better meet the occupational education needs of all students. It is a concept that proposes to correct this particular deficiency in our system without in any way replacing all that is now good and proper in that system.

At the present time, the concept of career education can be said to be in a developing stage. Clearly, further development of this concept is needed. The specific means for implementing this concept in American education remain largely undeveloped. The broad suggestions contained in this chapter represent only a beginning set of considerations. They do not, and are not intended to, represent final answers.

It is hoped, however, that even this beginning discussion has made clear that if career education is to be implemented as a part of American education, great change in our present structure will be required. Such change will be expensive in many ways. While the particular methodologies required for effecting such change are yet to be developed, the concept has reached a stage where its desirability as an educational goal can be judged. The American public must now decide whether or not they wish to endorse this concept and provide the support required for its implementation. The question really is one of commitment.

■5 Career Education: How to Get It

No matter how attractive as a concept, career education can emerge only from concrete efforts at implementation which must occur at two levels: (1) the policy level at which legislators, school boards, and administrators, perhaps influenced by public opinion, opt for a career education emphasis, and (2) the classroom level at which teachers and counselors choose to develop or revise specific materials outlining and facilitating career education and apply them in their instructional activities. The danger for career education is that too many endorse its concepts while waiting for someone else to push for implementation. It has been said that what is everybody's responsibility is nobody's responsibility. Any of the actors in the system could push for the required reforms, but no one has a clear assignment. This chapter addresses itself to specific procedures by which interested parties can set the career education process in motion.

Federal agencies can provide impetus to career education, but it is at the state and local levels that education is planned, teachers trained, curriculum developed, and students taught. Washington can call for a national response, but it cannot prescribe in detail how the local school system must respond. There is a rich mixture of creative energy in communities across the nation, just as there are unique resources in every region. While state and local systems may look to Washington for national leadership, it has been contrary to the traditions of American education for the federal government to do more than call attention to the national need, propose a logical response, cite examples, and perhaps suggest alternative models for local schools to consider in developing their own versions. The planning and implementation have occurred at the school and community level, though the local populace has looked to state and federal agencies for information, resources, and technical assistance.

This chapter explores the implementation role of federal, state, and local education officials and interested groups and suggests a framework within which local communities may create their own version of career education.

Need for National Leadership in Career Education

This book recognizes the weight of custom and law in assigning responsibility for education to state and local levels of education. The plurality of approaches and procedures which result from this local initiative has many worthwhile results. It is not notable, however, for the speed with which desirable innovations are implemented.

For career education of high quality to spread rapidly, national initiative is necessary. The results of these initiatives can and will be modified locally, thus preserving the best of national, state, and local action.

Development of Curriculum

Two approaches to the development of career education curricula deserve national attention. The first of these is to provide financial and technical aid to local schools so that they can develop curriculum materials which are then assembled, distributed nationally, and accepted, rejected, or modified by local schools. This approach is under way with funding by the Office of Education and the National Institute of Education of school-based, home-based, employer-based, and residential career education models, with universities and education laboratories assisting local schools and consortia of employees in developing procedures and materials which deserve to be disseminated. At the same time, one school in each state is working with its state education agency on a similar task.

The amount of involvement of each such agency ranges from very close interaction to an almost laissez-faire policy. Most of these efforts concentrate on kindergarten through twelfth grade, but a few are concerned with early childhood and post-secondary education.

The second approach to curriculum development at the national level has been used in physics, mathematics, biology, chemistry, industrial arts, and a number of other school subjects. Substantial funds are provided to a group of high-level specialists who prepare one or more versions of a school curriculum in consultation with teachers and experts outside education. The materials are tried out in the schools and revised repeatedly. A limited number of teachers are retrained, and the materials are published through regular commercial channels. Each local school is free to adopt, reject, or modify the materials which have been disseminated. This approach has not been used as yet for the whole of career education, though the Industrial Arts Curriculum Project courses, "The World of Work" and "The World of Manufacturing," fit well into the general career education framework.

Developments through the first approach are faster and cheaper (and they require less federal money), but widespread adoption comes slowly. The second approach results in more uniformity, and though several years are required for the preparation of the material, it has wider and quicker adoption once it reaches the publication stage. Both approaches need to be employed.

Research

To date, relatively few career education efforts, particularly at the school level, reflect an adequate research base. Too often teachers simply begin writing lesson plans and hope that the plans can be assembled into a coherent whole. At best these efforts are disjointed. Fortunately, some state and federal funds have been used for research, the results of which could and should be used in career education planning. Some educators draw together concepts from more basic research by career development specialists, philosophers, and educational psychologists to suggest a rationale for career education. Work is under way on various approaches to determine the desirability of occupational clusters. Home-, community-, and employment-based career education models are being explored. The major omissions of research are in career education programs for early childhood and for the post-secondary and adult education levels. This is unfortunate because of the importance of the home and family influence in shaping attitudes about work and careers. There are need and room for innovative models of career development at the community college level, where persons of both post-secondary and adult age can acquire skills for their first job or retrain for new career fields. National leadership is needed to see that these gaps are filled.

Evaluation

Most local efforts in career education attempt to include some type of evaluation. However, there is presently no accepted criteria for evaluating career education programs. There are two general approaches: First, evaluation ideally would concern itself with the long-range impact of career education on the career successes of its participants, compared to the experiences of similar groups of nonparticipants. However, such evaluation will take years, if not an entire generation. Second, long-term impact evaluations should be under way. In the interim, however, a general consensus is necessary as to components and practices found by past experience to be effective or to give strong assurance of success. Increases in the knowledge of the world of work and changes in work values and attitudes can be measures of short-range criteria. National leadership is needed to plan for evaluation of both the process of career education development and the outcomes of the program.

Training and Retraining of Education Personnel

Administrators, counselors, classroom teachers, coordinators, and community workers are key persons in the development and implementation of career education. Education personnel who are receiving preservice training in universities need to learn how to conduct, and how to relate to, career education programs. This requires the reeducation of many, if not most, trainers of university teachers. An even lengthier task involves the retraining of virtually every person in every educational institution in the nation, if they are to understand the philosophy and methods of implementing career education. Clearly, national leadership is needed in this task. Career education will not become a major force in American education unless education personnel are prepared to implement and teach it well. Fortunately, the balance between supply and demand for teachers in most fields requires an alternative to merely turning out large quantities of teachers to meet immediate demands, allowing attention to be given to improving the quality and adaptability of new and existing education personnel.

The book *Career Education and the Elementary School Teacher* devotes a full chapter to preservice and in-service teacher education which is applicable to all levels of the education system. Comments from the book are summarized here; the model for in-service training on pages 174 through 183 of that book should be studied carefully and adapted to the needs of the particular school or school district.

There is a clear need for reform in teacher education, with particular emphasis on giving prospective teachers and those who train them greater knowledge of and involvement in the world outside the school. Particularly for career education, the teacher trainer whose work values and knowledge of the world of work are limited to those occupations which cluster around educational institutions cannot be much help in broadening the exposure of prospective teachers. Probably the most practical approach is for teacher educators to have some noneducation work experience, be immersed in career education concepts, and institutionalize noneducation work experience into the requirements for teacher certification. At the same time, both modified certification requirements which credit work experiences at least equally with academic activities and the use in the schools of noncertified people with demonstrated subject matter and teaching competence can offset some of the limitations of teacher training institutions.

An immediate reform, important to and achievable by all teacher training, is to become involved in practice teaching early and continue that involvement throughout the teacher education years, rather than waiting until the end of the preparation process to find what teaching is really like.

Given the decreasing demand for teachers and the present drop in enrollments in colleges of education, however, the greatest impact in preparing teachers for career education must come from in-service training. There are eight generalizable approaches:

(1) *The working sabbatical approach,* in which teachers and other school personnel are released for a number of months of work

experience, guided in such a way as to extract generalizations supportive of career education

(2) *The planned, summer work experience approach,* in which employers agree to provide full-time summer employment (at school district expense) and assign one employee to each teacher as an "advocate" in learning what the workplace is all about

(3) *The intensive, summer workshop approach* of exposure to career education concepts and practice with career education techniques

(4) *The assured released time for planning approach,* in which school systems by flexible scheduling permit rotating groups of faculty and administrators to plan together for career education

(5) *The year-long, industry-visitation approach,* wherein school personnel receive college credit for supervised visitation to various workplaces

(6) *The addition of resource staff approach* to assign personnel with industrial experience or hire a retired member of the working community as school-community-career education liaison or to hire persons with successful work experience (retired persons, parents, workers wishing to return to school) as paraprofessionals to share with students a world with which the teacher may have limited familiarity

(7) *The conference approach,* in which brief "governors' conferences" for lay education policy makers — followed by in-service conferences for school personnel — provide exposure to and win support for career education concepts

(8) *The project* or *interdisciplinary approach,* where — following exposure to the concepts — teams of teachers and other personnel are given the released time and the supervision to develop career education materials and experiences for their students

Experience has shown that career education materials and projects are most likely to be used, and used imaginatively, if all those who use them are involved in their development.

Any school district which wishes to change teaching practices must work with people who are willing to change at the administration, counseling, and teacher levels. If an administrator wants to move into career education and the teachers are not ready, no amount of coercion will provide a relevant program. On the other hand, teachers who wish to integrate career education into their teaching practices will soon be stymied with red tape if the administrator is not supportive. A counselor's feeling about the program is yet another gauge on which to predict success.

Since administrative support and counselor (if there is one) support are important, anyone who seeks to become a change agent should begin at this level. These two groups must first understand what career education is. This is best accomplished through an informal meeting where all aspects of the program are clearly defined. Administrators and counselors should be allowed to ask questions and react during this meeting.

After this has been accomplished, those administrator-counselor teams who are interested in the program should *volunteer* to have their entire staffs exposed to the same type of meeting. Then, those teachers who wish to take the risk to teach their subject matter in a different way will become involved in in-service training. From this evolves a very practicable team from the school which not only will work together, but will reinforce each other's efforts. The administrator and the counselor become completely involved in the in-service training.

A group of four or five teachers in a school is an ideally sized group. If there are more teachers involved, then two or more groups should be formed. Administrators who would like to get their entire staff involved can be reassured that in consecutive years, other groups of teachers will want their turn. Eventually 80 to 90 percent of the staff will be teaching subject matter through the vehicle of career education.

The key of course is that as teachers become involved in development, they grow excited about implementation. Yet few teachers will have the built-in initiative to undertake development of their own career education materials, unless that development occurs within a structured in-service training and curriculum development program. Even within such a structural program, many will lack the imagination to develop materials, but they can be helped and inspired to adapt materials that others have developed to the particular needs of their classrooms and students. There will be some teachers in each staff who may never get involved, yet pressure will not encourage these teachers to integrate career education into their curricula. In other words, career education involvement has a spiraling effect. It begins with a core of interested, energetic teachers and then widens out year after year until most of the teachers in the school can no longer avoid the excitement generated by the students of those teachers.

An in-service teaching program should be based on the educational need of the learners in the school district, on the needs of the working community surrounding the school, and on creative endeavors of teachers, counselors, and administrators working together to initiate a program. The experts on which exploratory activities are appropriate for each grade level are the creative teachers in the classrooms. These teachers, working with someone to stimulate them to think about the world of work and to acquaint them with the resources available, can come up with the best program for their classrooms. Teachers, if provided the time, can create a career education program which is superior to any prepackaged plan in that it reflects the needs and resources of their communities and their students. Yet, since all teachers will not and cannot do this, it is useful to collect or develop tried career education learning experiences which can be adapted to particular needs.

Funding Career Education

Curriculum development and staff training will cost money. Funds may also be necessary to encourage and compensate employers and other community institutions which cooperate in career education. Beyond those functions, additional costs from emphasis on career education will be only those for general improvements — greater individualization through reduced teacher-student ratios, year-round school, etc. — which could and should be implemented, regardless of the advent of career education. The greatest danger in funding processes thus far has been that almost all of the federal monies allocated to career education have been drawn from the relatively modest funds available through the 1968 amendments to the Vocational Education Act of 1963. There are two dangers to this approach: (1) it confirms the charges of general educators that career education is a pseudonym for vocational education and the fear of vocational educators that it is a device to "rip off" their funds for general education purposes, and (2) available vocational education funds are not even adequate to support the vocational skills training component of career education, without trying to spread those monies over the other four components as well.

A few local education systems and a few state legislatures have made special appropriations for career education. This is important mostly as a declaration of support and priority. The past two federal budgets have included a relatively small $14 million item for career education, and its failure to receive approval is indicative of nonsupport. However, it is not new funds which are the primary career education need. Considering the massive investment in education currently made by American taxpayers, the need is for demonstration that current funding is being used in the most effective ways possible. There is no federal education legislation for which appropriations cannot be used with a career education emphasis. There are probably little or no state or local legal obstacles to the use of education funds for career education. While additional funds are always sought and welcomed by educators, the real need is for priority and commitment.

National Legislation

More important than additions to total funding is a legislative re-ordering of priorities. The trend in national vocational education legislation in the past ten years has clearly been in the direction of permitting more and more facets of career education to receive federal aid. As a result, in a few states, sizable programs of career education are under way. Illinois, for example, has more elementary school students in career education programs than it has in secondary school vocational education classes. In most states, however, federal funds are not used for elementary school career education. This occurs because the federal legislation declares no such priorities, and relatively little has been done to influence change. Decisions on expenditures are left to the states. New federal legislation would almost certainly extend the range of any career education that is encouraged. For example, industrial arts is now for the first time mentioned by name in new vocational education legislation.

Conflicts between the legislative and executive branches of the federal government have interfered with selling the career education program to Congress. Yet sections of the Education Amendments of 1972—

of which we show two — clearly indicate congressional sympathy with the concepts, if not the name. Section 1057, "Program Grants for State Occupational Education Programs," states the following:

(a) *Purpose of the program grants*
. . .

    (2) . . . design, establish, conduct programs of post-secondary occupational programs

    (3) . . . carry out progams of long-range strategy for infusing into the *elementary and secondary* schools occupational education including placement, career counseling, and guidance *for all age groups*

    (4) . . . develop an order of priorities for placing *high quality instructional* programs of post-secondary occupational education into operation

    (5) . . . preparation of teachers, administrators, and para-professional occupational education personnel [emphasis in the original]

Section 1058, "Assurances Judicial Review," focuses on the funding of the programs according to the amendments:

(a) *State administrative agency shall provide satisfactory assurance to Commissioner that:*

    (1) . . . the State Advisory Council on Vocational Education has had opportunity to *review and make recommendations* concerning grants

    (2) . . . federal funds will result in improved occupational education programs, and in no case supplant State, local, or private funds

    (3) . . . adequate provision has been made by such agency for programs described in section 1057(a)(3); (*elementary-secondary occupational* education) . . . [emphasis in the original]

Even larger changes in federal legislation are needed, however. Federal vocational education legislation does not permit expenditures for programs concerned with professions or with occupations which require a baccalaureate degree for entrance. Career education can have no such limitations. Even more important is the need to specify priority use of funds for career education. So long as the decision of whether or not to fund career education is left in the hands of the state boards of vocational education, little will be accomplished in many states. Most state boards of education will rightly reason that there is not enough money for vocational education; thus it would not be wise to divert existing funds to career education.

Needed is additional federal legislation, coordinated with the vocational education acts, but extending beyond them and earmarking present trends or providing priority for career education. A significant beginning toward outlining the kinds of provisions such career education legislation should contain was taken in a legislative resolution passed by the American Vocational Association's House of Delegates in their 1971 convention:

> BE IT FURTHER RESOLVED, that the American Vocational Association initiate a major legislative effort beginning in the second session of the 92nd Congress to implement a program of Education for Careers. Such legislation should provide support for:
>
> 1. Programs at the elementary, middle school, secondary school, and post-secondary levels and continuing education, designed to develop an awareness for the world of work, develop career orientation and exploratory programs, provide assistance in decision-making, provide specialized training for occupations and/or occupational clusters as needed at the secondary and post-secondary levels, and provide for training or retraining of adults for new careers.
> 2. Programs to be jointly sponsored by business and industry and the public school system.
> 3. Programs for the career of homemaking and recognition of the role of the family in Education for Careers.
> 4. Programs involving the efforts of employers to provide observational, work experience, and work-study programs for present and prospective workers.
> 5. Programs of vocational guidance activities at all levels of the educational structure.
> 6. Programs for placement activities.
> 7. Curricular development and the preparation of instructional materials for Education in Careers, and the education of professional personnel to use the newly developed curricular material.
> 8. Support for professional personnel development programs designed to prepare teachers, administrators, supervisors, guidance personnel, and others at the pre- and in-service levels, including undergraduate and graduate training, in-service institutes and work shops, and sabbaticals to allow for further education and/or work experience.
> 9. Research and development programs and for exemplary programs designed to develop new models of Education for Careers, and
> 10. National, State and Local Advisory Councils of Education for Careers.

National Policy

Education policy at the national level is set primarily by national associations and by the executive and legislative branches of the federal government. In career education, the national associations include the

American Vocational Association, the American Personnel and Guidance Association, the American Association of Junior Colleges, and the National Education Association and its more or less affiliated groups such as the American Association of School Administrators, the American Society for Curriculum Development, the National Association of Secondary School Principals, and the American Industrial Arts Association. The American Vocational Association has taken a leadership role in bringing these groups together in an attempt to work on both policy and legislation, committing itself at its 1971 convention to:

(1) Convening a national forum on Education for Careers to involve the joint participation of all segments of the educational, industrial, business, and labor communities, to define the goals of such education and the strategies for its implementation. Such forums would emphasize the convergence of the movements of vocational education, technical education, vocational guidance, vocational development theory, developmental tasks, practical arts, self-concept development, occupational structure, social stratification, and decision making into a comprehensive program of Education for Careers.

(2) Providing professional leadership to enable its affiliated organizations to sponsor similar forums at regional, state, and local levels.

(3) Preparing and disseminating publications and information on Education for Careers.

(4) Promoting a White House conference on Education for Careers.

Despite this self-assignment, none of the objectives was accomplished in the first two years. No such coordinating group is present in the Congress. The Senate Committee on Labor and Public Welfare and the Committee on Appropriations are key groups. In the House, three committees — Education and Labor, Interstate Trade and Foreign Commerce, and Appropriations — are all affected. To date, none has shown interest in or understanding of career education . . . perhaps because attention has been drawn away by administration efforts to transmit federal education grants to the states as non-earmarked "revenue sharing."

In the executive branch of government, responsibility for career education has been placed within a coordinating office under the Deputy Commissioner for Occupational Education in the Office of Education, reinforcing the appearance of vocational education dominance and cost. The major effect so far has been to further siphon off staff and funds from vocational education. Only limited aspects of career education appear to have the research interest of the National Institute of Education. Without major departures from past practice, new assistant secretaries and commissioners of education will want new crusades attached to their names for the sake of prestige. Continued federal leadership in career education may therefore be tenuous.

The best hope for national policy in career education presently seems to lie with the education associations, working in concert with the appropriate congressional committees to develop legislation which will establish policies and funding for career education. Eventually, a career education administration reporting directly to the chief education officer should be created. It should include career exploration, vocational education, professional development, career development, curriculum development, education personnel development, and research and evaluation components.

STATE BOARDS AND STATE DEPARTMENTS OF EDUCATION

Though planning and organizing career education must occur at the community level, little is likely to happen without commitment and aggressive leadership from the state boards of education in declaring policy and the state departments of education in carrying it out. The staffs of these two bodies of state government will know the strengths and weaknesses of the various local education agencies and those which are most likely to respond innovatively.

State agency responsibilities will include policy making, technical assistance, coordination, professional personnel development, and resource management. It is not unlikely that some career education concepts and practices will be inconsistent with existing state procedures and law. A number of states have very specific regulations covering such items as hours of attendance, off-campus field trips, and specialized course offerings. Other states by law may limit the integration of vocational and academic programs or restrict particular learning experiences to very carefully prescribed on-campus physical facilities. Where this is the case, the rationale for these laws should be examined, and changes should be sought where the laws interfere with progress.

Since career education represents a new and important national goal, every state education agency will probably wish to support this program actively. Each state education agency should also consider developing a set of guidelines to assist local school systems in their planning and organizing of career education programs. These guidelines should be addressed to administrative requirements, including the use of professional and noncertified personnel, financing, procedures for accrediting innovative learning experiences (particularly off-campus activities), the use of school facilities by the community, and any other administrative topics of significance, to guide local school districts to implement career education.

"Selling" career education is also in large part a state agency responsibility. School board members and chief state school officers have widespread political contacts and community influence. Local educators also look to state and school officials and state education supervisors for direction, and they have a unique opportunity to assist local school systems in introducing innovation and modernization.

Technical assistance will be required in understanding career education, relating it to current practice, and devising specific curriculum plans which adapt the concepts to the local setting. To provide such technical assistance, state personnel must become career education experts by participating in national and regional meetings, by keeping up with publications, curriculum guides, technological developments, and the entire flow of ideas, material, and apparatus currently so prevalent, and by adopting the best practice in and out of the state for dissemination throughout the state.

The activities required to keep the state staff abreast of new developments in career education cannot be left to accident. They must be systematically planned and carried out on a frequent basis. For this to happen, the responsible state leaders must go on record to specify this goal as a program priority. Communication between state and local educators and between educators and the larger community is part of both a technical assistance and coordination role because it is from such exchanges that most ideas will emerge. Evaluation is also a form of technical assistance. It should be a state function; it provides quality control and identifies strengths and weaknesses for replication or improvement.

The coordination function at the state level is composed of four principal activities:

(1) The identification and "spotlighting" of innovative practices at the local school level

(2) Information collection and dissemination among all participating school systems

(3) Facilitating cooperation in program planning, promotion, and resource sharing among local school systems

(4) Coordination of local school programs in other states and special national projects contracted out of Washington or federal regional offices

The state education agency can play a key if not central role as the facilitator of a system to assure the smooth flow of information, ideas, and data concerning career education developments as they originate in Washington, at the state level, or in local school systems.

Career education calls for a conceptual change throughout education rather than major additional components within education. Its need will not be so much new personnel as a major reorientation among existing professional education staff at every level and in every program component. To win the genuine support of school faculties, administrators, and other education personnel, a carefully conceived and methodical program of personnel development must be designed and initiated by state agencies in cooperation with teacher-training institutions and other organizations concerned with professional personnel development. Teachers who have grown accustomed to the traditions of subject specialization, a four-walled classroom environment, and learning experiences divided into uniform blocks of time may find it difficult to break out of their compartmentalized view of education.

How teachers learn to work with community resources and how interested citizens are used in a way that complements and supports the professional educator represent a new process in American education. The specific activities that make up successful practices deserve careful observation. In fact, these valuable observations should be recorded and studied, and those judged appropriate should be classified and disseminated. In this way, the most creative and imaginative practices will emerge and be made available to all parties interested in the success of career education.

The traditional structure and conventional procedures found throughout most schools are usually reflected and often perpetuated at the college and university levels. Teacher-training institutions are not noted for their innovativeness. It may be necessary for the state department to exercise its not inconsiderable leverage as major consumer to move universities and colleges of education into making career education part of every prospective teacher's training.

State agencies are in an excellent position to assist local school systems in the identification of available resources and the promotion of new resources. The state agency is also aware of the best procedures local schools might follow in developing a broader resource base. It should be a state responsibility to communicate to local schools the availability of program materials, new instructional resources, sources of funding, and perhaps most important of all, to identify those school systems where highly successful programs of career education might serve as models or islands of innovation that can be "spotlighted" at very little expense.

The resource management function of a state agency should also include promoting new sources of support for career education. The use of television, newspapers, and other media, when carried out at a state level, will reach far greater numbers than when initiated as a local activity. The state education agency can work with other state agencies and organizations which are not directly related to the schools, but which show an active interest in career education. This would certainly include the state departments of health, labor, industry, and natural resources. All of these state agencies collect information and publish materials that are relevant to major career fields.

The state education agency in addition to promotional activities and its role in identifying resources is itself a source of funding which can be viewed as existing and potential. Existing resources are those that can be used under existing legislation. "Potential resources" refers to the key role the state agency plays in representing public education before the legislature. Exciting, bold, and imaginative programs of career education may not require new funding. On the other hand, in some states current laws may have to be changed. Therefore, local school planners of career education programs will want to work closely with the state education agency to develop a legislative program that is consistent with state philosophy and policy and that is sufficiently comprehensive to cover as many as possible the action steps to be identified and discussed in the remainder of this chapter.

Role of State Leadership Organizations

How committed the state board of education and state education agencies are to career education and how effective that commitment is in bringing meaningful change will depend upon the prompting and the support those official bodies receive from influential persons and organizations throughout each state. Education itself has a large and well-organized power group consisting of many influential groups. Among them are: (a) groups such as parent-teacher associations with a general mission to improve all aspects of education; (b) professional organizations representing specialized subject matter areas such as industrial arts, vocational education, mathematics, and so forth, (c) professional associations structured along administrative lines such as administrators, guidance personnel, and teachers, and (d) student organizations. All of these should have a vital interest in the furtherance of career education and the power to help bring it about.

At least as potent and as vitally interested as these education groups are legislators, employer organizations, labor unions, trade associations, organizations representing agricultural interests, associations of public officials, service clubs, churches, and so on, through an almost endless list. Much of the potency and progressiveness of American society emerges from the phenomenon of private interest groups. What they as a whole or in major part make up their collective minds to do will happen. A crucial step in the implementation of career education is to gain the allegiance of such groups. The next most vital step is for them to organize to focus their power on the career education objective by:

(1) Using the organizations' own communications networks to make their memberships aware of the meaning and significance of career education

(2) Exercising a leadership role by encouraging their local constituents to actively promote career education in their respective communities

(3) Assisting local groups to identify and assess physical and human resources that can be used at both the state and local levels to initiate and expand career education

(4) Coordinating local organization activities across the state, and planning jointly with other state-level groups

(5) Developing legislative strategies to support the goals of comprehensive career education within the scope of the purpose and mission of their own organizations

One of the most potent ways in which the state-level commitment can be tested and the state-level movement can begin is by organizing and conducting a successful state conference on career education. Some states have already conducted career education conferences, but few if any have called for the participation of all the relevant education, labor, and employer groups who have expressed support of this concept at the national level. Under the combined leadership of the governor's office, the legislature, and the chief state school officer, and supported by other influential groups, such a conference can give powerful impetus to the implementation of career education.

The purpose of a state conference is threefold. First, it provides an excellent platform for recruiting individuals throughout the state who have the capability of implementing career education at the local level. Second, it instructs these people in the basic concepts of career education. Third, it establishes a framework for local initiative and innovation for program development. While career education will evolve at the local level in a variety of different ways, based on local resources and conditions, state-level organizations can support the state education agency in constructing a flexible framework that stimulates local efforts, while at the same time permitting and encouraging a cross-fertilization of ideas, procedures, and techniques among schools across the state.

The state conferences should provide a model that county and large school districts may wish to emulate when promoting career education at the local level. For this to happen, considerable preplanning will be required. Central to this planning will be a statement of objectives the conference planners will want to achieve. This should include qualitative and quantitative criteria, such as the number of people participating as well as the extent of their participation and the position they hold in a state organization. To maximize participation and interest, a number of preconditions must be established before the conference and well in advance of invitations — publicity being among the most significant preconference activities.

The use of radio and television should be coordinated with the state education agency and the advertising council or similar organizations in the state. In this way, film and other media available through the Office of Education can be used with maximum coverage. The regular newsletters, magazines, or journals published by state-level organizations represent a highly useful way of making the public aware of both the need for career education and the importance of beginning the implementation process with a state-level conference. The selection and recruiting of participants for the state conference should be directed to include those persons who occupy key positions or who have the ability to influence the direction of education and community affairs at the local level. This pool includes more than school personnel and school board members. It certainly should include trade union leaders, employers, officers of local service organizations and professional groups, and interested persons from the public at large.

The conference should be viewed as the first formal meeting of state organizations and representatives of local constituencies who are concerned with improving educational opportunity. But it should be planned and organized to accomplish the following objectives:

(1) Identify and recruit state-level decision makers to a forum where they can actively participate in designing a strategy and program of career education.

(2) Instruct these participants in the concepts of career education, the need for it in the local schools, and a procedure for getting it implemented in every school at every level across the state.

(3) Secure from each participant a commitment and set of specific suggestions as to how he or she as an individual and how his or her organization can assist its constituents in pursuit of local implementation.

(4) Train local community constituents and opinion makers so that they know precisely what to do when they return home to begin the process of career education implementation in the local school system.

The Superintendent and the Local School District

If a public school system is to successfully implement a comprehensive program of career education, the local district superintendent of schools and his or her board of education must identify career education as a high priority and adequately fund the program. The principal and faculty members in the local school system must know that career education is a performance priority. In meetings of central office administration and in discussion sessions with the principals of the school units in the system, the superintendent must express his or her concern and expectation that career education will be a high-performance priority in the goal structure and operational objective of the school district.

To be implemented in the elementary and secondary schools, career education must have the attention and support of the central office staff. The curriculum and instruction staff must build the program's scope and sequence. The student personnel leaders in the central office must give priority to developing adequate counseling programs. The teacher personnel office at headquarters must plan the in-service training programs for faculty members. The public relations office must assist in the vital communications task of gaining support and understanding through working with the press and others to explain the new crusade to make the educational program more relevant through career education. The school business office and budget department must plan funding priorities to support the effort.

The central office staff should develop specific, detailed, time-phased action steps to reach certain milestone events of accomplishment in career education. The local school units need the challenge of this type of performance expectation.

Changes in most school systems will not occur unless this level of direction and commitment is made from the central office structure of the school system. Extensive discussion and exchange of ideas to gain grass roots support in every classroom of the school system must emerge from the leadership activities of the superintendent and his staff. The gaps between what is and what should be can be identified by central office leaders working with groups of schools and groups of key leaders in each school.

The action steps for implementation that follow will be brought to fruition in the schools and communities only to the extent that local education agency leadership moves to support career education with staff resources, dollars, and administrative pressure to move the system.

ACTION STEPS FOR IMPLEMENTATION

Whether at the state, local school district, or individual school level, there are a number of specific action steps which must be undertaken if career education is to become a reality. Planners at all levels of education are usually concerned with three major factors: personnel, resources, and activities. An educational plan represents an orderly sequencing of one or more combinations of these factors in some kind of time frame. While hundreds of detailed steps will be required for most communities to implement programs of career education, the actual ordering of these detailed steps will depend upon the unique conditions of each community, as well as the skill and experience of those participating in the development of the program.

Detailed steps for disparate problems cannot be foreseen here. However, ten general action steps for implementing career education are shown in Figure 3 as a four-phase operation. Though the discussion is directed to the local level, parallel steps can and should occur at the state level. The action steps in the earliest phase are devoted to establishing the preconditions required for the new concepts and innovative processes to gain a footing. In this first phase, the emphasis is on defining the goals and developing a strategy for selling the program, as well as identifying the "shakers and movers" who can make the program a success. The second phase is given to organizing the resources in preparation for a program of action. There is no clear line of demarcation among any of the four phases. But it is possible to think of action steps four through six as beginning in phase II and continuing into phase III. Phase III is primarily concerned with accelerating activities started earlier and actually conducting many previously formulated programs and learning activities in career education. Full-scale and intensive implementation should be under way in phase III. The final phase is given to program evaluation, improvement, expansion, and program maintenance. The last three action steps are intended to tie back into the first action step; that is, these latter steps "close the loop," making it possible for this new system to grow and expand in response to new opportunities and changing local conditions. Full implementation should be seen as an

Phase I

1. Organize the appropriate interactive network of interested individuals and groups.
2. Gain an understanding of the concepts of career education and establish appropriate educational objectives.

Phase II

3. Study the current education system to determine the changes necessary to turn it into a true career education system.
4. Inventory and marshal all available resources.
5. Begin planning the career education system most appropriate for your community.

Phase III

6. Seek the cooperation of all necessary organizations, institutions, and individuals.
7. Implement the system.
8. Put the evaluative process in operation to determine how well the system is working.

Phase IV

9. Create a feedback system to use evaluation findings to adapt and improve career education programs.
10. Make provision for a program of maintenance to sustain the vital parts of the system and the initiative, and tie these activities into the interactive network.

FIGURE 3. Ten Action Steps for Implementing Career Education

attainable objective that requires an early start and frequent initiatives. Responsibility for starting these initiatives can be assigned by the local school board to the school administration, or interested citizens can begin the planning process on a voluntary basis. A combination of school, university, and community persons represents the most ideal model.

Action Step One: Organize an "Interactive Network"
of Interested Groups

Interest and personal commitment are the two most basic qualifications for participating in the planning and organization of local programs of career education. However, the design, development, and expansion of this new program will not achieve its full potential if local school systems or state education agencies work in isolation from each other or if the school functions apart from other groups or agencies in the community. The cross-fertilization of ideas and concepts and the transfer of successful methods and similarities of experiences are essential. The need for an approach built upon a foundation of local initiative and fostered and encouraged at the regional and national levels has already been recognized by leaders in education, business, and labor. Governors, state directors of vocational education, chief state school officers, and the U.S. Chamber of Commerce have all endorséd the concepts and principles of career education. The American labor movement at every level, from its national headquarters to its state federations and individual locals, has consistently supported an educational philosophy and program built upon the goals of preparation for useful employment, service to others, and personal satisfaction and fulfillment. University administrators say that their curricula are devoted to the preparation of teachers and other professionals who can be of maximum value to society. All of this support and momentum must be coordinated and fully used.

No completely new agencies need be organized to coordinate the energies or the flow of information and resources to be assigned to career education. What should be fostered is an interactive network that ties local schools and interest groups together on an informal basis. While it is useful to take time to learn what other schools are doing, it should prove more productive and rewarding to concentrate on organizing and fostering local activities to take advantage of local talent and resources.

A public information program should be designed to promote the concept, stimulate interest, and call for active participation by all parties in the community on the part of school and nonschool groups. The promotional program should be a joint undertaking carried out in cooperation with as many parties in the cmmunity as can be interested and recruited.

The U.S. Office of Education and other education agencies and organizations have developed useful informational materials that can be used to promote career education at the state and local levels. But promotional activities should reflect a local input and should be aimed at a local audience. A film "Career Education" has been prepared under the direction of the Office of Education and is available through state education agencies, the national Audio-Visual Center, and Olympus Publishing Company. It has been designed for use by commercial television and will meet the needs of local stations to provide public service programs. Radio stations have a similar public service responsibility and can be used as an excellent medium to promote career education. Local newspapers are always interested in school affairs.

The promotional activities should do more than create public awareness of career education. They should stimulate considerable interest throughout the community. Early in the promotional program, planning should begin for recruiting interested parties from the community to participate on a career education advisory committee. The particular interest groups that may wish to participate in the planning and organization of career education may prove to be unmanageable if viewed as separate entities. A pragmatic approach calls for organizing these numerous interest groups into five major categories. In certain instances, there may appear to be an overlapping of the five program components and the five principal groups or categories who should be recruited to move career education forward. The five groups are as follows:

(1) Parents and organizations with particular concern for the home and family

(2) Educators from all levels

(3) Employers, trade union leaders, and other parties representing business and labor

(4) Representatives from public agencies and elected officials

(5) Other organized groups in the community, such as service clubs and retired workers from all walks of life

Those who vote in school board elections or are active in such groups as the local parent-teacher associations are a useful measure of community interest in school affairs. The public has insisted for some time that the schools take on more and more of the responsibilities originally reserved for the home. As a result, the educational philosophy that the school should and could meet the needs of children that were not met in the home has gained wide acceptance. While this may have been first intended for a small number of children who required basic educational or nutritional supplements, the democratic nature of the school extended these services to include the needs of the "whole child," and soon schools were expected to extend these services to all children. Any desirable change in direction can probably be accomplished if broad-based community support can be promoted. Career education provides both the school and the home with an opportunity not only to reassess their respective roles, but to establish a healthy and viable partnership that will benefit the student and strengthen the tie between the home and the school in the bargain.

Parents, Home, and Family

Parents are the most natural allies, supporters, and champions of career education. They know of their own struggles and place a high premium on the ability of their children to "make out" in the world of work. They are likely to see career success as the primary objective of education, and they see nothing controversial in career education. Economic security is too vital to family solidarity for planners of career education programs to omit any institutions that are concerned for the home.

Education Personnel

Every person in the school system has a role to play in career education: school personnel (including professional, noncertified staff and students at all levels) and school board members. While the classroom teacher may spend most of his or her time with students in a classroom, the school counselor, the nurse, the custodian, gardeners, and education administrators can also bring to the planning of career education an infinite variety of skills, interest, and valuable resources. Teacher educators need help and can be of help, both in preservice and in-service programs for the local school staff.

Business and Labor

Business and labor leaders have been active in some specialized fields of education. Industry advisory committees have been helpful in vocational education in planning programs in newly emerging occupational areas or evaluating and upgrading programs in the established occupations and crafts. To inform and recruit representatives from business and labor to the cause of career education, we should approach them on two levels: (1) at the general or industry level, and (2) for their expertise in a specific industry or a particular occupational field. It should be self-evident that any program concerned with education for a career must make provision for active participation by persons familiar with the industrial and labor relations process and with the skill requirements of particular occupations. Of equal importance is the role industry can play in providing the school with opportunities to observe working situations or to engage in actual employment.

Elected Officials and Public Agencies

Every elected official is sensitive to the fact that education generally represents the largest single expenditure of local and state government. Career education should not be promoted on the basis that it will lower school costs. It is very likely to increase school budgets, at least in the short run, while increasing the quality of education. However, much of formal education has traditionally consumed substantial local resources without returning to the community any tangible results. The taxpayer is no longer indifferent. School budgets are under close observation by many community groups. A key feature of career education is that it can provide service to the community whenever and wherever such services provide a useful learning experience. It has the potential for serving all of the people while reducing welfare and manpower retraining costs. This service element can be implemented by joint cooperation between school and public agency leaders.

Participation by public officials in locating, facilitating, and monitoring these valuable learning and service experiences is of the utmost importance. Furthermore, their active participation in the planning and development of career education will provide wise and mature guidance to the program, while at the same time enlisting the support of a key group.

Service Clubs and Other Special Groups

Service clubs are always seeking opportunities to do good within the community. In addition, their members are also influential in many other walks of life. Their involvement can be doubly potent. Boy Scouts and other youth groups are anxious to improve the long-run welfare of their charges. Senior citizens in every community are anxious to be of service. Men and women with one career behind them represent a rich and valuable resource that can and should be utilized fully.

Many senior citizens have mastered skills and crafts that are in very short supply. Others have skills in the use of tools, materials, and processes that are no longer practiced in the modern labor market but which can still serve as the basis for children and young people to learn important job skills and recreational or leisure-time skills. Perhaps more important, senior citizens often require patient understanding and the need to be of service and to be wanted. Working with senior citizens and getting to know them and their special needs are positive learning experiences for any young person, child, or adult.

Career education is an expansion of the regular school curriculum, and as a bold and imaginative new concept, can profit from the experiences of these and other community groups. Each community will have unique characteristics and special groups that should be identified and recruited to this family-school-community-based program.

The fundamental principle underpinning the interactive network and perhaps its most attractive virtue can be briefly summarized. It calls for the sharing of information, materials, ideas, and technology in career education between schools and communities at all levels. It provides an alternative to creating new and possibly duplicating institutions. It taps those who are already the "shakers and movers" of the community and those with the most reason to develop commitment to a key issue of mutual interest — career education.

Action Step Two: Gain an Understanding of Career Education and Establish It as a High-Priority Objective

The intent of this chapter is to provide a basic framework for the design and implementation of career education at the local school and community level. Within this framework local ideas and energies will create a variety of career education programs that draw upon local interest, resources, and opportunities. Because communities differ, educational programs designed to equip people with salable skills will differ when it comes to the selection of specific occupations requiring specific skills training. On the other hand, many of the prevocational skills, attitudes, and understanding about the world of work and career decision making have general application. The precise response must reflect a community view, but the national perspective offers local school planners a sense of direction.

In order to provide intelligent direction to the energies and enthusiasm to the people recruited and organized as part of Action Step One, we must make them understand more than the definition and need for career education. They will require a working grasp of the components, the principal actions, and the program objectives. While this understanding of the major concepts can be at a general level, it is essential that the planners of career education reach agreement on the kind of model they hope to develop and the parts of the model they hope to emphasize. We can suggest a few examples, but these illustrations are intended to provide general rather than specific direction. Other literature such as items in the bibliography or observation of what others have done can supply further ideas, but ultimately each community and school must "do its own thing."

The second part of Action Step Two calls for establishing career education as an educational objective of high priority without slighting or deprecating the worth and importance of other sound educational goals. Educational objectives provide direction and benchmarks for measuring progress. While the first part of Action Step Two is concerned with the process of career education, this second part focuses on the need for defining objectives. Educational objectives are derived from policy, and educational policy is usually determined by school boards or the legislature. The following policy statements serve as examples of simplicity and brevity.

Assembly Bill No. 102 — Chapter 713

An act to add Section 7504 to the Education Code, relating to educational opportunities. Approved by Governor on August 24, 1971. (Filed with Secretary of State on August 24, 1971.)

The People of the State of California do enact as follows:

> The Legislature hereby recognizes that it is the policy of the State of California to provide educational opportunity to every individual to the end that every student leaving school should be prepared to enter the world of work; that every student who graduates from any state-supported educational institution should have sufficient marketable skills for legitimate remunerative employment; and that every qualified and eligible adult citizen should be afforded an educational opportunity to become suitably employable in some remunerative field of employment.

The Los Angeles School District resolution adopted October 28, 1971, supported this action to read as follows:

> We believe that it should be the policy of our school district to provide career education for all youths and adults of the district, to the end that no student drops out of school who is not prepared to enter the world of work, that no student graduates who does not have salable skills for productive work or college education, and that no adult is denied an educational opportunity to become properly employable.

These two statements clearly establish career education as a priority for large state and large city school systems. Both statements reflect a commitment and provide a sense of direction without defining an end product. The two statements suffice as statements of policy, but they have serious deficiencies as educational objectives.

To be useful, any educational objective should be practicable and attainable, and it should possess the following qualities:

(1) Simplicity of statement

(2) Ease of understanding

(3) Be able to be measured with acceptable accuracy

The proper preparation of educational objectives requires the skills of an experienced craftsman because it demands the instinct of a creative artist and the knowledge of sound principles of learning theory. The statement of educational objectives is the heart of the career education plan. It can be compared to a road map or navigation chart: The more detailed and comprehensive it is, the more certain the school and community can be in their new direction, and the more confident they can be of their progress.

Action Step Three: Study the Current Education System to Determine the Changes Necessary to Incorporate into It a True Career Education System

Many school systems conduct ongoing programs of self-study and evaluation for the purpose of improving the instructional and extra-curricular programs. Career education will provide these study groups an opportunity to engage in a reexamination of the purpose and functions of many existing programs and courses. In those communities where self-evaluation has not been carried out with any frequency, career education offers an opportunity to educators and community leaders to examine the schools in order to determine where improvements can be made, how the process and goals of career education can be implemented, and how the school can take advantage of off-campus community learning resources.

Sometimes there is a tendency to claim that the local schools already offer educational services and special programs that in fact do not exist for any significant number of students. Such claims are not meant to be false or defensive; they are in fact often based on a simple misunderstanding of new educational concepts. Career education is not simply a modification of industrial arts, nor is it meant to supplant many of the useful programs and courses found at every level of education. Career education represents a philosophical foundation for giving new direction and relevance to progams in the formal school and recognition to new forms of learning off the campus in the community. Its primary purpose is to prepare children, youth, and adults for productive and satisfying employment.

It may be true that your school is well on the way to offering a high-quality program of career education at every grade level, including adult retraining and career counseling. If this is the case, or if your school system is freshly embarking on career education, you will want to devise a set of instruments to help you and other members of the community examine just what educational opportunities exist that are intended to assist people to acquire salable skills and to make career decisions.

If the school provides all students with the tools they need to make effective career decisions, there must exist a well-defined and observable process that can be measured against some set of standards. A highly useful but simple tool to assess how well a local education system is performing is the graded scale of which two simple examples follow:

The career education program includes an orientation to job and work situations.

0	1	2	3	4
No students are exposed.	A minority of students are exposed.	A majority of students are exposed.	A substantial majority are exposed.	All students are exposed.

Applying job skills either in simulation or on the job is an element of the career education program.

0	1	2	3	4
No students are exposed.	A minority of students are exposed.	A majority of students are exposed.	A substantial majority are exposed.	All students are exposed.

A similar set of graded scales can be prepared to aid in assessing every facet of the school administration, faculty, instructional and guidance programs, extracurricular activities, and use of facilities, including classrooms, laboratories, shops, gymnasiums, and off-campus resources.

The open-ended question is the traditional method of recording observations and collecting information. Its weakness is the difficulty one encounters in assembling, understanding, and evaluating data collected. A recent national survey of career education used the open-ended question to identify possible exemplary programs of career education. While the following set of statements and questions represents only one facet of this national effort to assess selected programs, it was possible for all local school districts to respond to this self-assessment effort. These same questions and statements should prove useful for any local education system interested in determining the changes necessary to start a program of career education or expand its early efforts.

(1) What are the segments of your career education program? What percentage of the students in the school are directly involved in each segment?

(2) Briefly list and describe the main goals and objectives for the overall career education program and each segment in the program.

(3) How is the career education concept being assimilated into the educational program (e.g., strategies for installation)?

(4) Briefly list and describe those features particular to your career education program for the various segments at different grade levels.

(5) Briefly list and describe the curriculum changes which took place in implementing the career education program.

(6) What supportive services (e.g., guidance, counseling, placement, follow-up) are available to the students in each segment of the career education program? To what extent are these available to all students?

(7) What in-service training was provided for administrators, teachers, and staff in implementing the career education program?

(8) Identify and explain how community resources were used in planning, establishing, operating, and evaluating the career education program.

(9) What opportunities are available to students in the career education program for job preparation?

(10) Briefly list and describe the data that are being gathered as evidence of success or failure of each segment of the career education program.

(11) What provisions have been made for placing students in jobs or further educational programs when they leave school?

These questions were designed for kindergarten through twelfth grade. Additional questions are needed to establish linkages with early childhood and post-secondary educational programs, since these latter programs are usually conducted by different education agencies.

Action Step Four: Conduct an Inventory and
Marshal Community Resources

A number of conventional educational programs already make use of community resources for off-campus learning. Visits to museums, parks, and places of historical significance constitute a valuable but traditional part of most school programs. Work-study and cooperative education have been a part of vocational education for nearly half a century. What is innovative about the use of community learning resources for career education? That will depend upon the imagination of conceptualization, the intensity of use, and the practicability and career relevance of the experience. Needed resources consist of physical facilities such as space, equipment, and access to work stations, as well as a vast pool of human talent. There is in every community a growing number of retired persons with rich and valuable experience in almost every career field. Service clubs and similar organizations represent another form of human resources. Despite the extensive learning resources available in every community, very few schools have actually begun to make effective use of the many talented individuals residing in the community and willing to be of service to the schools.

Before these human resources or the off-campus learning resources can be used, they must be identified. A proper identification will record the availability of each resource and describe in some detail precisely how the particular facility, individual, or material might be used to provide an appropriate educational experience. Figure 4 is a simple form that can be used to collect the information on individuals who are available to serve in an expanded program of career education. This form has been successfully used in small towns and in neighborhoods in large cities; however, the unique characteristics of every community may require that a questionnaire be especially tailored to collect local data. The questionnaire can be adapted for use with firms and other organizations.

Professional educators and persons with training in the field of education should be involved in the resource identification process because they will be able to appraise the potential for learning experiences and can evaluate off-campus activities and resources. Marshaling these resources begins with the evaluation, classification, and analyses of the resource data collected. The actual marshaling of community resources is a continuous process, but in this step, the process begins by confirming the availability of those resources judged most appropriate for meeting program objectives.

Action Step Five: Design Preliminary Program of Career Education

With a general understanding of career education formulated at the local level and a detailed set of statements of desired goals and objectives,

The Career Education Advisory Committee is studying various ways of enriching the educational program of the _____ schools. One way to widen the students' educational opportunities, particularly in learning work skills, is to use the resources of the community. The purpose of this questionnaire is to find out what interests and talents the people of _____ would be willing to share with their young people. Once this information is on file, it will be possible to match an individual's special skill with a student's particular interest. Would you be willing to have this questionnaire kept on file at the _____ School so that in the event of a particular need or interest, you might be contacted?   YES   NO   (Circle one.)

Name _____

Address _____ Phone _____

Field of Interest (cite occupation or industry, public service, arts and crafts, science, public service, business, trade union) _____

_____

Special Skills: _____

What size group would you like to work with?
____(large: 20 plus)   ____(medium: 5-20)
____(small: 2-5)   ____(individual: one to one)

How much time would you be willing to give?
____Once a week   ____Number of hours
____Hands-on type training (every day for several weeks)
____Occasional (lecture or demonstration for a specific topic)
____other

Can you volunteer your services?_____ If not, tentatively how much would you expect to be paid?_____

I understand that this information is merely exploratory and does not bind me in any way. If there is a need for or interest in my services, I shall be contacted and further arrangements will be made.

Signed _____
Please return completed questionnaire to the person who gave it to you—or to John Doe Career Education Advisory Committee, Post Office Box 707, Random Town, U.S.A.

FIGURE 4. Community Resources Questionnaire

added to a knowledge of available resources, a community is prepared to begin to design new programs of instruction in school and to arrange for career learning experiences in the community. Program planning at this early stage should be as much exploratory as it is tentative. The emphasis should be more on experimentation than on long-term courses of action. But the design of career education programs will require considerable expertise in at least the following fields:

(1) Preparing instructional objectives

(2) Curriculum design and development

(3) Student personnel services, particularly in vocational guidance and counseling

(4) Educational professional development, especially for in-service teacher training

(5) Early childhood development

(6) Human ecology

(7) Community organization with experience in working with business and labor leaders and organizations wherever convenient

Some of this expertise will have to come from the present school staff. A great deal of the needed expertise can be and should be recruited from the community. In 1970, for example, there were more than 400,000 registered nurses who classified themselves as "full-time homemakers" distributed across the many communities of the country. They are an indication that every city and town and most neighborhoods have representatives from a variety of occupational categories and industries who can be helpful in designing educational experiences relating to the world of work and careers.

A local office of the state employment service represents another form of expertise that can form a partnership with the schools' guidance personnel in order to design informational packages and programs based on available and emerging areas of employment in the community and surrounding labor markets. Many additional examples could be cited to suggest who might cooperate in the design of career education programs. The shape of programs, their quality, and the rate of progress in achieving early goals will depend to a great degree on how much information is made available to the community and how successful planners are in using all relevant resources.

The emphasis of Action Step Five should be on developing a "plan for planning" more than on introducing programs of instruction. But this step represents a transitional activity. The first five steps have been concerned with establishing the preconditions necessary for implementing career education at the local level. The next series of action steps suggests procedures for moving into actual program implementation.

Action Step Six: Establish a Cooperative Relationship among the Participating Organizations, Institutions, and Individuals

The purpose of this step is to achieve cooperation among all of those in the community who are essential to the implementation of a program of career education. Five major groups have already been suggested in Action Step One, but every community will want to develop its own lists of "shakers and movers." To achieve this goal, a series of substeps is recommended. Emphasis is given to the use of nonschool talent and facilities.

This may be a new approach in education. The traditional character of the school and formal education in most communities suggests that a conservative approach to the planning of present change will meet with less hostility than a call for major surgery. The organization of interested individuals from the community represents an activity that can be structured according to conventional school and community patterns, yet at the same time be used to bring about dynamic change.

While the purpose of this step is to gain cooperation among the many diverse elements in the community, the suggested procedure for achieving this is through the formation of a school-community career education advisory committee. The purpose of this committee is to advise the local school board, the school administration, the faculty, and the community at large of recent developments, needs, and future plans concerning career education in their schools and community. Responsibility can be focused in the advisory committee. This means that the advisory committee will do more than advise. It can provide both the leadership and energy for moving all elements in the community toward the full implementation of career education. The following are minimum elements of a career education advisory committee:

(1) *Steering committee:* Functions as an executive body providing general direction, coordination, and reporting to official bodies

and agencies inside and outside the community. It calls for all advisory committee meetings and assigns major roles and tasks to the other working groups.

(2) *Visitation committee:* Contacts other schools and communities and visits other programs that are under planning or in actual operation. The visitation committee also collects information and reports on its observations and assessments.

(3) *In-school or on-campus committee:* Works with faculty, students, and community resources to introduce change into the existing program of instruction and determines how career education can best fit into the regular formal education system.

(4) *Off-campus committee:* Identifies learning resources in the community but outside regular school facilities. Its function is to make provisions for assessing these on-campus resources so that they can be available as useful learning experiences in career education. The off-campus committee makes its findings and recommendations available to the committee as a whole, thus providing alternatives to on-campus or in-school educational programs. Its first major task is the administration of the community census briefly described in Action Step Four.

The substeps leading to committee organization are simple and straightforward. Following a program of public information, when community interest is at a high point, community and school leaders can call for an organizational meeting to establish the career education advisory committee. Membership on the four subcommittees described above can be voluntary, or certain individuals may be assigned to specific committees in order to provide adequate balance and expertise. Those responsible for calling this organizational meeting will probably be the same persons who carried out the original study and planning activities described in the first five steps of this implementation plan. Because of this early experience, they will be in a position to develop a detailed agenda, including supporting materials and documents for use in the organizational meeting.

When the agendum and materials are prescribed at an open meeting, there should be opportunities for the audience to express their ideas. Provision should be made for those with expertise in career education to assist the first-time participants record their own interpretations and thoughts about career education. An easy method of accomplishing this is to make available an agendum that briefly outlines the general activities of the four working committees while leaving ample space to permit individual note taking as various items on the agenda are discussed. The results of this operation can be a set of committee-developed guidelines for planning and action.

Most likely the in-school and the off-campus subcommittees will attract the largest membership. This is important because they will be expected to carry out the most complex and numerous tasks. Of equal likelihood is the desire of local school systems to create their own committee structure and assign responsibilities accordingly. The committee organization reviewed here represents a model that has proved successful in a number of local school systems in various parts of the country over the past few years.

The steering committee functions in an executive capacity and the visitation committee in a narrowly defined role, but the functions of the two large working groups are varied and many. A few specific examples may illustrate the worth of the in-school and off-campus subcommittees.

In-School Subcommittee

The following is a model of the assignment which might be given to such a group:

The purpose of this subcommittee is to study the existing instructional program and on-campus resources to determine the most effective method for adopting appropriate elements of career education. Membership on this committee is open to students, faculty, school administrators, and interested parties from the community. The following is a tentative list of activities this subcommittee has been asked to investigate:

(1) A key task of this group will be the formulation of goals, objectives, and expected outcomes to be achieved through career education. Because of the experience and expertise of professional educators in the writing of educational specifications, it may be possible that the in-school subcommittee can provide examples of goal statements and precise objectives stated in measurable terms for use by all of the working committees.

(2) The identification of instructional resources for use on campus is an activity to be coordinated with other working committees. This activity will require the design of data collection instruments to properly record existing resources and to tentatively assess ongoing programs. Following the collection and analysis of information that describes existing resources, the in-school subcommittee, in cooperation with the steering committee, will begin the design of new programs.

(3) Having set new goals and having decided on the direction and general content of new programs, the subcommittee will have to make decisions covering a number of highly important program elements. So that these decisions will be made systematically and so that they reflect a broad consensus, attention should be given to the assignment of any working subgroup who may share responsibility for making recommendations on the following subtopics:

(a) What changes are required in existing courses, their organization, and content so that they will be more relevant to student career needs?

(b) What new courses should be offered?

(c) What changes are required in existing programs, including new and existing courses?

(d) Is it necessary to design totally new programs and all new courses?

(e) What consideration should be given to alternative staffing of existing courses and new courses?

(f) Is it possible to make use of vocational education personnel and academic instructors for cooperative teaching?

(g) Is it possible to make use of academic and vocational instructors for cooperative program planning?

(h) To what extent can the schools use nonschool personnel in regular courses of instruction?

Community or Off-Campus Subcommittee

The primary purpose of this subcommittee is the identification, organization, and development of career education learning experiences that are available out of school and off campus. Off-campus learning activities are not suggested as a means for eliminating traditional classroom and shopwork. They are recommended as a means to expand curriculum resources to include the wealth of human talents available in all communities, as well as to make greater use of local facilities and institutions where students can acquire useful skills while providing valuable services. Membership on this subcommittee should include a few educators who can provide a liaison role to the other working committees (particularly the in-school subcommittees) as well as provide professional advice to nonschool personnel.

The general goals and objectives developed by the in-school subcommittee and the steering committee can be used as guidelines for the off-campus subcommittee. It is possible that certain objectives can be best achieved through off-campus learning activities. For example, many of the service activities students undertake in the community may prove to be far more meaningful and comprehensive than anything the school might provide during regular classroom instruction. Assisting in a hospital ward or a child day-care center or working as a recreation aide with senior citizens provides young persons with the opportunity to explore three separate career fields while rendering valuable service to the community. Many of the off-campus learning activities will not include a major service component but will emphasize a particular academic or specific job skill. What these particular skills might include will depend upon the extent and quality of activities and learning resources the off-campus subcommittee successfully recruits to the career education program.

The most significant activity the off-campus subcommittee will undertake is the census of community learning resources. This census will classify and tentatively assess every identifiable off-campus community learning resource, including volunteer instructors (public and private) and any other situation that lends itself to learning skills and attitudes related to the world of work. The census form introduced earlier can be completed under the direction of the off-campus subcommittee, using parents, students, faculty, and any other interested parties capable of identifying community learning resources. The census should be viewed as a continuous process rather than a one-time affair. The results of this ongoing inventory of community learning resources can be made available to members of the in-school subcommittee to complement in-school projects as well as to tailor specific off-campus learning activities.

Action Step Seven: Implement the System

The title of this action step can be misleading. The actual process of implementing career education at the school system level begins with the first meeting of interested parties who decide to take action. A separate action step is suggested because it represents a crucial event in the planning process. The early steps are chiefly concerned with preparing the preconditions for implementation. Action Step Six describes how people from the community and school can work toward implementation. The recommended working committees need a target date that specifies when significant events and activities are to take place, and particularly when career education instruction will actually begin in the classroom and in the community. This means that when the calendar date for Action Step Seven comes up, the following substeps will have been completed.

(1) Contact will have been made with state educational agencies and available guidelines and state policy endorsed by local education authorities.

(2) A compendium of educational objectives will have been established at every level where career education is to be implemented in the first target year.

(3) The process of career education will have been examined by school personnel and community resource persons and experimental programs tried and evaluated on a limited basis.

(4) An evaluation of existing school programs and activities has been initiated, resulting in recommendations for changing specific parts of the curriculum.

(5) Professional personnel and some community education resource persons will have formulated new strategies and programs, and teachers will have received whatever in-service retraining is required.

(6) New programs and activities will be ready for implementation. Detailed descriptions will be available for every new course or learning activity concerned with career education.

(7) Estimates of faculty time and the need for special equipment and facilities will have been determined, and funds will have been provided.

(8) Detailed budgetary procedures will have been followed for determining the cost of new programs and activities.

(9) Cost-saving measures will have been recorded, particularly from those courses, programs, and activities that may have been deleted from the original program of instruction.

(10) Following an analysis of costs and benefits relative to new programs and activities, alternative strategies will be examined to permit the phasing of courses, programs, and activities of high priority into immediate operation, while assigning new implementation dates to activities of lower priority.

Each of the ten general substeps listed above are made up of specific tasks. The identification of tasks and their analysis (i.e., what is involved or required to complete the tasks) will provide the planner with information as to who should be assigned responsibility for completing the tasks, how it should be accomplished, what resources will be required (e.g., tools and facilities), how much time will be required, and what it will cost.

In brief summary, Action Step Seven is intended to establish a target date for implementation and should be regarded as a firm taskmaster. Such a date provides all parties with a common reference point for measuring their progress. A target date for implementation is also a "hidden persuader" that permits the planners and "implementers" an opportunity to systematically review the progress achieved in moving concepts and resources into action programs. A framework for reviewing this progress can be prepared by setting out a detailed set of questions and tasks that fixes responsibility, assigns resources including costs, and sets time constraints for their accomplishment. The specific questions and tasks will reflect the unique nature of each local program of career education.

Action Step Eight: Develop a Program of Evaluation

The purpose of this step is to permit career education planners, administrators, and participants to systematically assess and measure program progress and to determine what modifications or adjustments might be required to achieve program goals and objectives. As in several other steps, the evaluation planning and the evaluation of the process must begin earlier, but it is during Action Step Seven and afterward that evaluation of results must be carried out. The care and precision used in originally describing goals and objectives are a continuous process that begins just as soon as a planner understands the policy he is expected to implement, the direction he is to pursue, and the process to be used.

In designing a program of evaluation, planners of career education have an opportunity to reconsider program goals and objectives, if for no other reason than to restate these objectives in terms that permit their being measured. For example, an early goal statement might be ". . . provide for occupational competence." How can one measure the attainment of this goal? Preparing goal statements requires a degree of precision that permits one to measure effectiveness; that is, actual performance. Placement on the job and both satisfaction on the part of the new employee and satisfactoriness of the employee to his employer represent examples of measurable criteria.

Among the most common techniques for evaluating education and training programs are:

(1) Direct solicitation of the reactions of the participants, including students and community persons

(2) Individual and group tests to actually measure progress and achievements and attitudes in any phase of the program

(3) Performance tests or observation of a student actually demonstrating his ability in the use of a skill

(4) Comparison of results of new techniques and procedures with results over older or traditional methods

(5) Observation of the career education process to determine problems and find remedies

The ultimate evaluation of career education will not be achieved until enough persons have traversed the full system from early childhood throughout their working lifetime into retirement. Only then can society have a valid comparison of the old and new in career development. But in the meantime, interim evaluations are necessary to test and improve the system.

The design, development, and use of evaluation procedures can best be performed by those capable of organizing a logical framework for identifying goals and then measuring the progress made in achieving these goals. The close relationship among goal statements, evaluative criteria, and performance standards cannot be overemphasized. Efforts spent in refining goal statements are almost certain to be reflected in greater precision of measurement of progress achieved in attaining these goals.

Evaluation provides the planner with an opportunity to use objective criteria to supplement personal opinion. This is particularly true when instruments are designed and tested to reduce personal bias. The development of such tools can be done in the local school if a commitment is made early in the planning process. This commitment might take the form of establishing a special evaluation group that is encouraged to function relatively independently of other operational or working groups. In this way an element of objectivity can be built into the evaluative process.

Action Step Nine: Create a Feedback System to Use Evaluation Findings to Improve Career Education Programs

Evaluation determines how well the system is performing and pinpoints where improvement is required. Feedback is concerned with taking the results of an evaluation and applying them to correct or improve any part of the system requiring it.

Feedback systems have to be developed for every element in the system. When students are tested, the results of their achievement should be shared not only with the student himself but also with all of those persons directing the particular learning experience as a measure of the effectiveness of that activity. In this way the program can be monitored to determine where and how change might be introduced.

The school administration and local school board have legal responsibility for all elements of formal education in the community; however, they are not in the best position to provide detailed monitoring of program activities. The career education advisory committee can play a central role in the feedback process. For example, it can assign students, faculty, and community representatives to working committees, coordinating the work of educators so that every element of the program can be systematically measured, problem areas identified, and recommendations formulated to take action when and where required. These elements should include at least information on students, the instructional programs, and community resources.

Evaluation of Student Progress — Students

Perhaps the standard report card is the oldest and most conventional form of feedback. It records evaluation results (good or bad) and sends these data home and keeps them recorded in the formal system. In some schools there is very little explanation on the grade card that would explain to students or to anyone else the meaning of each grade or how progress can be made in the future. A student-based feedback system would diagnose student progress, record those areas where achievement is satisfactory and where improvement is required, and specify how a student can make these improvements.

Student Self-Kept Records

Because of the importance of skills acquisition and the need for students to develop the ability to make and act on career decisions, there is a special requirement for students to learn how to keep up-to-date records on their own personal achievements and how to interpret the data. This system of personal record keeping can begin in the early grades with very simple forms and in later years record the information the students need to reflect on what events, activities, and experience influenced their early career.

The Instructional Program

All of the key components of the instructional program and process that were assessed originally in Action Step Three and evaluated in Action Step Eight should be considered as potential information elements to be included in a feedback system. What actually is selected to go forward to the career education advisory committee as feedback data has to be predetermined by criteria that take into account at least the following questions:

(1) What information is needed to pinpoint problem areas?

(2) How should it be collected and recorded, and to whom should it be sent for utilization?

(3) What data are required to identify effective innovation and successful learning experiences for the purpose of replication in other parts of the system?

(4) What data standards and procedures need to be created to provide for a system of incentives to stimulate and reward improvement and expansion of career education opportunities?

Community Resources

The census of community resources identifies what is available at a particular period of time. The evaluation process measures the quantitative and qualitative factors associated with these resources. The feedback system should be concerned with upgrading the inventory of community resources and reporting to all relevant parties the results of any evaluation of use of these resources.

In summary, the actual design of a feedback system will have to be tailored to meet the specific information needs of planners, administrators, and participants of local programs while at the same time providing for two-way communication between the local schools, other schools, the appropriate state agencies, and all other concerned groups.

Action Step Ten: Make Provisions for a Program of Maintenance to Sustain the Vital Parts of the System

This final action step will close the planning and implementation loop so that selected early initiatives can become institutionalized within the local school system and community. Selection of these key elements should begin whenever it is possible to make judgments concerning the impact and contribution each element makes to the learning process. These elements will center on the administrative process, the instructional program, and counseling and guidance services. In this action step, these three groups of elements must be examined to determine how a local school system in partnership with its own community can cooperate and interact with other schools and state level agencies to improve and expand the career education process (Figure 5).

The administrative process is concerned with leadership, organization of resources, and overall program management. The instructional program is concerned with providing learning experiences in school and off campus in the community. The guidance function is intended to

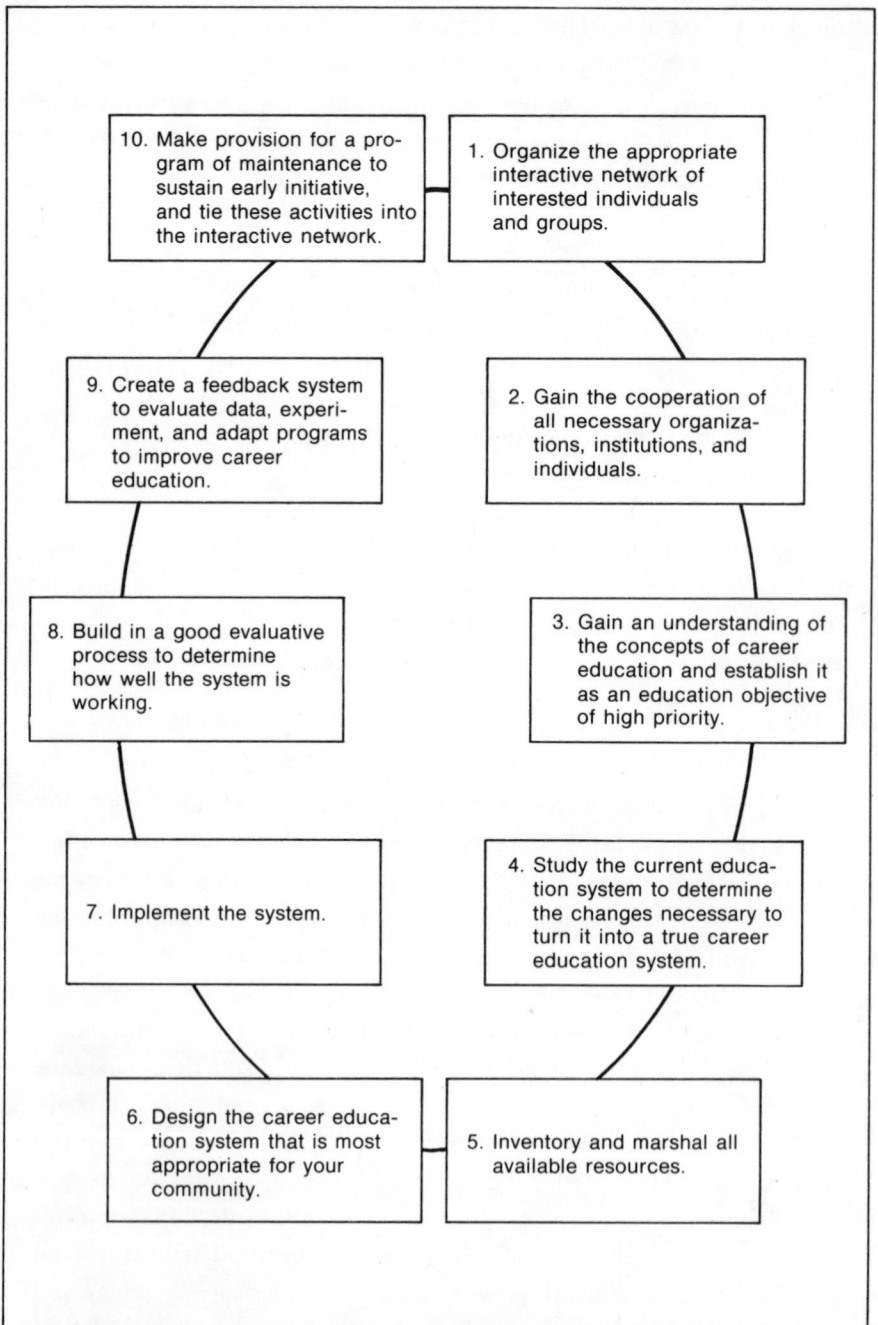

FIGURE 5. The Career Education Implementation Process

provide students with the experience and information they require to make and understand why they make particular career choices.

In Action Step Nine the emphasis was on communicating essential information back into the system for corrective action, for improving parts of the system, and for rewarding all effective facets of the system. In this final action step the emphasis is on expanding and maintaining the system. As information becomes available through evaluation and as it is communicated through the feedback system, it is directed to specific working committees or to individuals who have responsibility for taking action. These actions cannot be determined in advance, but it can be anticipated that they will be of a particular nature. For example:

(1) Some activities or programs, including students and resource personnel, may have to be dropped from the program for any number of reasons ranging from disciplinary difficulties to a simple lack of interest. Whatever the causal factors, it is essential that activities that do not meet student needs at a predetermined or adjusted level of performance be modified or eliminated.

(2) Other programs may have to be modified to accept additional students or to take advantage of available resources.

(3) New activities will have to be added if the program is to grow and meet additional student and community needs.

(4) If outside funds are used, there may come a time when these will disappear; thus plans should be made to incorporate vital features of the career education program in the regular budget as rapidly as possible.

In summary, the local level process of career education is not a one-time process but a continuing task of trying, learning, re-doing, and improving that will not end until every student can be given reasonable assurance of a successful lifetime working career.

6 Potential Contribution of Career Education

The major turnaround needed in our schools is a rededication to education as preparation for work as well as preparation for and part of living. To accomplish this objective, basic changes will be necessary at every level of education.

Some Basic Ingredients

One essential ingredient of career education development must be concern with changing attitudes of professional educators toward work and toward education as preparation for work. Provision must exist for all elementary and secondary school teachers to visit business and industrial settings, to acquire work experience in business and industry, and to reformulate their instructional objectives and programs to include a proper emphasis on education as preparation for work.

Equal attention must be given to providing school administrators with in-service education and bona fide work experience in the occupational world outside the structure of formal education. Special attention must be given to a program of reeducating school counselors, in both elementary and secondary school settings, to education as preparation for work, with appropriate attention directed toward changing counselor attitudes and providing counselors with a variety of kinds of work

216

experience and opportunities to interact with members of business, industry, and labor. In addition to providing multiple opportunities for educators to gain experience in and exposure to business and industry, each school should provide means for members of the business, labor, and industrial community to assume an active role in the schools' total program of career education. This will require some in-service education for such personnel, along with stipends and employer rebates that will make their active participation possible.

Simultaneously, a second essential ingredient will be drastic changes in the teacher education and professional education programs that now exist in the colleges and universities of the United States. There is little to be gained from a massive in-service education emphasis for those now in the field unless constructive efforts are aimed at changing the pre-service programs for those entering education as a career field. Part of this emphasis must be on helping prospective teachers see occupational implications of their subject area. Another part must be helping teachers learn how to help students plan, complete, and evaluate educational progress on an individualized basis. In addition, prospective teachers must be helped to acquire a greater understanding and appreciation of the total occupational society through a series of simulated or real work experiences outside the field of education as a basic part of their teacher education program.

✔ A third essential ingredient will be restructuring curricula and instructional materials to reflect a career development emphasis. The career implications of every subject should be emphasized in a variety of ways both through instructional materials and through instructional content. While this emphasis is needed throughout the curriculum, it will be especially important in the social studies parts of elementary and secondary education. Provision must be made for a multi-media approach to development and use of instructional materials. The technology for doing so is already present. Special emphasis must be given to development of materials appropriate for use in adult education.

A fourth ingredient will be effective programs of individual and occupational assessment as essential bases for programs of career education. It will be especially important that provision be made enabling students to have hands-on experiences as part of occupational exploration. The use of simulated work experience as a means of testing both aptitude and interest must be greatly expanded. Other simulation techniques must be developed, validated, and implemented for allowing persons to discover the abilities and interests with respect to programs of occupational education at the secondary and post-secondary levels. Follow-up studies of graduates of occupational education programs must be funded as part of this data base. Similarly, provision must be made for securing, analyzing, and disseminating job placement and occupational information pertinent to entry occupations available to those leaving schools with particular sets of skills. All forms of educational technology, including (but not limited to) the use of computers, must be included in this ingredient.

Fifth, an obviously essential ingredient must be provision for the education and employment of specialized career development personnel. This must begin with support for instructional personnel in occupational education. We must provide means by which qualifications for such personnel can be recognized and rewarded through their prior work experience backgrounds as well as through their formal academic education. This ingredient, if it is to be effective, must also include provision for a wide variety of support personnel, such as outreach and test technicians; occupational, career exploration, and placement specialists; job agents; and follow-up technicians. A clear pattern of relationships to professional career development specialists must be established, as well as concretely defined career ladders by which one may progress from one level to the next. Only by encouraging the use of such support personnel can a viable system that gives adequate individualized assistance to students be established and maintained.

At the same time, this ingredient must provide professional career development counselors at every level of the system. No system can be any stronger than the provision it has for helping each student make individual choices and decisions, and thus control his or her own destiny. Individual freedom of choice extends far beyond merely receiving a list of alternatives from which one can choose. The student has the right and the responsibility to be an active participant in formulating the total set of alternatives and to choose — based upon the best possible combination of information about himself or herself — those opportunities which he or she will follow. Career decision making can be facilitated by the active interaction of professional career development counselors with each student.

A sixth essential ingredient is support for research in extending our knowledge and competency throughout all of the areas of career education. Much remains to be learned regarding the theory of occupational choice and regarding occupational decision making, the dynamics of relationships between education and occupations, occupational assessment, the transition from school to work, and a host of other key concepts.

Finally, a seventh essential ingredient is provision of national, state, and local advisory councils for career education. Membership on such councils should include persons from education, business, industry, labor, the general community, and students (both youths and adults) who are currently enrolled in schools.

OBLIGATIONS OF THE SCHOOLS

At the elementary school level, the components of career education most needed should emphasize helping students acquire positive attitudes toward work, toward all levels of occupations found in the society, and toward themselves as prospective workers. These components should provide for introduction of some hands-on acquaintanceship with both tools and machines as an essential part of the curriculum. They should provide opportunities for elementary school students to visit in the occupational world, and for representatives from that world to visit students in their elementary schools.

At the junior high school level, there must be provision for career exploration in broad career fields for all students through a combination of classroom instruction, counseling, and actual experiences. It is here that the concept of work experience should be introduced as part of the program of career education. Here, too, all students should be exposed to the nature of and their potential for profiting from senior high school programs of occupational education through the kinds of simulated work experiences discussed earlier. Visits to senior high school education facilities and to business and industry should be an essential part of career education programs in the junior high school.

At the senior high school level, the emphasis on career implications of all courses should be especially emphasized. It is vital that those who, after finishing high school, will attend four-year colleges and universities be assisted in thinking about such decisions in terms of their career implications. It will be essential that comprehensive programs of occupational education be made available to every senior high school student either as part of a comprehensive high school or in a separate area vocational school facility. Such occupational education programs should be multipurpose. For some students, they will be used for further career exploration. For others, these programs will provide basic skills required for employment after they have left high school. Job placement and follow-up will be essential ingredients here. For still others, these programs will offer basic vocational training that will give students both a basis for choosing and a basis for succeeding in post-high school programs of occupational education.

At the post-high school level, programs of occupational education at less than the baccalaureate level should be available to all who desire and can profit from them. Support must be provided for such programs in a wide variety of settings, including residential vocational schools, community colleges, private business and vocational schools, and apprenticeships. For some students, it will be necessary to receive direct subsidies that will enable each to choose the particular school that best meets his or her needs. Participation should be limited to those institutions which are willing to provide valid product evaluation data regarding the occupational experiences of their graduates. The current process evaluation approach represented by traditional accreditation procedures must be supplemented by product evaluations for those institutions eligible to receive public support. Again, job placement and follow-up will be essential ingredients in this process.

It is especially important that every state establish at least one residential vocational school operating at the post-high school level serving citizens throughout the state. Such schools, while authorized by federal legislation, have never been supported by actual appropriations. They will be essential in a comprehensive system of career education. Every state has its sparsely populated areas where an extensive vocational curriculum cannot be offered. It also has students who seek preparation for unusual occupations in which only a few in the community are interested.

Educational Innovations

American education is currently undergoing unprecedented change. Innovations are widespread, though they yet involve only a small proportion of the immense total of the education system. One of career education's advantages is that it can be incorporated smoothly into the most traditional of classroom situations, or it can be an integral part of the most advanced of educational concepts. The traditional teacher lecturing 35 students in a traditional classroom can emphasize the career implications of the academic subject matter taught and can use world of work examples as illustrations of application — and motivation and learning can be increased thereby. However, innovation tends to encourage innovation. Career education is more likely to be adopted where the atmosphere encourages other experiments.

Among the many current educational innovations, five would be particularly supportive of career education. First, the year-round school in which both students and teachers attend classes on a staggered basis throughout the full twelve months of the year holds two particular advantages. It avoids dumping large numbers of graduates on the labor market every June, a practice that guarantees unemployment for some of them. Assuming that each teacher continues to teach the traditional nine months each year, the staggered approach enables teachers to gain hands-on experience in occupations outside the school without burdening employers with a concentration of teachers in the summer months.

A second and related idea is the community school concept, one aspect of which is to have the schools open during the evenings as well as in the daytime, six days a week. Among the payoffs would be greater flexibility in mixing work experience and work-study programs with school attendance. Schools could make a greater contribution to adult education, including the need for retraining and upgrading both unemployed and underemployed adult workers. It is time to cash in on the ten-year manpower training program experience by making career education for the adult worker an integral part of the education system. The longer school day and school week would allow more efficient use of school facilities and in particular, would allow expansion of vocational education without huge investments in new shops and laboratories.

Performance evaluation is a third current innovation with considerable promise for career education. Time spent in the classroom has traditionally been accepted as a surrogate for measured achievement in

education, as hours on the job have been for apprenticeship. Performance evaluation holds these multiple advantages for career education:

(1) The opportunity for college-bound students to explore occupational education without being locked in by strict Carnegie unit
requirements of so-called college "prep" courses

(2) The opportunity to extend educational credit for student learning that goes beyond the four walls of the school, without detracting from the worth of the credits granted

(3) The opportunity to allow students some voice in determining
their unique educational goals in a system under which they can
see how nearly they approximated accomplishing their goals,
not how they failed to meet goals established for them by others

The competency-based curriculum is a related concept, valid probably only for the later school years. It seeks to define the skills and knowledge required of and pursued by the individual, and attempts to design
a curriculum to provide those achievements. Its advantages for occupational preparation are obvious.

A fourth basic change — one which borders on the realm of being
essential to career education — is to make it possible for persons without
standard teaching certificates, but with needed knowledge and the
ability to impart it, to teach in elementary and secondary schools. The
bulk of the education process will undoubtedly remain in the hands of
the professional educator. However, there is no reason to deny the student access to needed knowledge and role models just to maintain pro-
fessionalization. The ways to gain knowledge are just as manifold for
teachers as for students. Realities of the world of work as well as most
occupational skills can be learned only by experiencing them. No professional teacher can have all the necessary experience. There is no argument for ruling from the classroom the survivors of the "school of hard
knocks" in deference to the graduates of the "school of hard books."
Both have their place, and the system must find a way of evaluating
teaching competence that is not limited to academic credentials.

Fifth, the concept of open/entry-open/exit, largely a contribution of
manpower training and post-secondary vocational education, should be
incorporated throughout the education system. In these times of rapid
technological change, it is no longer possible for most persons to honestly

say that they have completed their education. Some secondary school students will profit more from formal education if they are allowed to work full time for a while before they finish the twelfth grade. They should be able to do so without being labeled "school dropouts." Moreover, it should be possible for out-of-school youth and adults to return to the public schools to continue their education without being placed in special classes. There are many good reasons why our public schools nowadays must be prepared to serve adults as well as youth. The career education movement represents one of these reasons. Another is merely institutional survival. Given population trends — low birthrates and extended longevity — adult education and continuing education are likely to be where the action is in the foreseeable future.

Changing the Community's Role

While innovations in education can enhance career education, change in the business-industry-labor community is essential if the fourth component of career education, discussed in chapter 4, is to have practical reality. Those who comprise and control the world of work must be active participants, not just passive cooperators, if career education is to be a link between the school and the outside world. Major changes must take place in the business-industry-labor community if an immense expansion of opportunities for observation, work experience, and work-study programs advocated by career education is actually to occur. Observation experiences have been made available to elementary school students on an infrequent and sporadic basis in the past. Programs of work experience and work-study carried out cooperatively with school systems have been limited primarily to some vocational education students.

The career education concept calls for observation, work experiences, and work-study to be made available to all students during their kindergarten through twelfth grade public school years. At the same time, it calls for similar opportunities to be made available to teachers, counselors, and school administrators. When one considers that this is to be done, in part, through exchange programs between school personnel and persons from the business-labor-industry community, he realizes that the challenges for change take on a mind-boggling dimension. Yet exchange roles will be imperative — if the career education concept is really to work.

The business-labor-industry community must be willing to work with school personnel in establishing and operating comprehensive placement programs designed to help students make a successful transition from school to work. A career education program that would help students who want to work, equip them with job skills, and then do nothing about job placement would surely be a farce. We have seen the ratio of youth to adult unemployment rise persistently until a three to one relationship has been established. Career education is charged with the responsibility of reserving this trend. If reversal is to be accomplished, comprehensive job placement programs, carried out cooperatively between schools and the business-labor-industry community, must be established. Public education and the business-labor-industry community cannot continue to merely blame each other for the failure of many former students to make a successful transition from school to work. Change is essential, and persons from schools, from business, from industry, and from labor are the only ones who can accomplish it.

An additional basic change must consist of conscious and conscientious efforts by the business-labor-industry community to improve both physical and psychological conditions in the workplace itself. One reason some employers say they have "lousy" workers is that the employers have so many "lousy" jobs to be performed. A wide variety of means — now readily available — can help workers gain more personal pride, satisfaction, and feeling of accomplishment from the tasks they are asked to do. In far too many employment settings, these new approaches have not yet been considered, to say nothing of being adopted. We know that racism and sexism are still significant and powerful forces in both hiring and promotion practices existing in the occupational sphere of our society. Career education cannot in good conscience try to help more students want to work unless it is willing to devote considerable attention to these problems. The solutions must of course take place in the business-labor-industry community.

All of these needed changes might discourage an attempt at implementing career education. But none are prerequisites. They are concomitants — not only things which should or must happen, but things that will happen in the process of selling and implementing career education's advantages.

SUMMARY

The term "career education" means the sum total of those experiences of the individual associated with his or her choice of, preparation for, entry into, and progress in a sequence of jobs and unpaid work throughout his or her lifetime. Career education is crucial in a society such as ours — a society that has been built and continues to operate essentially in accordance with a strong work ethic, combined with firm protection of choice for the individual.

The needs of all in society, both youths and adults, in these times for individual and continuing assistance in career preparation and development are great — and are becoming greater. Much of the current societal dissatisfaction with the service it receives from its schools exists because of a lack of emphasis on career education for all, an overemphasis on college degrees which are in reality available to relatively few, and the failure to recognize that college, too, along with its other purposes, is a component of career education. It is time that career education needs of all our citizens be recognized and provided for.

A harmful societal attitude that must now be eliminated is the false notion that a four-year college education is the only respectable preparation and the best route to successful employment. Public education has been a major contributor to this misleading philosophy and has a major responsibility to remedy it. But at the same time, college education will continue as a major path, both for career preparation and for intellectual and esthetic satisfaction, probably for a slowly rising proportion of the total population. It must be available to all who want and can profit from it, and it must be as meaningful as it is possible to make it.

Finally, it is important to note that in asking for career education, we base our requests on the needs of all citizens, including the more than four-fifths of the populace — both youths and adults, both in school and out of school — who will never attain a four-year college degree. It is time that education gives as much concern to serving this majority of our population as the concern it has directed toward the college-educated minority. It is noteworthy that the education needed is not of a single variety, serving a particular small segment of American education. What is needed is not more elementary and secondary education, more guidance, more vocational education, or more community colleges. We need a comprehensive program of career education that covers all levels of education for all citizens. With rising longevity, changing technology, and newly emerging opportunities and challenges, adults have as much right as youth to, and indeed a growing need for, a path to remedial education, occupational upgrading, and preparation for new phases of their lives. There should be career education for the adult worker, the labor force reentrant, and the retired person.

There you have it! We have described what career education is, explored why it is needed, and traced something of its development. We have given some inklings of how to do it in the classroom and the community, and suggested strategy for getting it implemented politically. We have dissected it into seven concepts, five components, three stages, and seven ingredients, ten planning steps, and twenty questions until it is a remarkable reader who is not confused by the anatomy.

What more is to be said? There is a substantial job ahead in reorienting teacher training institutions, in retraining the current administrative and teaching corps, and in training new teachers, changing certification requirements, establishing home-school-community linkages, identifying learning environments outside and linking them with the classroom, writing new prospectuses, teaching guides, and curriculum — the list is almost endless.

All that is termed "career education" in the near future will not be. The temptation will be to continue doing the familiar while calling it by a new name. Training, technical assistance, supervision, and incentives will be needed over a sustained period of time to bring positive change. Research, experiment, planning time, and substantially increased resources are necessities. It will be difficult to convince the taxpayer, now often "turned off" on education, that something new is coming which will meet his approval if he will just advance more money. Employers will need a long-range focus to look past the current bother of coordinating with schools and having students and teachers in the workplace.

Somewhat surprisingly, elementary educators appear to be moving faster than the rest of education in endorsing and implementing career education. Their integrated classrooms and project-oriented techniques can be modified relatively easy for transfer to the home for early childhood education.

The junior high appears next most ready, but has little experience upon which to build. The high schools have had vocational education and can move from that base to coordination and merger with the more academic. However, that which exists may stand in the way of something new. The much-maligned vocational educators, criticized for their narrow concentration on traditional job skills, now prove to be among the most ready to change, often even at high cost to their own budgets and protected positions. Academic teachers with their focus on subject matter disciplines and college entrance requirements may find it most difficult to endorse and implement the merger into career education.

The best of community colleges — those really serving their communities with open-entry/open-exit practices, zero-reject entrance, and linkages to all community institutions — are already doing career education. The rest are just junior colleges, yearning to grow up to be senior, get selective, and grant higher degrees. The colleges are farthest away, still allocating the education dollar through selection practices to those who need it least and rejecting those who need education most, trying to remain "pure" by ignoring the world, and in their most vocational aspects, the graduate schools, perpetuating artificial and irrelevant entrance requirements to some of the better paid occupations. Colleges of education — once centers of innovation as well as protectors of quality in education — are now more likely to be perpetrators of the status quo and defenders of stodginess. The number of institutions which must be changed is almost overwhelming, but the prize is worth the effort.

Work values can be restructured. People can find joy in achievement, in the labor market, in voluntary service, and in productive avocations. The manpower needs of industry and the society can be met while maintaining and increasing individual freedom of choice and providing challenging and well-paid employment. Dignity can be given to workers in all occupations. Meaning can be given to abstract concepts, the value of which students often do not recognize until too late. Motivation to learn can emanate from that recognition. Opportunities to learn from experience as well as from instruction can be provided. The concept of dropout can be abolished and replaced with a variety in learning environments. New occupations can become available as old ones disappear or lose their challenge. Progress in existing careers can be speeded by upgrading.

But these are what can be, not necessarily what will be. Putting career education in place will be a long and arduous task requiring federal and state legislation and appropriation; national leadership from the Office of Education; state and local education agency leadership at their levels; political pressuring from national, state, and local interest groups and public officials; cooperation from employers and labor organizations; innovation and dedication from classroom teachers, counselors, and administrators; and response from students. Some schools will not accept the challenge, and some students will not respond.

Only part of the frustrations of life arise and can be stilled in a workplace. Deeper philosophical or theological restlessness may be untouched. Economic dislocation, environmental pollution, ill health — all of the perils of personal life and society — will not go away if career education is implemented. There will still be dull and grubby jobs which must be done. But no sensible person expects panaceas.

Marginal improvements constantly made are achievement enough, and career education's promise is one of life's basic aspects. To make work possible, meaningful, and satisfying to each individual is challenge enough. Career education can do that, but only if we all do career education.

Selected Bibliography

Bailey, Larry L.; and Stadt, Ronald. *Career Education: New Approaches to Human Development.* Bloomington, Illinois: McKnight and McKnight Co. 1973.

Begle, Elsie P.; *et al. Career Education: An Annotated Bibliography for Teachers and Curriculum Developers.* Palo Alto, California: American Institutes for Research. January 1973.

Bell, T. H. *Your Child's Intellect.* Salt Lake City: Olympus Publishing Company. 1972.

Berg, Ivar. *Education and Jobs: The Great Training Robbery.* New York: Praeger. 1970.

Bottoms, Eugene; and Matheny, Kenneth B. *A Guide for the Development, Implementation, and Administration of Exemplary Programs and Projects in Vocational Education.* Atlanta, Georgia: Atlanta Public Schools.

————; *et al. Career Education Resource Guide.* Morristown, New Jersey: General Learning Corporation. 1972.

Bruner, Jerome S. "Some Theorems on Instruction (Illustrated, with Reference to Mathematics)." *Theories of Learning and Instruction.* Edited by Ernest R. Hilgard. Chicago: University of Chicago Press. 1964.

Combs, Janet; and Cooley, W. W. "Dropouts: In High School and After School." *American Educational Research Journal* (October 1970), vol. 18, no. 1.

Cottingham, Harold F. *Guidance in Elementary Schools*. New York: McKnight and McKnight Co. 1956.

Crites, John O. *Vocational Psychology*. New York: McGraw-Hill Book Company. 1969.

Dunn, James A.; *et al. Career Education: A Curriculum Design and Instructional Objectives Catalog*. Palo Alto, California: American Institutes for Research. April 1973.

Dwyer, J. *Teaching Children through Natural Mathematics*. New York: Parker Publishing Co. 1970.

Education Amendments of 1972. Title X, Part B. Vocational Education Act of 1963. Public Law 92-318.

ERIC Clearinghouse on Vocation and Technical Education. *Career Education Practice*. Columbus: Ohio State University, Center for Vocational and Technical Education. December 1972.

Evans, Rupert N. *Foundations of Vocational Education*. Columbus, Ohio: Charles E. Merrill Publishing Co. 1971.

————. "Rationale for Career Education." *National Association of Secondary School Principals Bulletin* (March 1973), vol. 57.

————; and Terry, David R. (Editors). *Changing the Role of Vocational Teacher Education*. Bloomington, Illinois: McKnight and McKnight Co. 1972.

————; Mangum, Garth L.; and Pragan, Otto. *Education for Employment: The Background and Potential of the Vocational Education Amendments of 1968*. Ann Arbor: University of Michigan, Institute of Labor and Industrial Relations. 1969.

Feldman, Marvin. *Making Education Relevant*. New York: The Ford Foundation. 1966.

Feirer, John. *Going Metric for Career Education*. Kalamazoo: Western Michigan University, Center for Metric Education. 1973.

Galloway, Joel. "Males in Process of Incarceration in the Illinois Penal System." Champaign: University of Illinois. 1971. Unpublished paper.

Goldhammer, Keith; and Taylor, R. *Career Education: Perspective and Promise*. Columbus, Ohio: Charles E. Merrill Publishing Co. 1972.

Green, Thomas. *Work, Leisure, and the American School*. New York: Langmans, Green & Co.

Greer, Colin. *The Great School Legend*. New York: Basic Books. 1972.

Gribbons, Warren D.; and Lohnes, P. *Emerging Careers*. New York: Teachers College Press, Columbia University. 1968.

Havighurst, Robert J. *Human Development and Education*. New York: David McKay Co., Inc. 1953.

Herr, Edwin L. *Review and Synthesis of Foundation for Career Education.* Washington, D.C.: U.S. Government Printing Office. 1972.

————; and Cramer, Stanley H. *Vocational Guidance and Career Development of the Schools: Toward a Systems Approach.* New York: Houghton-Mifflin Company. 1972.

Herrick, Neal Q. "Who's Unhappy at Work and Why." *Manpower* (January 1972).

High, Sidney C., Jr.; *et al. Bibliography on Career Education.* Washington, D.C.: U.S. Office of Education, Division of Vocational and Technical Education, Program Development and Operations Branch. 1973. Mimeographed.

Hill, George E.; and Luckey, Eleanore B. "Vocational Guidance." In *Guidance for Children in Elementary Schools.* New York: Appleton-Century-Crofts. 1969.

Hoppock, Robert; and Novick, Bernard. "The Occupational Information Consultant: A New Profession." *Personnel and Guidance Journal* (March 1971), vol. 49.

Hoyt, Kenneth B. *Career Education: A Newsletter Series* (1 through 4). *SRA Guidance Newsletter* (September-October, November-December 1972; January-February, March-April 1973). Science Research Associates, Inc. 1973, 1972.

————. "The Community College Must Change." *Compact* (August 1970), vol. 4.

————; *et al. Career Education and the Elementary School Teacher.* Salt Lake City: Olympus Publishing Company. 1973.

Illich, Ivan. *Deschooling Society.* New York: Harper & Row. 1971.

Inhelder, Barbara; and Piaget, Jean. *The Growth of Logical Thinking from Childhood to Adolescence.* New York: Basic Books, Inc. 1958.

Jencks, Christopher; *et al. Inequality.* New York: Basic Books. 1972.

Keller, Louise J. *Career Education In-Service Training Guide.* Morristown, New Jersey: General Learning Corporation. 1972.

Leonard, George. *Education and Ecstasy.* New York: Dellacorte. 1970.

Levitan, Sar A.; and Johnston, William B. *Work Is Here to Stay, Alas.* Salt Lake City: Olympus Publishing Company. 1973.

McClure, Larry; and Buan, Carolyn (Editors). *Essays on Career Education.* Portland, Oregon: Northwest Regional Educational Laboratory. April 1973.

McMurrin, Sterling (Editor). *Functional Education for Disadvantaged Youth.* New York: Committee for Economic Development. 1971.

Mangum, Garth L. *Reorienting Vocational Education.* Ann Arbor: University of Michigan, Institute of Labor and Industrial Relations. 1968.

"Marland on Career Education." *American Education* (November 1971).

Maslow, Abraham H. *Motivation and Personality.* New York: Harper & Row. 1954.

Morgan, Robert L.; and Shook, Mollie W. (Editors). *Career Education Monograph Series.* Raleigh: North Carolina State University. 1973.

National School Public Relations Association. *Vocational Education: Innovations Revolutionize Career Training.* Washington, D.C.: National School Public Relations Association. 1971.

Olympus Research Corporation. *Career Education: A Handbook for Implementation.* U.S. Department of Health, Education and Welfare, Office of Education. Washington, D.C.: U.S. Government Printing Office. February 1972.

Osipow, Samuel H. *Theories of Career Development.* New York: Appleton-Century-Crofts. 1968.

O'Toole, John (Editor). *Work in America.* Cambridge: M.I.T. Press. 1973.

Pucel, David J. "Variables Related to MDTA Trainee Success in Minnesota." Minneapolis: University of Minnesota. 1968.

Pucinski, Roman C.; and Hirsch, Sharlene R. (Editors). *The Courage to Change.* New York: Prentice Hall. 1971.

Tiedt, Sidney W.; and Tiedt, Eric. *Elementary Teacher's Complete Ideas Handbook.* Englewood Cliffs, New Jersey: Prentice-Hall, Inc. 1965.

U.S. Department of Labor. *Dictionary of Occupational Titles.* Washington, D.C.: U.S. Government Printing Office. Various years.

Venn, Grant. *Man, Education and Manpower.* Washington, D.C.: National Education Association-American Association of School Administrators. 1970.

"Vocational Education: The Bridge between Man and His Work." Publication 1, Highlights and Recommendations from the General Report of the Advisory Commission on Vocational Education, U.S. Department of Health, Education and Welfare, Office of Education. 1967. Multilith. Reprinted in Evans, Rupert N.; Mangum, Garth L.; and Pragan, Otto. *Education for Employment: The Background and Potential of the Vocational Education Amendments of 1968.* Ann Arbor: University of Michigan, Institute of Labor and Industrial Relations. 1969.

Wernick, Walter. *World of Work Resource Units for Elementary Teachers.* DeKalb: Northern Illinois University, ABLE Model Program. 1971.

Williamson, E. G. *Vocational Counseling.* New York: McGraw-Hill Book Company. 1965.

Wool, Harold. "What's Wrong with Work in America?" *Monthly Labor Review* (March 1973).

Index

A

absenteeism in the labor market, 53
accountability, demand for, 75–78
Act
    Economic Opportunity, 90
    Manpower Development and
      Training, 90, 133, 137
    Vocational Education, 84, 91, 94,
      97, 161, 175
action steps
    1: organize interactive network,
      190–94
    2: gain understanding and
      establish high-priority objec-
      tive, 194–96
    3: study system to determine
      needed changes, 197–99
    4: conduct inventory and marshal
      community resources, 199–200
    5: design preliminary program,
      200–03
    6: establish cooperative relation-
      ships, 203–08
    7: implement system, 208–09
    8: develop program of evalua-
      tion, 209–11
    9: create feedback system,
      211–13
    10: provide program of mainte-
      nance, 213–15
adult education, 63–64, 72–73, 90, 91

Advisory Council on Vocational Edu-
    cation, 91
aged's economic role, 48, 53
Albuquerque, New Mexico, 147
all education is not career education,
    33–35
American
    Association of Junior Colleges, 179
    Association of School Admin-
      istrators, 179
    Personnel and Guidance Associa-
      tion, 179
    Society for Curriculum Develop-
      ment, 179
    Vocational Association, 94, 178,
      179
"American Industries" project, 85, 86,
    87, 88
Anne Arundel County, Maryland, 110,
    116, 121
approaches
    for training and retraining of
      education personnel, 172–73
    to career education emphasis in
      the classroom, 111–15
Arizona, 97; State Department of Edu-
    cation, 96
Assembly Bill No. 102, 195–96
"Assurances Judicial Review," 177

Atlanta, Georgia, 97
attitudes regarding college, 58–63, 65, 66–68

B

baccalaureate and graduate degrees, 134–35
Baltimore, Maryland, 121–22, 148
basic understandings of career education, 136–38
biases in the labor market as a social ill, 54–55
Bismarck, North Dakota, 96
Boy Scouts of America, 90
Bridgeport, Michigan, 121
Bureau of Adult Vocational and Technical Education, 95
business-labor-industry
    changes in, 162–63
    component, 29, 146–53
    forerunners of career development, 90
    interactive network, 193
    personnel as school instructors, 63
    relevance to children, 48

C

career
    alternatives component, 28–29
    choice, timing of, 42–43
    clusters, U.S. Office of Education, 31–32, 95
    development, nature of, 138–42;
        personnel in programs, 144–46;
        understandings of, 136–38
Center for Occupational Education, North Carolina, 95, 97, 110
Center for Study of Vocational-Technical Education, Ohio, 95
Central Michigan University, 88
changes
    business-labor-industry community, 162–63
    child labor laws, 162–63
    counselors, 163–64
    home and family, 164–65
    needed, 64–80
    organizational and administrative structure in education, 165–66
    parent attitudes, 156–57
    required, 158–67
    teacher education, 166–67
    vocational education, 160–62
changing significance of work, 41–42

child labor laws, 162–63
Clearwater, Florida, 121
clusters
    as linkages, 124–26
    fifteen occupational, 31–32, 95
Cobb County, Georgia, 110
Cogswell Polytechnical College, 89
college as the only preparation for a career, 58–63, 65, 66–68, 72
Colorado, 97
committees for action step six, 203–04
community
    resources, action step nine, 213
    subcommittee, 206–08
comparison
    curricula, 66–68; according to sex, 68–69
    employment risk of graduate and nongraduate, 49
    general and vocational curricula, 79, 80
    high school graduates in the labor force, 47, 65
    lengths of compulsory education, 73
    measurable criteria, 77
    occupational instruction and general education, 79
    white- and blue-collar workers, numbers of, 47
competition among education, welfare, and manpower programs, 64
components (five) of career education, 24–30
    A: career implications of substantive content, 104–17
    B: vocational skills training in formal education, 117–35
    C: career development as part of career education, 136–46
    D: contributions of employers, employees, and labor organizations, 146–53
    E: role of home and family, 153–58
compulsory education, 73–74
concepts (eleven) of career education, 22–24
conference approach, 173
conflicts in goals, 78–80
congressional committees, 179
continuing education. *See* adult education

cooperation of
  business-labor-industry com-
    ponent, 29, 146–53
  home and family component,
    29–30, 153–58
correctional institutions, 65, 71–72
counselors, changes in, 163–64

D

Dallas Independent School District,
  96–97
decisions, implementation of, 142–44
decline of labor force participation, 53
definition. *See also* description
  career education, 15, 100
  economic efficiency, 80
  exploring, 100
  leisure, 19
  Marland's, 13–14
  random, 15
  U.S. Office of Education refrained
    from, 13
  vocational educator, 14
Delaware, 96
demand for accountability, 75–78
description of career education
  Marland's, 13–14
  U.S. Office of Education's, 14
  vocational educator, 14
development of curriculum, 169–70
Dictionary of Occupational Titles, 139
dignity of workers, 42
dissatisfaction with educational
  practices, 45
District of Columbia, 97–98

E

early childhood education, 69–71, 108
Eastern Illinois University, 109
ecological destruction as a social ill, 51
Economic Opportunity Act, 90
education's successes, 57–58
elected officials in interactive network,
  193
eleven concepts of career education,
  22–24
energy crisis, 47–48
ERIC clearinghouse, 110
evaluation of
  career education, 171
  student progress, action step nine,
    212
executive branch responsibility, 180

Exemplary Programs branch of
  U.S. Office of Education, 109–10
Explorer program, 90

F

failure to explore work ethics, 69–70
family structure shrinkage as a social
  ill, 48
fifteen occupational clusters, U.S.
  Office of Education 31–32, 95;
  as linkages, 124–26
fifth component of career education,
  29–30
first component of career education,
  25–26
Florida, 121
Ford Foundation, early experiments, 85
fourth component of career education,
  29
funding, sources of, 40–41, 175–76

G

Georgia, 96, 97, 110
goals, conflicts in, 78–80
graduate degree, 134–35
graduation once a year, 74

H

Hackensack, New Jersey, 97
Hazelton, Pennsylvania, 122
home and family
  changes in, 164–65
  component, 29–30, 153–58
  living, teaching of, 154–56
  objectives, 192
  shrinkage of structure, 48
homework as work, 18
Hotel and Restaurant Foundation, 90

I

implementing decisions, 142–44
Indianapolis, Indiana, 121
individualized instruction, 65–66
industrial
  evolution as a social ill, 47–48
  revolution, 47
Industrial Arts Curriculum Project,
  88, 170
industry-business-labor. *See* business-
  labor-industry
in-school committee, 204; subcommittee, 205–06
instructional program, action step nine,
  212–13
interdisciplinary approach, 173

236

J

Jefferson County, Colorado, 97
job
    dissatisfaction as a social ill, 52–53
    enrichment, 53
Job Corps, 90, 133
Junior Achievement, 90
junior high school level, vocational
    skills training, 119–24

K

Kansas, 123

L

labor-business-industry. *See* business-
    labor-industry
labor market trends, 53–56
learning environment, nature of, 66–68
Liberal, Kansas, 123
linkages, clusters as, 124–26
Los Angeles, California, 97; School
    District resolution, 196

M

manpower
    individualized instruction, 65
    needs of society, 78–79, 83
    programs, demand for, 55
    remedial programs, 90
    trainees, 65
Manpower Development and Training
    Act of 1962, 90, 133, 137
Maryland, 90, 110, 116, 121, 148
Mesa, Arizona, 97
Michigan, 97, 121
migration to cities, 54–55
mini-models, 109–10
Mississippi, 96

N

national
    legislation, 176–78
    policy, 178–80
National Advisory Council in Voca-
    tional Education, 94
National Association of Secondary
    School Principals, 33, 95, 179
National Institute of Education, 98,
    169
nature of
    career development, 138–42
    learning environment, 66–68

needed
    basic changes, 64–80
    changes in teacher education,
      166–67
need for
    change in traditional school
      practice, 43–44
    skills training, 43
New Jersey, 97; State Department of
    Education, 85
New Mexico, 147
new technology's demands as a social
    ill, 54–55
Norfolk, Virginia, 121
North Carolina State University, 95,
    97, 110
North Dakota, 96
Nova schools in Florida, 85, 86, 87

O

objective of career education, 24
OCCUPACS, 109
occupational alternatives
    component, 28–29
    student, 78–79, 83, 90
    trainee, 80
occupational clusters, fifteen, 31–32, 95
off-campus committee, 204; subcom-
    mittee, 206–08
Ohio State University, 95
on-campus committee, 204
operational problems for classroom
    teachers, 115–17
organized labor, 79, 83, 146–53, 162
originality of career education, 39–40

P

parent
    attitudes, changing of, 156–57
    interactive network, 192
    participation, 157–58
"Partnership Vocational Education
    Project," 88
Pennsylvania, 122
personnel in career development
    programs, 144–46
phases of career education, 30–32
pollution as a social ill, 51
Pontiac, Michigan, 97
post-secondary, less than baccalaureate,
    131–34
poverty as a social ill, 46, 50, 51, 55
"Pre-technical Program," 89
prisons, 65, 71–72

problem
  1: serving as a source of informa-
     tion, 147–48
  2: serving as a source of observa-
     tion, 148–49
  3: work experience and work-
     study programs for students,
     149–50
  4: work-study programs for edu-
     cators, 150–51
  5: education and training in the
     occupational community,
     151–52
  6: making work meaningful to
     workers, 152
  7: job-placement programs,
     152–53
process of career education, 103–04
"Program Grants for State Occupational Education Programs," 177
"Project FEAST," 89; "TALENT," 83
propositions of definition, 100–01
Protestant (Puritan) work ethic, 19,
  69, 101–02
public agencies in interactive network,
  193
Puerto Rico, 97–98

R

Racine, Wisconsin, 121
reduced commitment to work, 53
relationship to
    post-secondary education, 35–37
    vocational education, 37–38
released time approach, 173
research, 170–71
resource staff addition approach, 173
revision of child labor laws, 162
"Richmond Plan," 89
roadblocks in structure of education,
  60–64
role of state leadership organizations,
  184–86

S

San Diego School Board, 97
San Francisco City College, 90
San Mateo Unified School District, 87
school
    for schooling's sake, 60, 65, 103
    responsibility component, 25–26
scope of career education, 33–35
second component of career education,
  27–28
segregation, 68–69

self-kept records, students, action
  step nine, 212
senior high school level, vocational
  skills training, 126–30
service clubs in interactive network,
  194
sex segregation, 68–69
Skills Centers, 90
skills training, need for, 43
socioeconomic segregation, 68–69
sources of
    funding, 40–41, 175–76
    social unrest, 46–53
specialization in the urban society,
  48–49
Sputnik, 84, 85
state boards and departments of education, 180–88
steering committee, action step six,
  203–04
Stout State University, 85
student options. See occupational
  alternatives
subcommittees for action step six,
  206–08
summer work experience approach, 173
superintendent's role, 187–88

T

technological power as a social ill, 50
"Technology for Children," 85, 86
Texas, 76
third component of career education,
  28–29
time
    allocation of, 80
    as a roadblock, 62–63
    constraints, 66–67
timing of career choice, 42–43
training and retraining, 171–75
twelve-month school year, 63, 74

U

understandings of career development,
  136–38
unemployment
    as a social ill, 52–53
    rates of college graduates, 55–56
unions. See organized labor
university. See college
U.S. Chamber of Commerce, 98, 190
U.S. Office of Education
    description of career education, 14
    fifteen occupational clusters,
      31–32, 95

V

Virginia, 121
visitation committee, action step six,
    204
vocational education
    changes in, 160–62
    national legislation, 176–78
    three goals, 83
    unified system of, 92–94
Vocational Education Act of 1963,
    84, 91, 94, 97, 161, 175
vocational maturation, 31
vocational skills training
    at junior high school level, 119–24
    at senior high school level, 126–30
    component, 27–28, 117–25

W

wealth as a social ill, 50
work ethic
    and the family structure, 48

changing significance of, 41–42
encouraged development of tech-
    nology, 49
failure to explore, 69–70
inculcation in elementary schools,
    82
Protestant (Puritan), 19, 69,
    101–02
youth's rejection of, 77
working sabbatical approach, 172–73
will career education work?, 44
Wisconsin, 121
Wyoming, 96

Y

youth
    career education for, 106–11
    inadequately prepared to earn
        living, 77
    in labor market, 48–49, 53, 55
    rejection of work ethic, 69